Classic Country
Collection

GW01071984

Lady Flo Bjelke-Petersen was born in Brisbane, Queensland, and married Sir Joh Bjelke-Petersen in 1952. Elected to the Senate in 1981, Lady Flo retired in June 1993, after serving as a senator for 12 years.

Sir Joh and Lady Flo live on their property 'Bethany', in Kingaroy, and have four children and many grandchildren.

Classic Country Collection

Lady Flo Bjelke-Peterson

REED EDITIONS

Published 1996 by Reed Editions
a part of Reed Books Australia
22 Salmon Street, Port Melbourne, Victoria 3207
a division of Reed International Books Australia Pty Limited

Copyright © for this collection Lady Flo Bjelke-Petersen 1996

All rights reserved. Without limiting the rights under copyright
above, no part of this publication may be reproduced, stored in or introduced into a retrieval system, or transmitted in any form
or by any means (electronic, mechanical, photocopying, recording or
otherwise), without the prior written permission of both the copyright
owner and the publisher.

National Library of Australia
  cataloguing-in-publication data:

Bjelke-Petersen, Flo, Lady, 1920-.
    Classic country collection.

    Includes index
    ISBN 1 86345 117 X.

    1. Cookery. 2. Baking. 3. Home economics, Rural - Australia. 4.
    Home economics - Australia 5. Country life - Australia. I. Bjelke-
    Petersen, Flo, Lady, 1920- . Classic country cooking. II. Bjelke-
    Petersen, Flo, Lady, 1920- . Classic country baking. III. Bjelke-
    Petersen, Flo, Lady, 1920- . Classic country wisdom. IV. Title. V.
    Title : Classic country cooking. VI. Title : Classic country baking. VII.
    Title : Classic country wisdom.

641.5

Printed and bound in Australia
by the Australian Print Group

I dedicate this Classic Country Collection to my
dear husband, Joh, and all my family, who have given me
tremendous support and encouragement over the years
the three books in the Collection have been published.

Contents

Foreword

I am happy that my publisher, Reed Books, has decided to bring out the Classic Country Collection, comprising my three books published over the past three years – Classic Country Cooking, Classic Country Baking and Classic Country Wisdom.

I have appreciated the tremendous support I have received for these books from so many people throughout Australia, but particularly from so many friends in Queensland.

Having been the wife of the Premier of Queensland for nineteen and a half years, and a Queensland Senator for twelve and a quarter years, I have been glad of the opportunity to meet many friends as I have travelled around promoting the three books. Now that they are together in the Classic Country Collection, I look forward to meeting many of you once again, and trust the Collection will appeal to you all.

My Favourite Grace

For health and food
For love and friends
For everything your goodness sends
Father in heaven we thank you

Classic Country Cooking

CONTENTS

SOUPS, SNACKS, SALADS AND VEGETABLES

MY THOUGHTS ON COOKING

Cooking is one of the great joys of this world, and I would have to admit that eating is pretty enjoyable too.

I have always been interested in cooking right from the time I made sure my family had something to eat when they came home from school, and I have found cooking to be a relaxing hobby. These days of course my time is somewhat limited, and I am lucky to have the time to cook my famous, or should I say infamous, Pumpkin Scones for Joh on our day off on Sundays. I have to admit that I prefer a homestyle of cooking, with plenty of delicious recipes which have been handed down from my mother. Indeed, it was her Pumpkin Scone recipe which made me somewhat of an authority in the kitchen. If she were alive today I'm sure she would be quite amused to see that her recipe has created such interest.

PEA SOUP

1 cup split peas
4 or 5 bacon bones
2 teaspoons salt or to taste
pinch of pepper
2 onions
1 carrot
4 level tablespoons plain
  flour
2 level tablespoons
  chopped mint

Wash peas and soak in cold water overnight. Drain peas and put into large pan with bacon bones, salt, pepper and 3 L water. Peel and chop vegetables and add to pan. Bring soup slowly to boiling point, then simmer gently for 2–3 hours. Remove bones and rub soup through fine sieve or strainer. Return to saucepan and heat to boiling point. Blend flour with 1 cup cold water. Stir into soup and boil gently for 3 minutes. Add chopped mint and serve hot.

OXTAIL SOUP

1 oxtail
2 stalks celery
1 carrot
1 onion
1 white turnip
5 cups beef stock
2 cloves
pinch nutmeg
salt and pepper
parsley

Wash oxtail pieces, remove excess fat. Place in saucepan with stock, peeled and chopped vegetables and seasoning. Bring slowly to boil and simmer for 4 hours. Strain and allow to cool. Remove fat when set. Cut meat from bones and chop finely. Bring soup to boil, add meat and serve garnished with parsley.

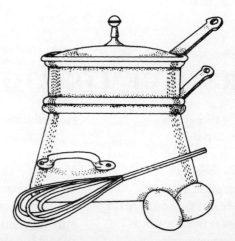

SCOTCH BROTH

4 tablespoons pearl barley
1 kg mutton necks, shanks
   or soup bones
3 carrots
2 turnips
2 stalks celery
1 large onion
1 small parsnip
salt and pepper
parsley

Wash barley. Place in saucepan with 6 cups water and meat. Prepare and dice vegetables finely. Boil all together for 2½–3 hours. Add salt and pepper to taste and some of the parsley. Remove bones and skim any fat from top. Serve hot with parsley sprinkled on top.

CLEAR SOUP STOCK

2 kg beef bones
2 teaspoons salt
1 carrot
1 turnip
1 onion
2 sticks celery
12 peppercorns
12 cloves
1 blade mace

Trim fat from bones and wash. Put bones, salt and 3 L water into large saucepan or boiler. Bring slowly to boil. Cut up vegetables coarsely. Add vegetables, peppercorns, cloves and mace to saucepan. Simmer gently for 4 hours. Remove bones and strain. Allow to cool and remove fat.

CREAM OF TOMATO SOUP

500 g tomatoes
1 small onion
1 bacon rasher, chopped
1 teaspoon salt
1 teaspoon sugar
1½ dessertspoons butter
1 dessertspoon flour
½ teaspoon salt
1 cup milk

Roughly chop tomatoes, onion and bacon and place in saucepan with salt, sugar and ½ dessertspoon butter. Cook gently until soft. Rub through a sieve to make a soft mixture. Put dessertspoon butter into large saucepan and melt. Remove from heat and stir in flour and salt. Add milk and stir until smooth. Return to heat and boil for 3 minutes, stirring continuously. Add tomato mixture, mix through and reheat but do not allow to boil.

ASPARAGUS SOUP

1 large tin asparagus,
   drained
900 mL vegetable stock
1 onion
2 level dessertspoons
   butter
2 level teaspoons salt
600 mL milk
4 level tablespoons
   cornflour, blended in
   a little milk

Reserve tips of asparagus for garnishing and put remainder of tin into saucepan. Add stock, chopped onion, butter and salt. Simmer for approximately 30 minutes. Add milk and blended cornflour. Allow to boil for 2–3 minutes. Rub through a sieve, then return to saucepan and reheat. Serve garnished with asparagus tips.

HEARTY TOMATO SOUP

500 g tomatoes
1 onion
1 teaspoon butter
2 cups vegetable stock
1 bacon bone
1 dessertspoon sago
salt and pepper
chives

Scald and peel tomatoes then cut up roughly. Peel and chop onion. Heat butter and sauté vegetables, without browning, for a few minutes. Add stock and bacon bone, stir until boiling and simmer for 30 minutes. Rub through sieve, return to saucepan, add sago and simmer gently until clear. Skim, if necessary, and adjust seasoning. Serve with a dollop of yoghurt and sprinkle with chives.

PUMPKIN SOUP

My daughter Helen's recipe for pumpkin soup which, in warm weather, is delicious served chilled.

30 g butter
2 onions
2 medium potatoes
750 g pumpkin
600 mL chicken stock
1 cup milk
salt and pepper
1 cup cream, optional
chives or parsley

Chop onions, peel and dice potatoes and pumpkin. Heat butter and sauté onions until golden brown. Add potatoes, pumpkin, stock and milk. Cover and simmer gently for about 30 minutes, or until vegetables are tender. Sieve, or puree in processor or blender and add salt and pepper. Add cream if desired and reheat gently. Serve garnished with chopped chives or parsley.

CREAM OF CAULIFLOWER SOUP

4 cups water
1 small cauliflower, broken
    into small florets
60 g butter
3 tablespoons flour
2 cups chicken stock
¼ teaspoon nutmeg
salt and pepper
2 egg yolks
⅓ cup cream
chopped parsley

Bring water to the boil in a saucepan. Drop in cauliflower florets and cook for about 10 minutes. Drain, reserving cooking liquid. Reserve about 2 cups cooked florets and puree remainder with 1 cup reserved liquid. Melt butter in a saucepan, blend in flour and cook, stirring, until a pale straw colour. Remove from heat and add remaining reserved cooking liquid and stock, stirring until mixture is smooth. Add cauliflower puree, return to heat and stir until boiling. Simmer for about 15 minutes, stirring occasionally. Add reserved cauliflower florets, nutmeg, salt and pepper and simmer for a further 5 minutes. Beat egg yolks with cream. Stir in a ladle of hot soup, then add this mixture to remaining soup, stirring. Heat gently without boiling, then pour into bowls and sprinkle with parsley.

OMELETTE

2 eggs, separated
salt and pepper
1 teaspoon butter

Beat egg whites until stiff, add yolks, 2 tablespoons water, salt and pepper and beat well. Heat butter in pan. Pour in egg mixture. Cook until set and brown on bottom. Turn with egg lifter and brown other side or brown under griller. Fold in half and serve immediately. Use any of the following fillings: grated cheese, cooked asparagus, mixed herbs, mushrooms, sliced tomato, bacon, finely chopped parsley.

MEAL-IN-ONE OMELETTE

Serves 4

2 tablespoons butter
1 large onion
1 tin crabmeat or 1 cup
  diced ham, cooked
  chicken, mushrooms
  or asparagus
1 cup shredded lettuce
8 eggs
salt and pepper
2 tablespoons grated
  Parmesan cheese

Melt butter in saucepan. Chop onion, add to butter and cook until tender. Add crabmeat (or substitute) to pan. Add lettuce. Beat eggs and add to mixture with salt and pepper. Cook gently. When almost set sprinkle with cheese and place omelette under hot grill until cheese melts and browns. Serve while hot. Substitutes such as sliced zucchini, corn or cold potatoes may easily be used.

SCRAMBLED EGG

2 tablespoons milk
1 teaspoon butter
1 egg
salt and pepper
¼ teaspoon chopped
  parsley

Boil milk and butter. Beat egg well, add salt and pepper. Pour milk slowly onto beaten egg. Stir over gentle heat till thick but do not allow to become hard. Remove from heat, add parsley, pile on hot buttered toast, and serve on a hot plate.

MACARONI CHEESE

1 cup macaroni
salt and pepper
½ cup grated cheese
2 cups White Sauce
   (see page 53)
cayenne
breadcrumbs
chopped parsley
extra grated cheese

Sprinkle macaroni into large saucepan half filled with boiling water (salted). Boil until tender, 15–20 minutes. Drain and pour boiling water over macaroni to remove excess starch. Stir grated cheese into freshly made White Sauce, season to taste. Mix macaroni into cheese sauce, pour into greased ovenproof dish. Top with layer of grated cheese and breadcrumbs. Brown in oven and garnish with chopped parsley.

POTATO FRITTERS

3 medium sized potatoes
2 eggs, beaten
½ cup plain flour
½ teaspoon salt

Peel and grate potatoes, rinse in colander to remove excess starch, squeeze water out. Place potato in a bowl, stir in flour and salt. Mix to a smooth dough. Grease frypan, cook until golden brown. Any or all of the following may be added for variety: onion, cheese, ham, parsley, sweet corn.

DEVILS ON HORSEBACK

prunes
strips of bacon
squares of bread

Remove stones from prunes. Roll each prune in a small strip of bacon. Place on squares of bread and bake for about 20 minutes in moderate oven (180°–200°C).

ANGELS ON HORSEBACK

oysters
lemon juice
salt and pepper
strips of bacon
toothpicks

Sprinkle oysters with lemon juice, salt and pepper. Wrap each oyster in a small strip of bacon and secure with toothpick. Place under hot griller or in frypan, cook quickly until bacon is lightly browned. Serve immediately.

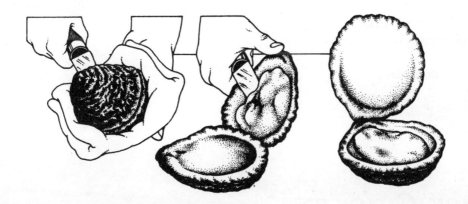

FRENCH TOAST

eggs
milk
pinch salt
butter
sliced white bread
maple syrup

For each egg use ¼ cup milk. Beat eggs, milk and salt together. Dip each slice of bread into this mixture and fry in melted butter on both sides until golden brown. Serve immediately with maple syrup.

WELSH RAREBIT

4 slices bread
1 cup grated cheese
3 tablespoons milk
½ teaspoon mustard
½ teaspoon salt
dash of pepper
1 teaspoon Worcestershire
    sauce

Toast bread and butter it. Keep hot, preferably over boiling water. Put grated cheese, milk, mustard, salt, pepper and sauce in saucepan. Heat very gently or stand saucepan in boiling water until ingredients are all well blended and mixture is creamy. Pour over toast and serve immediately.

NUTS AND BOLTS

1 kg salted peanuts
375 g packet stick pretzels
375 g packet circle
    pretzels
375 g packet Nutri-grain
3 packets french onion
    soup mix
1 dessertspoon curry
    powder
½ teaspoon chilli powder
½ cup oil

Mix oil into ingredients until mixture is well coated. Put mixture on 2 large trays. Bake in moderate oven (180° – 200°C) until brown and crunchy. Any or all of the following may be added for variety: dried fruits, sultanas, noodles.

MOCK CHICKEN

Ideal for seasoning meat.

1 small onion
1 ripe tomato
½ cup grated cheese
1 cup breadcrumbs
1 teaspoon mixed herbs
salt and pepper to taste
1 tablespoon butter

Chop onion finely. Pulp tomato. Add onion, tomato and cheese to breadcrumbs, together with herbs, salt and pepper. Melt butter and add to other ingredients, mixing well. Place mixture in a saucepan and stir over a low heat until cooked. When cooled, this dish can be stored in an airtight container for quite some time.

CAULIFLOWER AU GRATIN

To keep cauliflower sparkling white, add a little milk to the cooking water.

1 cauliflower (cooked)
1 cup White Sauce
(see page 53)
½ cup grated tasty cheese
1 tablespoon dried
breadcrumbs
1 tablespoon butter

Place cauliflower in an ovenproof casserole dish. Mask with White Sauce. Sprinkle with grated cheese and breadcrumbs. Dot butter in small pieces on top. Bake in a moderately hot oven (180°–200°C) until a golden brown, 10–15 minutes.

STUFFED TOMATOES

4 large tomatoes
salt and pepper
1 cup finely chopped cold
meat
4 tablespoons fresh
breadcrumbs
1 tablespoon chopped
parsley
1 pinch grated nutmeg
1 tablespoon butter

Cut tops off tomatoes, scoop out and save the pulp. Sprinkle tomatoes with a little salt and pepper. Mix meat with 1 tablespoon breadcrumbs, parsley, nutmeg, pepper, salt and 2 tablespoons of tomato pulp. Fill tomatoes with mixture. Sprinkle remainder of crumbs on top. Place a small piece of butter on each. Replace tops on tomatoes. Bake in a moderate oven (180°–200°C) for 15–20 minutes. Serve on slices of toast.

BEANS WITH LEMON BUTTER

500 g green beans
60 g butter
2 tablespoons lemon juice
salt and pepper

Top and tail beans and add to saucepan of boiling water. Boil 5 minutes. Drain. Place beans in cold water and leave until cold. Drain. Heat butter in pan. Add beans, toss in butter for 2 minutes while still on stove. Add lemon juice, salt and pepper. Toss beans over high heat until all lemon juice has evaporated and beans are well coated in butter.

MUSHROOMS

500 g mushrooms
2 tablespoons butter
1 cup milk
pepper and salt
1 tablespoon flour
1 slice bacon

Wash and peel mushrooms. Gently cook mushrooms in butter until tender. Add milk, pepper and salt and thicken with flour. Serve hot and garnished with grilled bacon pieces.

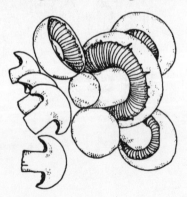

ASPARAGUS MORNAY

½ tin asparagus cuts
³/4 cup White Sauce
   (see page 53)
salt and pepper
1 hard boiled egg
4 tablespoons soft fresh
   breadcrumbs
4 tablespoons grated
   cheese
1 tablespoon butter
parsley

Mix well-drained asparagus cuts with freshly made White Sauce. Season with salt and pepper. Fold in chopped egg. Pour into greased ovenproof dish. Top with breadcrumbs mixed with grated cheese. Dot with butter. Bake in a hot oven (230°C) until top is brown. Garnish with parsley. Serve with brown bread and butter.

CHOKOES

Because we grow a lot of chokoes, we use them extensively.

Peel chokoes, cut them in half and remove seeds. Then cut into even-sized pieces and cook in boiling, salted water until tender. Serve with melted butter or white sauce.

BOILED BEETROOT

Cut tops off beetroot. Wash thoroughly. Place beetroot in saucepan and cover with boiling water. Boil with lid on until tender. Drain. Remove skin. Serve hot or use cold for salads.

BEETROOT FOR SALADS

⅔ cup white vinegar
3 cloves
2 teaspoons salt
1 tablespoon sugar
6 peppercorns
1 bunch Boiled Beetroot
  (see above)

Put vinegar, cloves, salt, sugar and peppercorns in saucepan. Bring to boil and simmer 3 minutes. Drain and cool. Slice beetroot and pour over mixture.

PUMPKIN

This is one of Joh's favourite vegetables, especially if it's mashed.

Peel pumpkin and cut into even-sized pieces, removing seeds. Cover with boiling, salted water and cook until tender. Drain, add butter and pepper and mash well.

Pumpkin may also be baked with roast meat; just chop and cook with potatoes.

POTATO SALAD

When boiling eggs, place a piece of lemon rind in the saucepan to prevent staining.

4 cups diced raw potato
1 onion
2 tablespoons chopped
**   mint**

Dressing:
1 hard boiled egg
**   (chopped finely)**
1 tablespoon sugar
⅔ cup cream
⅓ cup vinegar
salt and pepper to taste

Cook potato until just tender, drain and add finely chopped onion and mint. Mix together and add dressing, mix carefully. Serve chilled.

Dressing:
Mix all ingredients well.

SCALLOPED POTATOES

1 kg potatoes
90 g butter
salt and pepper
1 cup milk
nutmeg
60 g cheese, finely sliced

Peel and finely slice potatoes. Dry slices thoroughly. Smear a shallow ovenproof dish with 30 g butter. Carefully arrange potato slices in layers in the dish, seasoning each layer with salt and pepper. Scald milk and add a little nutmeg, salt and pepper. Arrange cheese on top of potatoes. Carefully pour milk over and add rest of butter, cut into small pieces. Bake in a preheated moderate oven (180°C) for 40–45 minutes or until tender and golden.

THREE BEAN SALAD

**1 cup dried red kidney
  beans**
1 cup dried haricot beans
1 cup dried butter beans
6 cups chicken stock
3 bay leaves
3 sprigs parsley
1 onion, peeled
3 cloves
salt and pepper
**1 red pepper,
  seeded and diced**
6 spring onions, sliced
**3/4 cup French Dressing
  (see page 17)**
chopped parsley

Soak kidney, haricot and butter beans separately overnight in water to cover. Next day, drain and put in separate saucepans. Put 2 cups stock, 1 bay leaf, 1 parsley sprig, ⅓ of the onion, 1 clove and salt and pepper in each pan and bring to boil. Simmer until beans are tender, about 1¼ hours for kidney beans and 1½ hours for haricot and butter beans. Drain, removing seasonings, and chill. Combine beans, spring onions and red pepper in a serving bowl, toss with French Dressing and garnish with chopped parsley.

COLESLAW

Revive a shrivelled capsicum by cutting it in half and removing the seeds. Place capsicum in a jar of water in the refrigerator and it will quickly become smooth and crisp again.

heart of a young cabbage
1 capsicum
1 apple
1 tablespoon chives
stick celery
salt and pepper to taste
1 teaspoon sugar
**French Dressing
  (see page 17)**

Wash and dry cabbage. Shred finely and place in bowl. Chop or cut other vegetables and fruit finely, and mix with cabbage. Add salt, pepper and sugar. Pour dressing over vegetables and mix lightly.

MUSHROOM SALAD

250 g mushrooms
1 red pepper
1 green pepper
4 shallots
1 tablespoon chopped
  parsley
1/4 cup French Dressing
  (see page 17)
salt and pepper

Slice mushrooms. Seed red and green peppers, chop finely. Chop shallots. Combine parsley, French Dressing, salt and pepper. Mix well. Add to vegetables. Toss well.

GREEN SALAD

If lettuce is at all limp, put it into the refrigerator until crisp.

lettuce, or selection of
  salad greens
1/3 cup French Dressing
  (see page 17)
1 clove garlic, crushed
  (optional)
fresh herbs (thyme, chives,
  mint, parsley)

Pull lettuce leaves apart. Wash well, dry thoroughly and tear into bite size pieces. Chop and mix fresh herbs. Place salad greens, herbs and garlic into a salad bowl. Just before serving, sprinkle French Dressing over leaves and toss lightly.

CUCUMBER SALAD

1 large cucumber
1 onion
salt
2 teaspoons lemon juice

Peel cucumber and score down length with fork. Cut into thin slices. Peel onion, slice thinly. Sprinkle salt over cucumber, stand 30 minutes. Drain. Combine cucumber, onion and lemon juice. Mix well.

QUICK SALAD DRESSING

1–2 teaspoons mustard
1 teaspoon salt
1 x 400 g tin condensed milk
an equal amount of vinegar

Mix mustard and salt with a little of the vinegar, add condensed milk. Using the same tin, measure in an equal amount of vinegar, stirring all the time. Allow to stand for a few minutes after it is thoroughly mixed. This dressing keeps for months in the refrigerator.

FRENCH DRESSING

2 tablespoons oil
2 tablespoons vinegar
salt and cayenne to taste

Place oil in container. Add vinegar drop by drop, beating and shaking vigorously till smooth. Season.

EASY HOME MADE MAYONNAISE

1 x 400 g tin condensed milk
an equal amount of olive oil
⅔ of that amount of vinegar
1 teaspoon mustard
½ teaspoon crushed garlic
¼ teaspoon chilli sauce
½ teaspoon salt
2 egg yolks

Beat together all ingredients and store in jars in the fridge. Will keep for months.

MEAT, FISH AND SAUCES

SUNDAY FAMILY DINNER

Every second Sunday, when we have church at eight o'clock in the morning, I love to have our Kingaroy families come home for lunch. Helen and Lester have three children and Ruth and John have three children, so there are twelve of us for midday dinner.

I usually serve roast lamb. I dry cook it by putting a little bit of flour and salt on it and put it on a stand in the baking dish.

I always serve it with roast potatoes, which I cook in very hot vegetable oil in my frypan. I'm very fortunate to have a non-stick frypan, which makes the potatoes lovely and crisp and crunchy.

Joh loves his mashed pumpkin and we also have chokoes, which we grow, and a few carrots and beans.

I make the gravy in the baking dish, draining off the surplus fat and putting in plain flour and gravy mix. I pour in boiling water, mix it all together and let the gravy simmer on the hotplate. I also serve mint jelly with the roast.

To follow that, in summertime I make fruit salad. We have pawpaw and banana, oranges, strawberries if they're in season, ice cream and jelly. My grandchildren just love that.

In wintertime I make apple crumble and custard, with perhaps a little ice cream to suit the grandchildren ... and myself as well!

That's our Sunday dinner and I try to make it on a regular basis whenever I can.

FLO'S BEEF CASSEROLE

A good standby if you are going out for the day. By the time you get home, your meal is almost cooked.

**1 kg round or chuck steak,
    cut into small pieces**
3 tablespoons plain flour
2 onions
2 tomatoes
1 tablespoon soy sauce
**1 tablespoon
    Worcestershire sauce**
1 tablespoon tomato sauce
salt and pepper to taste
2 tablespoons gravy mix

Put steak into a plastic bag with 1 tablespoon of flour and shake well. Put steak into a crockpot. Add finely chopped onions, chopped tomatoes, sauces, salt and pepper. Finally add 1½ cups of water. Cook on high until boiling, then turn down to low. Leave to cook very slowly for about 8 hours. Finally, thicken casserole with a mixture of 2 tablespoons plain flour, 2 tablespoons gravy mix and a pinch of salt blended in a small amount of water.

BEEF NAMBOUR

A recipe from my daughter Meg and called 'Nambour' because two ingredients (the ginger and the pineapples) are grown around the Sunshine Coast/Nambour area. This scenic spot is where Meg lives at present.

500 g diced beef
1 tablespoon plain flour
2 rashers of bacon
1 packet french onion soup
**1 x 440 g can pineapple
    pieces or half a fresh
    pineapple**
**1 pinch ginger or small
    amount of fresh ginger**

Coat beef with plain flour. Brown beef and bacon in a pan. Put beef and bacon in a casserole dish. Add rest of ingredients to casserole dish including the balance of flour. Add water and stir to give a smooth consistency. Cook in a moderate oven (180°–200°C) for 1 hour or until meat is tender. Garnish with parsley and serve with rice or mashed potato.

CORNED BEEF

1 piece corned beef
1 teaspoon vinegar
6 cloves
12 peppercorns

Wash corned beef to remove some of the salt. Weigh and allow at least 40 minutes cooking time for each 500 g. Place meat in a saucepan of warm water, cover and bring to simmering point. Add vinegar, cloves, peppercorns. Boil gently until tender. Serve on a hot plate with parsley, mustard or onion sauce as an accompaniment. If serving cold, allow to cool in water in which it was cooked.

TANGY SWEET CURRY

Serves 6

1 kg lean steak
4 sticks celery
2 large carrots
1 cooking apple
1 large onion
1 large tablespoon plain
   flour
1 dessertspoon curry
   powder
1 teaspoon salt
1 x 440 g tin condensed
   tomato soup
1 tablespoon golden syrup
juice ½ lemon

Cut steak into small pieces and place in saucepan. Dice celery, carrot, apple, and onion. Add to meat. Blend flour, curry powder, salt, tomato soup, golden syrup and lemon juice. Add to meat. Cover saucepan and simmer for 2 hours, or until meat is tender. Serve with rice. This recipe can also be cooked in a pressure cooker.

SAVOURY CURRY

The Queen Mother discovered this dish when on tour of South Africa.

1 kg topside steak, minced
pinch salt
1 onion
1 tablespoon butter
2 tablespoons plain flour
½ cup (approximately) milk
1 dessertspoon curry powder
½ teaspoon mustard
1 tablespoon Worcestershire sauce
1 tablespoon tomato sauce
1 teaspoon vinegar
grated cheese

Place topside in saucepan with salt, chopped onion and a little water. Simmer until cooked, stirring now and then. Melt butter in a saucepan. Add flour and stir for a few minutes. Add sufficient milk to make a thick paste. Mix curry with a little water. Add mustard, Worcestershire sauce, tomato sauce and vinegar. Add to paste and stir. Pour over meat and stir. Place in casserole dish and top with grated cheese. Place in a moderate oven (180°–200°C) until mixture is heated through and cheese topping is brown. Serve with rice and green vegetables.

GOULASH

500 g topside steak
1 tablespoon plain flour
1 onion
1 tablespoon butter
1 cup beef stock or tomato puree
1 small clove garlic
1 teaspoon paprika
½ teaspoon salt
pinch pepper
1 potato

Cut meat into cubes and roll in flour. Peel and slice onion. Brown onion in pan with butter. Add meat and brown. Add stock or puree and balance of ingredients except potato. Cover and simmer for 1½ hours. Peel and cut potato into cubes. Add to dish and cook a further 20 minutes or until potato is cooked. Serve with green vegetables.

SWEET AND SOUR BEEF

1 kg topside beef
1 tablespoon butter
1 onion
½ cup brown sugar
1 dessertspoon
   Worcestershire sauce
salt and pepper to taste
1 x 440 g tin condensed
   vegetable soup
1 dessertspoon soy sauce
¼ cup white vinegar
1 x 440 g tin pineapple
   pieces

Cut meat into squares and brown in a pan with melted butter. Dice onion. Add all ingredients with the exception of the pineapple to meat and simmer until tender, approximately 30 minutes. Then add pineapple and serve with rice.

CORNED BEEF PIE

1 x 375 g tin corned beef
2 tablespoons flour
½ L milk (approximately)
1 medium onion
2 cups grated cheese
6 medium sized potatoes

Keep corned beef in fridge overnight. Slice corned beef and layer in bottom of casserole dish. In a small saucepan, mix flour to a paste with a little milk, then add rest of milk while stirring. Bring to the boil stirring continuously. Add chopped onion and simmer for 5 minutes. Add grated cheese, saving a little for top. Pour cheese sauce over corned beef and place in a slow oven (150°C). Boil potatoes and mash. Place on top of sauce, flatten with fork. Sprinkle remaining cheese on top and bake until lightly brown. Serve with a choice of vegetables.

ROAST BEEF

1 piece beef
vegetables of your choice,
   e.g. potatoes, pumpkin,
   parsnip

Prepare oven. Wipe meat over with a damp cloth. Weigh and allow 30 minutes cooking time for each 500 g. Place in baking dish. Add 1 to 2 tablespoons of fat if very lean. Place in a moderate oven (180°–200°C) and cook gently, basting regularly, for the required time. Bake vegetables under and around the joint for 40 to 45 minutes. When cooked, serve on a hot plate, accompanied by Yorkshire Pudding (see page 56), horseradish sauce or brown gravy.

SAVOURY MINCE PIE

500 g minced steak
2 pinches salt
2 pinches pepper
1 large onion
2 level tablespoons plain
   flour
2 tomatoes
Simple Shortcrust Pastry
   (see page 115)
milk for glaze

Place minced steak, salt, pepper, chopped onion and ½ cup water in saucepan. Allow to cook slowly until meat and onion are thoroughly cooked. Thicken with flour blended in a little water and then allow to cool. Cut pastry into 2 pieces, one a little larger than the other. Roll out larger piece to line a large pie dish. Fill with cooked mince and top with slices of tomato. Cover mince with remaining pastry, first having moistened pastry edges with water. Press edges together firmly. Make a small hole in centre. Brush over with milk. Bake in a moderate to hot oven (200°–220°C) for 30 minutes. Serve hot.

BEEF STROGANOFF

To improve the flavour of parsley and make chopping easier, wash it in hot water beforehand.

500 g rump steak
2 tablespoons oil
2 onions
125 g mushrooms
1 tablespoon flour
1 tablespoon tomato puree
salt and pepper to taste
250 mL beef stock
125 mL sour cream
1 tablespoon chopped
   parsley

Cut steak into 3 cm strips. Fry in oil till brown. Add chopped onions, mushrooms, flour, tomato puree, salt, pepper and stock. Simmer 20–25 minutes. Add cream and heat through. Serve sprinkled with parsley.

SHEPHERD'S PIE

A new version of an old favourite.

3 or 4 rashers of bacon
500 g potatoes, boiled and
    mashed
¼ teaspoon nutmeg
500 g minced meat,
    cooked
2 tomatoes
1 onion
45 g grated cheese
¼ cup breadcrumbs

Fry bacon until crisp. Crumble and add to mashed potatoes, together with nutmeg. Put a layer of cooked mincemeat in an ovenproof dish and cover with sliced tomatoes and grated onion. Add another layer of meat, tomato and onion. Spread potato mixture evenly over and top with cheese. Sprinkle with breadcrumbs. Cook in moderate oven (180°–200°C) until cheese is toasted a golden brown.

CROWN ROAST

12–16 lamb rib chops
    (cutlets left in one piece)

Form chops into circle and tie. Place meat into a greased baking dish. Cover chop ends with foil. Bake in a moderate oven (180°–200°C) allowing 20 minutes for each 500 g. When serving, vegetables or stuffing can be placed in centre.

RISSOLES

Dip rissoles in cold water before rolling them in flour. This will prevent them from cracking.
A tasty recipe for good old minced beef!

1 or 2 onions
500 g minced beef
1 cup breadcrumbs
1 egg
salt and pepper to taste

Chop onions. Combine all ingredients well. Shape mixture into rissoles and fry until well-cooked and nicely browned. I just grease my frypan. Perhaps you might like to roll them in flour and cook in hot vegetable oil.

CASSEROLED MEAT BALLS

125 g minced steak
60 g sausage mince
1 tablespoon finely minced onion
salt and pepper to taste
1 tablespoon plain flour
½ tablespoon gravy powder
1 tablespoon tomato sauce
½ tablespoon Worcestershire sauce
1 medium potato

Mix meats, onion, salt and pepper. Shape into balls, roll in flour mixed with gravy powder. Place in greased casserole. Mix ⅔ cup water with sauces and pour over meat balls. Peel and slice potato, place in casserole. Cook with lid on 35–40 minutes in a moderate oven (180°–200°C).

MINCE CASSEROLE

A favourite dish from my daughter Helen.

500 g mince meat
1 beef stock cube
1 onion
½ cup cooked rice
1 x 440 g tin condensed
    tomato soup
1 cup breadcrumbs
½ cup cheese

Mix together mince meat, stock cube, diced onion, rice and soup. Place in a medium sized casserole dish. Sprinkle breadcrumbs and grated cheese on top of the meat. Cook in a moderate oven (180°–200°C) for 1–1½ hours or until tender. Serve with mashed potatoes and greens.

STEAK DIANE

To tenderise steak, rub with lemon juice, Worcestershire sauce or French salad dressing about an hour before cooking.

4 thin slices of fillet or
    rump steak
2 tablespoons butter
salt and pepper
2 teaspoons chopped
    parsley
1 tablespoon
    Worcestershire sauce
parsley and cooked peas

Beat steak with rolling pin. Heat a thick frying pan, drop in 1 tablespoon butter and, while foaming, put in steak. Cook quickly on both sides, keeping steak flat. Put on to a hot dish, salt and pepper lightly. Reheat frying pan and drop in remaining tablespoon butter. While foaming, add chopped parsley and Worcestershire sauce. Pour over steaks, serve at once and garnish with parsley and peas.

STEAK AND KIDNEY PIE

1 kg chuck or blade steak
2–3 sheep's kidneys
1 tablespoon flour
salt and pepper
½ teaspoon
**   Worcestershire sauce**
¼ teaspoon nutmeg
Rough Puff Pastry
**   (see page 116)**
1 egg, beaten

Cube steak and core and chop kidneys. Sprinkle with flour, salt and pepper. Spoon into a heavy saucepan and cover with water. Cover saucepan tightly and simmer gently over low heat for about 2 hours or until meat is tender. If necessary add a little more water. When cooked, stir in Worcestershire sauce and nutmeg. Spoon mixture into a pie dish, mounding it up in the centre, and allow to cool. Roll out pastry to 2.5 cm larger all round than top of pie dish. Place an extra strip of pastry around rim of pie dish, brush with a little beaten egg and cover with pastry lid. Press to seal and trim edge. Cut air vent in lid and chill for 30 minutes. Brush with egg glaze and bake in a hot oven (200°C) for 20–30 minutes. Reduce heat to 180°C and bake a further 30–30 minutes.

BRAISED STEAK AND ONIONS

750 g braising steak
seasoned flour
1 tablespoon oil
1 tablespoon butter
3 onions, sliced
1 clove garlic, crushed
1½ cups beef stock
1 bouquet garni
salt and pepper

Cut beef into bite sized pieces and dredge with seasoned flour. Brown, a few pieces at a time, in hot oil and butter in a heavy saucepan. Remove meat. Add onions and garlic and cook gently until beginning to brown. Pour off surplus fat, leaving about 1 tablespoon. Add stock and bouquet garni and bring to the boil, stirring once or twice. Add meat, cover tightly and simmer gently for 1½–2 hours or until meat is tender. Remove bouquet garni, adjust seasoning and serve with mashed potatoes.

BEEF POT ROAST

1–1½ kg piece braising
    beef
1 tablespoon oil
1 tablespoon butter
2 large carrots, diced
2 large onions, chopped
2 sticks celery, chopped
1 small turnip, diced
1 bouquet garni
1½ cups beef stock
salt and pepper

Brown meat in hot oil and butter in a casserole. Remove meat. Add vegetables, cover and cook gently for 5 minutes. Place meat on vegetables, add bouquet garni and stock, and season lightly with salt and pepper. Cover and cook in a moderately slow oven (160°C) for 2 hours or until meat is very tender. Remove meat from casserole. Boil down gravy until it is syrupy, then strain. Slice meat, arrange on a heated platter and spoon gravy over.

APRICOT STEAK CASSEROLE

Serves 8–9

¾ cup dried apricots
2 kg topside steak in one
    piece
1 tablespoon cooking oil
salt and pepper to taste
1 dessertspoon grated
    lemon rind
1 cup diced celery
1 onion
2 teaspoons cornflour

Wash and soak apricots in 1 cup water overnight. Heat oil in a large pan and brown meat on all sides. Drain. Season meat and place in casserole with 2 tablespoons water, lemon rind, celery and sliced onion. Cover and cook in a moderate oven (180°–200°C) for 2 hours or until tender. Add soaked apricots together with liquid and cook for a further 10 minutes. Lift meat and apricots from casserole. Thicken gravy in casserole dish with cornflour. Blend in a little water and add seasoning to taste. Replace meat and cook for a further 10 minutes.

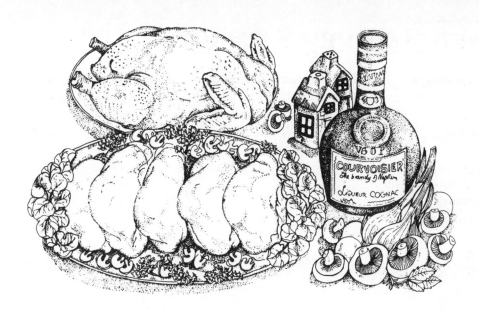

WIENER SCHNITZEL

4 veal steaks
salt and pepper
2 tablespoons plain flour
1 egg
4 tablespoons
    breadcrumbs
oil for frying
lemon slices

Flatten steaks will rolling pin until very thin. Season with salt and pepper. Dip into flour, then into beaten egg and, finally, into breadcrumbs. Heat oil in pan. Cook veal until golden brown. Serve with lemon slices.

PORCUPINES

1 roll of packaged sausage
    meat
½ cup rice
1 medium onion
1 x 440 g can condensed
    tomato soup

Place sausage meat in a large bowl. Half cook rice, rinse with cold water. Add rice and finely diced onion to meat, mix well. Roll mixture into rissole size balls. Roll porcupines in flour to prevent sticking if desired. Place in a casserole dish. Mix tomato soup with same amount of water and pour over porcupines. Cook in a moderate oven (180°–200°C) for about 1 hour. Serve with vegetables.

BRAISED SAVOURY SAUSAGES

½ kg cooked sausages
2 tablespoons butter
2 large onions
2 large tomatoes
1 teaspoon sugar
salt and pepper to taste
½ teaspoon crushed garlic
½ teaspoon mixed herbs
1 dessertspoon cornflour

Melt butter in pan. Add finely chopped onion and cook until tender. Add finely chopped tomatoes, sugar, pepper, salt, garlic and herbs. Cook until tomatoes are soft. Blend cornflour with ¼ cup water. Add to mixture. Add sausages and warm again. Serve with mashed potatoes.

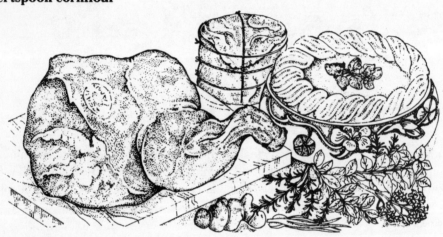

CURRIED SAUSAGES

8 sausages
1 large onion, chopped
¼ cup diced celery
1 cooking apple, peeled
    and diced
1 clove garlic, crushed
1–2 tablespoons curry
    powder
2 tablespoons flour
2 teaspoons tomato paste
2 cups chicken stock
salt and pepper

Prick sausages, place in a baking dish and bake in a preheated moderately slow oven (160°C) for 15–20 minutes or until well cooked. Drain sausages, reserving 3 tablespoons of fat. Place fat in a saucepan and fry onion, celery, apple and garlic until soft. Add curry powder and fry for 2 minutes. Blend in flour and tomato paste, then gradually add stock, stirring constantly until boiling. Season with salt and pepper. Add sausages to sauce and simmer until heated through.

TOAD IN THE HOLE

1 cup plain flour
½ teaspoon salt
2 eggs
1 cup milk
750 g sausages
60 g mushrooms
30 g butter

Stir flour and salt together. Place in blender with eggs and milk, blend for 30 seconds or until well combined. Leave to stand 1 hour or overnight. Put sausages in saucepan with cold water to cover, bring to boil, simmer 5 minutes then drain. Prepare a hot oven 230°C. Grease a 7 cup ovenproof dish. Wipe mushrooms with damp cloth and then slice. Melt butter in small pan and sauté mushrooms over low heat for 2–3 minutes. Blend batter once more. Arrange sausages in dish and pour in batter. Top with mushrooms and bake in oven for 50 minutes or until the batter has risen well and has a golden crust. Serve hot with vegetables.

SWEET AND SOUR PORK

500 g pork
1 egg, beaten
½ cup cornflour
oil for frying

Sauce:
oil for frying
½ teaspoon green ginger
1 cup pineapple pieces
½ cup red capsicum
½ cup cooked carrot
   pieces
2 tablespoons lemon juice
1 tablespoon sugar
1 dessertspoon tomato
   sauce
1 dessertspoon cornflour
1 teaspoon soya sauce
½ cup chopped shallots
½ cup cooked beans

Cut pork into bite sized pieces, dip in beaten egg, then roll in cornflour. Fry in oil until browned and cooked through. Keep hot.

Sauce:
In a pan, fry ginger, pineapple, chopped capsicum and carrots together in oil. Mix all other ingredients, except shallots and beans, in a bowl until smooth. Add 1½ cups water, then add this mixture to the mixture in the pan. Simmer, stirring continuously, until all ingredients are cooked. Finally add shallots and beans. Pour sauce over pork pieces and serve.

PORK FORK DINNER

500 g pork fillet
1 tablespoon oil
1 small onion, chopped
2 cups chopped celery
¾ cup rice
**½ green capsicum,
    chopped**
**1 x 440 g can condensed
    cream of mushroom
    soup**
**1 x 440 g can condensed
    cream of chicken soup**

Cut pork into bite sized pieces and brown in oil. Add all other ingredients to pan plus 1½ soup cans water and mix together. Cook very slowly for approximately 1½ hours. Stir occasionally to prevent catching and make sure that moisture is not absorbed too rapidly.

SCOTCH EGGS

When boiling eggs, to prevent shells from bursting, add a dash of vinegar or a piece of lemon to the water.

5 eggs
500 g pork sausage meat
breadcrumbs
oil for frying

Hard boil 4 eggs and beat up the fifth. Peel boiled eggs and cover entirely with well-seasoned sausage meat. Dip in beaten egg and breadcrumbs and fry in deep oil for 10 minutes. Serve hot with good gravy or cold with salad.

PORK CHOPS IN ORANGE SAUCE

6 pork chops
plain flour
salt and pepper to taste
3 tablespoons butter
2 oranges
pinch ginger
1½ tablespoons sugar

Coat trimmed chops with seasoned flour. Brown chops in butter in a large pan. Grate the orange's rind and squeeze juice. Combine rind, juice, sugar and ginger. Pour over chops. Place in a covered casserole dish. Bake in a moderate oven (180°–200°C) for 1 hour. Serve with vegetables.

PICKLED PORK

Delicious served as part of a cold meat platter.

1½ kg pickled belly pork
2 carrots, sliced
1 onion, sliced
6 black peppercorns
2 cloves
2–3 stalks parsley
3 tablespoons wine vinegar

Soak pork in cold water for 3–4 hours. Drain, put in a saucepan with fresh cold water to cover and add remaining ingredients. Bring to simmering point, skimming off scum, then cover pan and simmer gently for 1½–2 hours or until very tender. Drain pork, cool slightly and slip out bones. Place in a flat dish, cover with plastic wrap and press with a weight until cold. Chill, then remove to a fresh plate or cover with fresh wrap. Serve in thin slices with hot English mustard and vinegar.

PORK CHOPS CASSEROLE

Serves 8

8 pork chops
½ teaspoon salt
½ teaspoon sage
4 cooking apples
½ cup seedless raisins
½ cup brown sugar
2 tablespoons plain flour
1 tablespoon vinegar

Brown chops in hot oil. Place in casserole dish and sprinkle with sage and salt. Peel and core apples and slice into rings. Place apple rings and raisins on top of chops and sprinkle with sugar. Add flour, vinegar and 1 cup hot water to oil in pan. Blend and cook until thick. Pour over chops. Bake uncovered in a moderate oven (180°–200°C) for 1 hour.

BAKED LOIN PORK

To ensure a crisp crackling on pork, dampen the rind and rub with salt before cooking in a hot oven.

2 kg pork loin
vegetable oil
potatoes
onions
pumpkin

Score skin with sharp knife. Brush with vegetable oil. Bake in moderate oven 180°C for 40 minutes. Add vegetables, all peeled and quartered, to roast. Cook for further 1½ hours. Serve with gravy.

POTATO, ONION AND HAM DISH

8 large potatoes
4 large onions
1½ cups of shredded ham
   or small pieces of ham
   offcuts
salt and pepper to taste
600 mL cream

In an ovenproof dish layer finely sliced potatoes, finely sliced onions and ham. Sprinkle with pepper and salt. Pour cream over dish. Bake in moderate oven (180°–200°C) for 1 hour.

EGG AND BACON PIE

2 sheets Rough Puff Pastry
   (see page 116)
6–8 eggs
250 g bacon
2 tablespoons parsley,
   chopped
milk for glaze

Line base of 20 cm pie plate with 1 sheet of pastry. Break eggs into pie plate. Add chopped bacon and parsley evenly through eggs, being careful not to break egg yolks. Place remaining pastry on top and trim edge. Brush milk over top. Bake in hot oven (240°–250°C) for 15 minutes, reduce heat to moderate (180°–200°C), cook for further 15 minutes or until well browned. Serve hot or cold.

IRISH STEW

If soups or stews are too salty, add some potato.

4 lamb neck chops
2 tablespoons flour
salt and pepper to taste
4 potatoes
1 onion

Wipe chops with damp cloth and remove skin, gristle and fat. Mix flour, salt and pepper on a plate. Dip each chop in seasoned flour. Place ¼ cup water in a saucepan and pack chops into it. Sprinkle any remaining seasoned flour over the chops, add a further 1 cup water and bring quickly to simmering point. Cook gently for 45 minutes. Peel and cut potatoes into pieces about 5 cm square, slice onions into thin rings. Place onions on meat, potatoes on top. Allow to simmer gently 1 hour longer. Serve on a hot plate, first lifting potatoes out, then chops. Pour gravy over.

ROAST LAMB

This is Joh's favourite baked dinner.

1 leg of lamb (size depending on people catered for)
seasoning if desired (herbs, garlic, rosemary)
salt and pepper

Trim meat if necessary and remove shank. Coat leg with required seasoning and place in baking dish with approximately 2½ cm water in the base. Water will evaporate as meat is cooking and will be replaced with juices and dripping from lamb. Bake in a moderate oven (180°–200°C) for 50 minutes to each kilogram (thick joints) or 40–45 minutes (thin joints). Turn meat when half cooked.

Vegetables such as potatoes or pumpkin may be baked with meat. Allow from ¾ to 1 hour for these to cook. When meat and vegetables are done lift meat onto a hot serving dish. Drain vegetables on absorbent paper and sprinkle with salt and pepper. Keep hot while making Brown Gravy (see page 52) and serve. Mint Sauce (see page 54) can also be used as an accompaniment.

BRAISED LAMB SHANKS

Serves 4

4 lamb shanks
1 clove garlic
1 tablespoon plain flour
2 tablespoons oil
1 cup vegetable stock
1 bay leaf
salt and pepper
4 medium carrots
2 onions
1 cup chopped celery
2 tomatoes
1 cup peas
**1 tablespoon chopped
   fresh mint**

Insert slivers of garlic into each shank with a sharp knife, dust each with flour and brown in oil in heavy based pan. Add stock, bay leaf and seasoning to pan. Bring to boil then lower heat and simmer until shanks are tender, approximately 1½ hours. Add sliced carrots, chopped onions and chopped celery to pan 30 minutes before serving; add peeled and chopped tomatoes, mint and peas 15 minutes before cooking is finished. Adjust seasoning if necessary. Serve with steamed new potatoes.

BOILED CORNED LEG OF MUTTON

Serves 4–6

1 leg of mutton (corned)
6 peppercorns
4 cloves
1 tablespoon vinegar
1 tablespoon brown sugar
1 bay leaf
4 small onions
2 medium carrots
1 swede
1 parsnip

Wash meat and trim if necessary. Use a saucepan large enough to immerse meat. Place in pot with water to cover, add flavourings. Bring slowly to boil and simmer with lid on until cooked. Allow 2 hours for joints under 1½ kg and 2½–3 hours for joints over 1½ kg. Prepare vegetables, cut into serving pieces and add to pot ½ hour before serving. Lift meat and vegetables onto serving dish. Serve with mashed potatoes and broccoli or cabbage with root vegetables. Mustard Sauce (see page 51) may be served separately.

Note   If joint is to be served cold, allow to cool in the liquid it was cooked in.

Boiled Leg of Lamb

1 leg of lamb
1 tablespoon vinegar
4 peppercorns
1 carrot
4 small onions
1 turnip
salt to taste

Trim meat. Bring enough water to cover meat to the boil. Immerse meat in boiling water, add vinegar and peppercorns, bring to boil again, cover with lid and reduce heat. Simmer for 2½–3 hours. Prepare vegetables, cut into bite sized pieces and add, with salt, ½ hour before serving. Serve with Parsley Sauce (see page 53).

Lamb Casserole

2 tablespoons butter
6 lamb chops
2 onions
1 cup rice
1 x 425 g tin tomatoes
chicken or beef stock (may
    be made with cubes)
salt and pepper to taste
1 tablespoon brown sugar
2 slices bread
½ cup grated cheese

Heat 1 tablespoon butter in a big pan. Remove fat from chops. Brown chops on both sides and put aside. Fry sliced onions until just cooked. Remove. Place rice in greased ovenproof dish, drain tomatoes, add sufficient stock to tomato liquid to make up 2 cups. Bring stock to boiling point. Add to rice. Add salt and pepper. Place chops on rice, top with cooked onion, tomatoes and brown sugar. Cover and cook in moderate oven (180°–200°C) for 35 minutes or until chops and rice are tender. Cut bread into small pieces. Combine bread, cheese and remaining butter, sprinkle over chops and bake in oven until cheese is melted.

ECONOMICAL TASTY LAMB DISH

2 kg neck lamb chops
1 x 500 g jar pasta sauce
¼ cup Worcestershire
  sauce
¼ cup soy sauce
¼ cup barbeque sauce
½ teaspoon crushed garlic
½ teaspoon dried Italian
  herbs
1 dessertspoon sugar
2 large onions, diced

Trim fat from chops and put in large non-stick boiler. Add all ingredients and stir to mix. Bring to boil and simmer gently for about 1 hour or until chops are tender. Serve with pasta, rice or boiled or mashed potatoes.

TANGY CHOPS

Very tasty.

1 tablespoon butter
6 lamb stewing chops
¼ cup vinegar
¼ cup brown sugar
½ teaspoon salt
¼ teaspoon pepper
½ teaspoon ground ginger
1 dessertspoon cornflour
½ cup orange juice
1 teaspoon grated orange
  rind
1 teaspoon grated lemon
  rind

Melt butter, brown chops in frypan. Add vinegar, sugar, salt, pepper, ginger. Cover and simmer for 30 minutes. Remove chops. Add 1 cup of water to pan. Blend cornflour with juice and rind. Add to pan and stir until mixture thickens. Pour sauce over chops and serve with rice or mashed potatoes.

DELICIOUS SAVOURY CHOPS

My mother-in-law's favourite.

6 lamb stewing chops
1 tablespoon vegetable oil
2 onions
2 carrots
**2 tablespoons tomato
    sauce**
2 tablespoons vinegar
2 tablespoons plain flour
1 teaspoon sugar
½ teaspoon curry powder
½ teaspoon ground ginger
½ teaspoon mustard
½ teaspoon mixed spice

Brown chops in pan with vegetable oil. Put chops in casserole. Add chopped carrots and onions. Mix tomato sauce, vinegar, flour, sugar, curry powder, ground ginger, mustard, mixed spice with 2 cups of water. Pour over chops. Cook in a moderate oven (180°–200°C) for 1½–2 hours or until tender. Serve with mashed potatoes.

CHICKEN IN WHITE WINE

1 chicken
½ cup plain flour
1 teaspoon thyme
salt and pepper
oil
250 g mushrooms
8 small onions
1 small carton cream
¾ cup white wine

Cut chicken into pieces. Roll in flour seasoned with thyme, salt and pepper. Fry in oil until chicken is brown. Place chicken pieces in a large ovenproof dish. Arrange mushrooms and onions around chicken. Mix together wine and cream. Add mixture to chicken. Cover dish and bake in a moderate oven (180°–200°C) for 40 minutes. Turn chicken once during cooking. Serve with mashed potato.

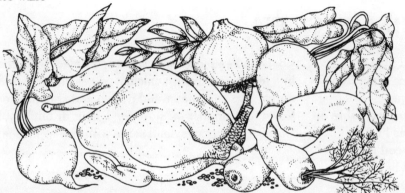

LAZY CURRIED CHICKEN

1 kg chicken pieces
1 dessertspoon mild curry
    powder
1 x 440 g tin skimmed
    evaporated milk
1 x 440 g tin mushroom
    soup

Put chicken pieces into ovenproof dish. Blend curry powder with small amount of milk. Add remainder of milk and mushroom soup stirring well. Pour over chicken pieces. Bake in a moderate oven (180°–200°C) for 1 hour. Uncover dish and brown for 15 minutes. Serve with rice.

BAKED CHICKEN

A tablespoon of sugar sprinkled over a chicken before roasting will help to make the skin lovely and crisp.

1 chicken

Stuffing:
1 small onion
1 cup white breadcrumbs
pinch herbs
1 tablespoon butter
¼ teaspoon salt
pinch pepper
1 tablespoon chopped
    parsley

Fill chicken with stuffing. Bake in a moderate oven (180°–200°C) for 1½ hours or until tender. Vegetables may also be added to meat ½ hour into cooking. Serve with Brown Gravy (see page 52).

Stuffing:
Chop onion and place in bowl with balance of ingredients. Mix well.

SPICED CHICKEN

1 kg chicken pieces
2 tablespoons plain flour
salt and pepper
2 tablespoons vegetable oil
2 tablespoons butter
2 cloves minced garlic
pinch mixed herbs
2 large tomatoes
parsley

Coat chicken pieces with seasoned flour. Heat oil and butter in a heavy pan. Brown chicken pieces all over. Add garlic, herbs, 1½ cups water and peeled and chopped tomatoes. Cover and simmer on stove for 1 hour or until cooked. Garnish with parsley and serve with rice or mashed potato.

Sweet and Sour Chicken

To make a boiling fowl tender, cover with cold water in which a dessertspoon of bicarbonate of soda has been dissolved. Leave to stand overnight, then dry and bake in the same way as a young chicken.

½ cup vinegar
4 tablespoons sugar
1 tablespoon soya sauce
3 rounded dessertspoons
   cornflour
salt and pepper
4 onions
1 red capsicum
2 tablespoons chutney
1 chicken, cooked and cut
   into pieces
cashew nuts

Place vinegar, sugar, soya sauce, 2 cups water, cornflour, salt and pepper in saucepan. Stir over heat until mixture has thickened. Add chopped onions and capsicum. Then add chutney and cook for 2–3 minutes. Heat chicken pieces and put into serving dish. Pour sauce over chicken and serve hot, sprinkle with cashew nuts.

Chicken Marengo

1 kg chicken pieces
2 tablespoons plain flour
salt and pepper
2 tablespoons vegetable oil
2 tablespoons butter
2 cloves minced garlic
pinch mixed herbs
1 ½ cups dry white wine
2 large tomatoes
mushrooms
parsley

Coat chicken pieces with seasoned flour. Heat oil and butter in heavy pan. Brown chicken pieces all over. Add garlic, herbs, white wine and peeled and chopped tomatoes. Cover tightly and cook for 30 minutes. Fry whole mushrooms in a separate pan then add to chicken and gently cook for another 30 minutes. Garnish with chopped parsley when serving.

APRICOT CHICKEN CASSEROLE

1 large chicken
⅓ cup oil
1 packet french onion soup
¼ cup plain flour
1 x 470 g tin apricot
   nectar
2 chicken stock cubes
salt and pepper
cream, optional
parsley

Cut chicken into pieces. Brown in pan with oil. Remove chicken pieces. Add onion soup and flour to pan. Stir until flour is golden brown. Remove pan from heat. Add apricot nectar, 2 cups water, chicken stock cubes, salt and pepper to taste. Return pan to heat, stir until sauce thickens. Stir in cream. Pour sauce over chicken and put in casserole dish. Bake in a moderate oven (180°–200°C) for 1 hour. Garnish with chopped parsley.

CHICKEN CASSEROLE

1 kg chicken pieces
1½ level tablespoons flour
2 level tablespoons butter
2 rashers bacon
1 onion
1 level teaspoon salt
pepper
mushrooms
parsley

Roll chicken pieces in flour and brown slowly in butter in large frypan. Remove from pan and place in large casserole. Put chopped bacon and onion into frypan and cook over a low heat until glossy and transparent. Pour over chicken. Add salt and pepper and sliced mushrooms. Cover and cook in moderately slow oven (160°C) until tender — about 2 hours. Remove any excess fat from casserole. Garnish with chopped parsley. Serve with rice and freshly cooked vegetables and salad.

Flo's Homestyle Tuna Mornay

Serves 6

1 x 425 g tin of tuna
1 cup breadcrumbs
juice of 1 lemon
4 hard boiled eggs
½ cup grated cheese
salt and pepper to taste

Sauce:
60 g butter
1 onion
4 tablespoons plain flour
2½ cups milk

Topping:
4 tomatoes
¼ cup fresh breadcrumbs
½ cup grated cheese
2 teaspoons dried basil
1 tablespoon butter

Drain tuna and flake in bowl. Add breadcrumbs, lemon, eggs (cut into quarters), cheese, salt and pepper to taste.

Sauce:
Melt butter in large frying pan. Add chopped onion and cook in pan until transparent. Stir in flour and cook for 1 minute. Remove pan from heat and stir in milk. Return pan to heat and bring mixture to the boil, stirring until thickened. Add tuna mixture. Pour mixture into a greased ovenproof dish.

Topping:
Slice tomatoes on top of mixture. Sprinkle with breadcrumbs, cheese and basil. Dot with butter. Bake in a moderate oven (180°–200°C) for 20 minutes. Serve with vegetables.

Smoked Cod or Scotch Haddock

250 g scotch haddock or
   smoked cod
juice 1 lemon
1 teaspoon butter

Place fish in a pan and cover with water. Bring to boil and simmer for 10 minutes or until tender. Serve with lemon juice and a dob of butter. If desired White Sauce may also be added (see page 53).

Baked Fish

1 whole fish or 1 small fish
   per person
butter
salt and pepper
lemon

Clean fish. Coat fish with melted butter and then sprinkle with salt and pepper. Cut lemon and put slices on fish. Wrap fish in foil. Cook in a moderate oven (180°–200°C) for 20 minutes or until fish is tender.

STEAMED FISH

1 whole fish or 1 fish fillet
   per person
juice of 1 lemon
salt and pepper
lemon
parsley

Clean fish and wash well. Dry and place on greased plate. Sprinkle fish with salt, pepper and lemon juice. Cover with another greased plate. Place over saucepan of boiling water. Steam for 10 minutes or until tender. Serve with White Sauce (see page 53) and garnish with slices of lemon and chopped parsley.

FISH IN BREADCRUMBS

Joh prefers vegetables, so that's what I usually serve with this dish. Serves 2

2 fish fillets
1 egg
1 cup breadcrumbs
1 cup vegetable oil
1 slice lemon

Beat egg in mixing bowl, dip fish in egg then roll in breadcrumbs. Fry in very hot vegetable oil until golden brown. Serve with lemon and salad or hot vegetables.

FISH PUFFS

½ cup self-raising flour
1 large tablespoon finely
   chopped parsley
1 egg
½ cup milk
salt and pepper
1 cup flaked salmon or
   other cooked fish, cold
2 teaspoons lemon juice
oil for frying

Sift flour and add parsley. Beat egg well and add milk. Stir into flour. Season salmon or other fish with lemon juice and mix through batter. Season with salt and pepper. Drop dessertspoons of mixture into smoking oil and fry until nicely browned. Drain on paper. Serve with Parsley Sauce (see page 53).

TUNA CASSEROLE

This dish is a fast and easy one to prepare for dinner guests and these are the comments my daughter Meg made when she sent me the recipe:

Despite the image of tuna, over the years I have found it to be a popular dish and one that doesn't fail. My husband is a clergyman and we often seem to have guests for meals. When the children were very young there was not a lot of time for elaborate preparations. However, I didn't realise just how often I did use this dish for guests until one day as I was busily opening the tuna and soup my young son casually asked, 'Who's coming to tea tonight, Mum?' After that it became the standard family joke.

1 cup cooked rice
1 teaspoon diced onion
½ cup grated cheese
1 x 425 g tin of tuna
1 x 440 g can of creamy asparagus soup
1 x 150 mL tin of evaporated milk
1 tablespoon butter
3 cups crushed cornflakes

Place rice, onion, cheese, tuna, soup and milk in casserole dish and mix thoroughly. Stand to one side and prepare topping by melting butter and pouring it on top of cornflakes. Spread topping on ingredients in casserole dish and cook in a moderate oven (180°–200°C) for 30–40 minutes.

FISH CAKES

500 g cooked fish
30 g butter
250 g mashed potatoes
2 eggs
salt and pepper
breadcrumbs

Remove skin and bones from fish and chop coarsely. Heat butter in saucepan. Add fish, potatoes, 1 egg, salt and pepper. Stir over heat then allow to cool. Shape into flat cakes. Brush over cakes with beaten egg and cover with breadcrumbs. Bake in a hot oven (200°–230°C) for approximately 20 minutes.

SALMON MORNAY

45 g butter
45 g flour
470 mL milk
125 g cheese, grated
salt and pepper
1 x 250 g tin salmon,
    flaked
breadcrumbs
a little extra grated cheese

Melt butter in saucepan. Remove from heat and stir in flour to make a smooth paste. Add milk and return to heat. Cook gently, stirring all the time until sauce begins to thicken. Add cheese and continue to stir until sauce is thick and smooth. Add flaked salmon and mix well. Pour into buttered ovenproof dish, cover with breadcrumbs and a little extra cheese. Brown in a moderate oven (180°–200°C) for 15 minutes.

TUNA PASTA SALAD

350 g pasta shells or bows
1 x 200 g tin tuna, drained
2 small onions, finely
    sliced
2 ripe tomatoes, peeled
    and quartered
2 hard-boiled eggs,
    quartered
10 black olives, stoned
chopped parsley

Dressing:
1 tablespoon tarragon
    vinegar
1 tablespoon sherry
salt and pepper
2 tablespoons chopped
    spring onions
2 tablespoons chopped
    parsley
4 tablespoons olive oil

Cook pasta in boiling salted water until tender. Drain well and cool. Flake tuna lightly with a fork. Mix with cooked pasta, onions, tomatoes, eggs and olives.

Dressing:
Combine vinegar, sherry, salt, pepper, spring onions and parsley in a bowl. Add oil in a stream, beating dressing until it is well combined. Pour dressing over salad and toss gently. Sprinkle with chopped parsley.

DEVILLED KIDNEYS

8 lamb kidneys
2 tablespoons butter
1 medium onion
pinch cayenne
salt
1 tablespoon
   Worcestershire sauce
1 tablespoon chutney
parsley

Soak kidneys in cold, salted water. Skin, remove core then dice. Place butter in saucepan, add finely chopped onion, cayenne and salt to taste. Sauté for a few minutes then add kidney, cook for 5 minutes. Add sauces and 2 tablespoons water and cook for further 10 minutes. Blend well together, adjust seasoning. Serve on buttered toast garnished with chopped parsley.

BAKED LAMB OR OX HEART

hearts (1 per serve)
fresh breadcrumbs
1 onion
1 teaspoon mixed herbs
salt and pepper
1 egg

Wash hearts and soak in cold salted water for ½ hour. Chop onions. Mix all ingredients, excluding hearts, together well. Dry hearts and stuff with mixture. Bake in a moderate oven (180°–200°C) until tender. Serve with vegetables. Hearts may also be sliced and fried.

LAMBS FRY

1 lambs fry
2 tablespoons flour
½ teaspoon salt
pinch pepper
oil for frying
250 g bacon
parsley

Wash liver well. Dry liver and cut in slices about 1 cm thick. Mix flour, salt and pepper on plate, coat each slice of liver in seasoned flour. Heat oil in frying pan. Fry slices of liver slowly for 8–10 minutes, turning frequently. Remove liver, drain on absorbent paper, and pour nearly all oil out of pan. Cook bacon, remove and keep hot. Sprinkle remainder of seasoned flour into frying pan. Stir well until browned, add 2 cups water, and stir until boiling. Strain gravy if necessary and return to pan, add fried liver, and simmer gently 7–10 minutes. Serve liver and gravy on a hot plate, and garnish with bacon and chopped parsley.

TRIPE AND ONIONS

500 g tripe
1 large onion
1 teaspoon salt
1½ cups milk
1 teaspoon butter
pinch cayenne
1½ tablespoons cornflour
1 tablespoon chopped
　parsley

Blanch tripe by covering with cold water in saucepan, bring to boil. Pour off water then add fresh water, sliced onion and salt. Cook until tender (approximately 1½ hours). Strain off water, cut tripe into pieces (2 cm). Add, with milk, butter and cayenne, to saucepan, bring to boil. Add cornflour (blended in a little milk), stir until thickened and cook for 2 minutes. Add parsley. Serve on hot plates with triangles of toast.

BRAINS

This is something that Joh really enjoys.

1 brain per person
salt
lemon juice or vinegar

Wash brains under running water. Soak in cold or tepid water, with salt, for 1 hour. Change water several times during soaking. Divide lobes of brains carefully with a knife. Remove skin very carefully with fingers. Place in a saucepan of cold water. Add a little lemon juice or vinegar. Simmer very gently for 20 minutes. Drain off water. Serve with Parsley Sauce (see page 53).

BRAINS AU GRATIN

cooked brains
　(see above)
1 dessertspoon butter
1 dessertspoon plain flour
½ cup milk
salt
parsley
1 cup brown breadcrumbs

Melt butter in a saucepan. Add flour and mix into a paste. Gradually add milk and stir over heat until thickened. Boil for 1 minute. Cut cooked brains into small pieces and place in sauce. Add salt to taste and a little chopped parsley. Pour into a buttered pie dish, sprinkle with breadcrumbs and place in a moderate oven (180°–200°C). Bake for 20 minutes.

FRICASSEED RABBIT

250 g rabbit
1 small onion
½ teaspoon salt
pinch pepper
1 tablespoon plain flour
⅓ cup milk
parsley

Trim fat. Dice onion. Put meat and onion into saucepan with sufficient water to barely cover them. Add salt and pepper, bring to boil, then simmer gently for 1½ hours. Blend flour smoothly with a little of the milk. Remove meat and onion from saucepan and measure liquid. Return ⅓ cup of liquid to saucepan and add remaining milk. Stir in blended flour carefully, return meat and onion to saucepan, and cook 3 minutes. Serve on a hot plate, and garnish with parsley.

MUSTARD SAUCE

½ cup water in which meat
  has boiled
1 tablespoon mustard
1 egg
1 tablespoon sugar
½ cup vinegar

Mix egg, mustard and sugar together. Add vinegar and water. Heat gently without boiling. Serve with either hot or cold lamb.

BROWN GRAVY

roast meat drippings
2 teaspoons plain flour

Drain almost all fat from baking dish in which meat has been cooked. Mix in flour and allow to brown. Add ⅔ cup of water and stir until boiling.

TARTARE SAUCE

⅓ cup mayonnaise
½ teaspoon finely chopped parsley
1 teaspoon chopped gherkin

Mix all together. Serve with fish.

HOLLANDAISE SAUCE

4 tablespoons vinegar
1 bay leaf
8 peppercorns
3 egg yolks
pinch cayenne
pinch salt
3 tablespoons butter

Put vinegar with bay leaf and peppercorns on to boil. When reduced to half quantity, set aside to cool slightly, then pour on to yolks, slightly beaten. Add cayenne and salt. Return to double saucepan, and stir with wooden spoon, working butter in gradually. Serve with boiled fish, asparagus and grills.

APPLE SAUCE

2 apples
1 teaspoon lemon juice
2 teaspoons butter
1 tablespoon sugar

Peel, core and slice apples. Put in saucepan with lemon juice, 1 tablespoon water, butter and sugar. Simmer till tender. Beat with a wooden spoon until smooth. Serve with roast pork.

BASIC WHITE SAUCE

If your white sauce is too thin, cream an extra tablespoon of flour with 1 tablespoon of butter and stir into the hot sauce. The sauce will thicken without lumps. (Casseroles and gravies can be thickened in the same way.)

2 level tablespoons butter
4 level tablespoons flour
600 mL milk
salt to taste

Melt butter in saucepan. Remove from heat and mix in flour, using a wooden spoon. Add a little of the milk and mix well. Return to stove and gradually add remainder of milk, stirring continuously. Boil for 2–3 minutes. Remove from heat and add salt. Use your basic mixture for any of the following:

PARSLEY SAUCE

Make up Basic White Sauce and then add 2 tablespoons of finely chopped parsley.

ONION SAUCE

Make up Basic White Sauce. Boil 2 white onions in salted water until tender. Drain, chop finely and add to white sauce, mixing well. This is a very good sauce to serve with corned meat.

CHEESE SAUCE

Make up Basic White Sauce then add a pinch of cayenne and 2 tablespoons finely grated cheese. Serve with cauliflower or fish.

HORSERADISH SAUCE

1 root horseradish or
   1 tablespoon powdered
   horseradish
3 tablespoons cream
2 tablespoons milk
1 teaspoon prepared
   mustard
2 teaspoons sugar
¼ teaspoon salt
pinch white pepper
1 tablespoon vinegar

Scrape horseradish finely and mix with cream, milk, mustard, sugar, salt and pepper. Work vinegar in a drop at a time.

CREAM ONION SAUCE

2 tablespoons butter
1 onion
1 dessertspoon plain flour
salt and pepper
1 teaspoon sugar
pinch nutmeg
2 cups milk
1 dessertspoon cream (if
   desired)

Melt butter in saucepan. Add finely chopped onion. Cook until translucent. Take off heat and stir in flour, salt, pepper, sugar and nutmeg. Gradually stir in milk. Return to heat and stir until boiling. Add cream if desired. Serve with steak, chicken, lamb or corned meat.

MINT SAUCE

Fresh mint should be washed well and dried before chopping.

3 tablespoons finely
   chopped mint
2 tablespoons sugar
½ cup vinegar
pinch salt

Place mint, sugar and 2 tablespoons boiling water into a jug. Cover and allow to cool. Add salt and vinegar. Stir well. An excellent accompaniment to roast lamb.

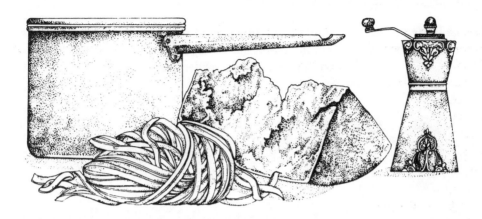

BOLOGNAISE SAUCE

From my daughter-in-law, Karyn.

2 small onions
500 g mince
1 dessertspoon cooking oil
**2 x 440 g tins condensed
    tomato soup**
2 teaspoons curry powder
½ teaspoon salt
2 tablespoons cornflour

Fry onion and mince in heavy pan with cooking oil until brown. Add soup, curry powder and salt to mince. Blend cornflour and ½ soup tin of water together. Add to mixture and simmer for 40 minutes. Serve over pasta.

GARLIC BUTTER

125 g butter
1 clove garlic

Crush garlic then cream butter and garlic together. Use as garnish for grilled chops, roast or steak. Also, spread on a crusty loaf to make garlic bread.

PARSLEY BUTTER

1 tablespoon butter
½ tablespoon parsley

Chop parsley finely and mix with softened butter. Beat until smooth and creamy. Shape into small balls. Makes an excellent garnish for grilled chops or steak.

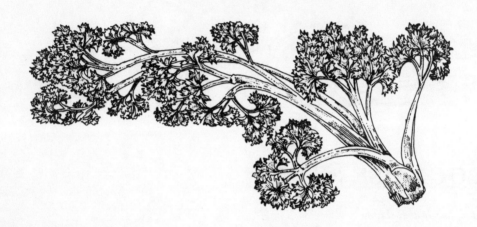

BOILED RICE

Lemon juice added to boiling rice will both whiten and separate the grains.

pinch salt
½ cup rice

Boil 5 cups water and salt. Wash rice if necessary. Add rice to boiling water. Cook until tender, approximately 15 minutes. Strain.

YORKSHIRE PUDDING

1 cup flour
½ teaspoon salt
2 eggs
½ cup water
½ cup milk
1 tablespoon oil

Sift flour and salt into basin. Beat eggs and add to flour. Combine ½ cup water with milk. Gradually mix flour, adding water and milk a little at a time. Beat well with electric beater. Allow mixture to stand for 30 minutes. Heat oil in an ovenproof dish, pour mixture in and bake in hot oven 220°C for 20 minutes or until centre is set and top browned. Cut into squares to serve. Delicious with roast beef.

DESSERTS

LADY FLO'S STOVE

When we were first married, Joh thought it would be nice to give me everything I needed, so he decided to give me two stoves — an electric stove and a wood and coke stove.

Wintertime came and I thought, oh yes, I'll use the wood stove. I tried my hand at cooking on it and it was all right when I was using the top, but when I tried baking things in the oven, they just didn't seem to rise. It was terrible; I just couldn't cook anything properly.

Gradually I started to move over to using the electric stove where I knew exactly what was happening. I said to Joh, 'This wood and coke stove's no good, I'm afraid. I don't think it's working properly.'

After a long time when it was hardly ever used, I decided to sell the wood stove and make a bit more space in the kitchen. A lady down the road, Joyce Snell, said, 'Well, if you're going to sell it, I'll buy it.'

So we sold it to her. And, I hate to say this, but she entered shows and won many first prizes with the cooking she did in the oven of that stove! So I came to the conclusion that it wasn't the stove, it was me!

BASIC FAMILY PUDDING

1 cup self-raising flour
pinch salt
½ cup sugar
1 tablespoon butter
1 egg
½ cup milk

Sift flour and salt into basin. Add sugar. Melt butter and add to flour with egg and milk. Beat at a slow speed until smooth. Use your basic mixture for any of the following:

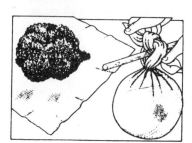

STEAMED PUDDING

Steam Basic Family Pudding for 1 hour in pudding basin with 1 tablespoon jam or golden syrup in bottom of basin. Or steam for 1 hour with choc bits folded through mixture.

FRUIT SPONGE

Pour Basic Family Pudding mixture over stewed fruit, e.g. apples, pears, plums, peaches, and bake in a moderate oven (180°–200°C) for 30 minutes.

BAKED PUDDING

Bake Basic Family Pudding in a moderate oven (180°–200°C) for 30 minutes after sprinkling with a mixture of sugar and cinnamon.

SUNNY DAY PUDDING

Brown sugar will not harden if stored in a plastic container in the freezer.

2 tablespoons butter
¼ cup sugar
pinch salt
½ cup raisins
½ cup milk
1 egg
1½ cups self-raising flour
1 cup brown sugar

Beat butter and sugar. Add rest of ingredients, except the brown sugar, mixing well. Pour mixture into greased ovenproof dish. Dissolve brown sugar in 1½ cups water on stove. Pour over mixture and bake in a moderate oven (180°–200°C) for 30–40 minutes.

BAKED CHOCOLATE PUDDING

If brown sugar hardens, cut up one apple or one slice of bread into cubes and place on top of the sugar.

1 cup self-raising flour
2 teaspoons cocoa
60 g butter
½ cup castor sugar
1 egg
½ cup milk
6 drops vanilla

Sauce:
½ cup brown sugar, firmly
   packed
1 tablespoon cocoa

Grease an ovenproof dish well. Sift flour and cocoa. Cream butter and sugar until light and fluffy. Beat in egg. Add milk to which vanilla has been added and sifted flour alternately. Place in dish. Combine brown sugar and cocoa for the sauce. Sprinkle this on top of the mixture in dish, pour 1¼ cups boiling water gently over all. Bake in a moderate oven (180°–200°C) 45–50 minutes. Serve with custard, cream or ice cream.

LEMON AND ORANGE PUDDING

3 eggs, separated
½ cup sugar
1 cup milk
1 tablespoon self-raising
   flour
2 teaspoons grated orange
   rind
¼ cup lemon juice
¼ cup orange juice
1 extra tablespoon sugar

Beat yolks with sugar until light and creamy. Beat in milk, sifted flour, orange rind, orange and lemon juice. Beat egg whites until soft peaks form. Add extra sugar to whites and beat until dissolved. Fold into mixture. Pour into a greased 1 L ovenproof dish. Stand in a shallow pan of cold water. Bake in moderate oven (180°–200°C) for 1 hour.

SYRUP SPONGE PUDDING

A quick and easy steamed pudding.

1 tablespoon butter
2 tablespoons golden
  syrup
½ teaspoon bicarbonate of
  soda
½ cup milk
¾ cup self-raising flour
pinch salt
desiccated coconut,
  optional

Cream butter and syrup together. Add bicarbonate of soda dissolved in hot milk. Add sifted flour and salt, fold into mixture. Grease a pudding basin with butter. Sprinkle with coconut if desired. Pour in the mixture. Cover with a double thickness buttered greaseproof paper, folding a pleat in this to allow pudding to expand as it cooks. Secure paper with string. Place pudding in a steamer over a saucepan half filled with simmering water, or place basin on an upturned saucer in a saucepan, and fill with boiling water two-thirds up side of basin. Cover pan with a tightly fitted lid and steam for 30 minutes. Serve with hot custard.

IMPOSSIBLE PIE

Absolutely delightful and so simple.

4 eggs
½ cup plain flour
1 cup sugar
2 teaspoons vanilla
½ cup butter
2 cups milk
1 cup desiccated coconut

Blend all ingredients. Pour mixture into a 26 cm greased pie plate. Bake in a moderate oven (180°–200°C) for 1 hour, or until centre is firm. The flour settles to form a crust, the coconut forms a topping and centre is an egg custard filling.

STEAMED CUSTARD

1 egg
1 dessertspoon sugar
¾ cup milk
¼ teaspoon vanilla

Beat all ingredients together, place in a small greased basin covered with foil and steam in saucepan (water half way up basin) for 15–20 minutes.

PERFECT BAKED CUSTARD

Delicious for a dinner party. Can also be kept in fridge and used for desserts for 3–4 days.

1 x 400 g tin condensed
   milk
1 x 400 g tin coconut milk
300 mL cream
8 eggs
1 teaspoon vanilla essence
nutmeg

Add milk, coconut milk, cream, eggs, vanilla and 1 condensed milk tin of hot water to bowl and beat well. Pour into a greased ovenproof dish. Sprinkle with nutmeg. Stand dish in a baking dish of chilled water which reaches half way up the side of the custard dish. Bake in a moderate oven (180°–200°C) for 1 hour, or until set. Use this Perfect Baked Custard mixture for any of the following:

COCONUT CUSTARD

Make up Perfect Baked Custard. Cover base of custard dish with 1 cup desiccated coconut before pouring custard mixture in.

SULTANA CUSTARD

Make up Perfect Baked Custard. Sprinkle base of custard dish with ¾ cup of sultanas.

RICE CUSTARD

Make up Perfect Baked Custard. Sprinkle base of custard dish with 1 cup of cooked rice.

BOILED CUSTARD

6 cups milk
2 dessertspoons sugar
3 tablespoons cornflour
pinch salt
3 teaspoons butter
3 eggs
½ teaspoon vanilla essence

Place milk, sugar, cornflour, salt and butter in a saucepan. Beat eggs in a bowl and add to milk mixture slowly. Bring slowly to the boil, stirring continuously until thick. When cold, flavour with vanilla.

BREAD AND BUTTER CUSTARD

Joh's very fond of this and complains bitterly that since the family has grown up I don't make it as often as I used to.

2 or 3 slices buttered
 bread
½ cup sultanas
½ cup desiccated coconut
2 cups milk
3 eggs, beaten
2–3 dessertspoons sugar
½ teaspoon vanilla
1 tablespoon butter
nutmeg

Grease a pie dish. Into bottom of dish place bread buttered side up with or without crusts, according to your preference. Sprinkle with sultanas and coconut. In a saucepan bring 2 cups milk to boil. Remove from heat and stir in beaten eggs, sugar and vanilla. Pour over bread and butter, sprinkle with nutmeg and dobs of butter. Place in a baking dish of hot water and cook in a slow to moderate oven (150°–180°C) for 30–45 minutes, or until set.

BAKED SAGO CUSTARD

A recipe given to me by my mother and also popular with my children.

1½–2 dessertspoons sago
2 cups milk
1½ dessertspoons sugar
pinch salt
2 eggs
½ teaspoon vanilla essence
nutmeg
1 tablespoon butter

Soak sago in 2 cups water for at least 2 hours. Drain and add 1 cup milk. Boil until thick — approximately 10 minutes. Add further cup of milk, sugar and salt and bring to boil. Beat eggs and vanilla and add to mixture. Put mixture into greased pie dish. Sprinkle with nutmeg and dobs of butter. Stand pie dish in a baking dish of hot water. Cook in a moderate oven (180°–200°C) until set, approximately 30 minutes.

DATE PUDDING

1¼ cups self-raising flour
3 tablespoons sugar
1 cup dates or mixed fruit
1 cup milk
1 teaspoon baking soda
1 large tablespoon butter
1 large tablespoon jam

Mix flour, sugar and fruit together. Dissolve soda in milk with melted butter and jam. Add to mixture. Grease pudding basin, pour in mixture. Stand bowl in a steamer of water and boil for 3 hours. Serve with custard.

SAGO PLUM PUDDING

Sir Joh's favourite dessert.

2 tablespoons sago
1 cup milk
1 tablespoon butter
1 cup brown sugar
1 egg
1 cup raisins
1 cup fresh breadcrumbs
1 teaspoon bicarbonate of
   soda, dissolved in
   1 tablespoon milk
pinch salt

Soak sago in milk overnight. Beat butter and sugar. Add egg, soaked sago, raisins, breadcrumbs, bicarbonate of soda in milk and salt. Mix well. Put mixture in buttered pudding basin and steam for 3 hours.

HINTS FOR BOILED PUDDINGS

1. Pudding can be covered with a cloth.
2. Cloth should be clean and well floured before use. Lay cloth over top of basin and tie with string under the rim.
3. The water should be boiling rapidly when pudding is put in and then should simmer gently.
4. As water boils away, boiling water must be added.
5. Pudding should be allowed to stand for a couple of minutes before being turned out in order that some of the steam can escape, causing pudding to shrink and thus be less liable to break.

STEAMED PLUM PUDDING

This pudding can be enhanced by the addition of a few chopped almonds or walnuts.

2 large tablespoons butter
½ cup brown sugar
2 eggs
grated rind of 1 lemon and juice, or grated rind and juice of an orange
½ cup milk
1 tablespoon golden syrup
1 heaped cup plain flour
1 teaspoon mixed spice
½ teaspoon cinnamon
1 teaspoon baking powder
2 tablespoons desiccated coconut
1 cup sultanas
1 cup raisins
small quantities of mixed peel and glacé cherries
1 teaspoon bicarbonate of soda

Cream butter and sugar. Add eggs 1 at a time, beating each well into mixture. Add lemon or orange rind and juice. Warm milk and syrup together over a low heat until syrup is dissolved. Add to mixture, beating well. Mix flour, spices, baking powder and coconut and add to mixture. Then add fruit. Dissolve bicarbonate of soda in a small quantity of water or milk and add to mixture. Place mixture into a well-buttered pudding basin and steam for 3 hours.

SUPER PLUM PUDDING

Can also be used as a Christmas pudding.

½ cup butter
¾ cup sugar
4 eggs
1 heaped cup breadcrumbs
1 cup raisins
1 cup sultanas
2 tablespoons plain flour
½ teaspoon baking powder
½ teaspoon mixed spice
½ teaspoon nutmeg
1 tablespoon brandy or
    rum
1 tablespoon golden syrup
1 tablespoon jam or
    marmalade
2 tablespoons lemon peel

Cream butter and sugar. Add eggs 1 at a time, beating well. Add breadcrumbs, fruit, sifted flour and baking powder, spices, brandy, syrup, jam and lemon peel. Mix well. Transfer to a well-greased basin, cover and steam for 6 hours. Leave pudding in basin. Replace cover with a clean, dry, well-floured cloth laid over top of basin and tied with string under the rim. Wrap in greaseproof paper and store in a cool place. Steam a further 2 hours on the day of using. Serve with Hard Sauce (see page 79).

CHRISTMAS PUDDING

I'm not very good at cooking Christmas pudding in cloths, so I'm particularly happy with this pudding cooked in a steamer.

500 g butter
500 g brown sugar
4 eggs, beaten
3 tablespoons brandy
500 g mixed fruit
500 g sultanas
125 g raisins
125 g mixed peel
125 g almonds
125 g breadcrumbs
125 g self-raising flour
pinch salt
¼ teaspoon bicarbonate of
    soda
1 teaspoon nutmeg
1 teaspoon mixed spice

Cream butter and sugar. Add beaten eggs and brandy and mix well. Stir in fruit and almonds. Add breadcrumbs, sifted flour, salt, soda, nutmeg and spice. Mix well. Put mixture into a well-buttered pudding bowl and steam for 6 hours. Serve with custard.

APPLE TART

I'm rather partial to apple tart.

4–6 cooking apples
¾ cup sugar
½ cup water
cloves to taste

Pastry:
185 g plain flour
1 level teaspoon baking
   powder
pinch salt
90 g butter
2 level dessertspoons
   castor sugar
1 egg
⅓ cup milk
extra milk for glaze

Place peeled, cored and sliced apples and sugar in saucepan with water. Stew gently until soft. Add cloves to taste. Drain off any surplus liquid before adding to tart.

Pastry:
Sift flour, baking powder and salt into bowl. Rub in butter. Add sugar and mix in. Blend egg with milk and gradually add to mixture. Mix into a dry dough. Turn onto a lightly floured board and knead until smooth. Cut dough into 2 pieces. Roll out 1 piece to line a greased tart plate. Pour in apple mixture. Roll out second piece of pastry to cover apples. Moisten edges of pastry with water and press together to seal. Brush top with milk, prick with a fork and cook in a moderate to hot oven (200°–220°C) for 30–40 minutes. Serve with cream or custard.

BAKED APPLE PUDDING

Another of Joh's favourites.

4 cooking apples
1 cup dates
½ cup sugar
1 dessertspoon apricot jam
1 dessertspoon rum
slivered almonds

Peel and core apples. Stuff with chopped dates. Boil ½ cup water and sugar until sugar dissolves. Add jam and rum and boil a little longer. Place apples in a buttered pie dish, sprinkle with slivered almonds. Pour rum mixture over them and cook in a moderate oven (180°–200°C) until apples are tender. Serve with whipped cream, custard or ice cream.

APPLE PUDDING

Delightful and easy to make and a very nice recipe for winter.

4 cooking apples
1 tablespoon butter
2 tablespoons self-raising
　flour
¾ cup sugar
2 tablespoons desiccated
　coconut
pinch salt

Peel, core and halve apples. Place in a greased pie dish with cut side up. Rub butter into sifted flour. Add sugar, coconut, salt and 1 cup cold water. Mix well. Spoon over apples. Cook for 35 minutes in a hot oven (230°C). Serve hot or cold with custard, cream or ice cream.

APPLE CHARLOTTE

stale bread
1 tablespoon melted butter
1 tablespoon marmalade
500 g apples
½ cup sugar
rind and juice of 1 lemon
1 teaspoon castor sugar
1 teaspoon cinnamon

Cut bread into very thin strips, dip in melted butter, then line pie dish by laying them over bottom and sides, with edges overlapping. Spread marmalade over bread. Partially stew apples with sugar. If there is much juice with apples, strain off most of it before putting fruit into pie dish. Put fruit into dish, add lemon juice and scatter in a little of the grated rind. Cover with bread dipped in melted butter. Bake in moderate oven (180°–200°C) until golden brown (30–40 minutes). Turn carefully onto hot dish, sprinkle with castor sugar and cinnamon. Serve with cream or custard sauce.

APPLE CRUMBLE

A delicious dessert which I make often.

6 cooking apples
6 dessertspoons sugar
2 tablespoons brown sugar
3 tablespoons self-raising
　flour
3 tablespoons desiccated
　coconut
1 tablespoon butter

Peel, core and slice apples. Put in saucepan with sugar and small amount of water and cook until tender. Place apples in a greased pie dish. Put dry ingredients into a bowl, rub butter through the mixture. Sprinkle over apples. Cook in a moderate oven (180°–200°C) for 20–30 minutes or until topping is a golden brown.

BAKED APPLES

When measuring syrup or honey, stick the spoon in boiling water first.

4 apples
½ cup sultanas
125 g sugar
30 g butter
2 tablespoons plain flour
1 tablespoon golden syrup

Peel and quarter apples. Place in greased ovenproof dish with sultanas. Mix sugar, butter, flour and syrup in 1 cup hot water. Pour over apples and bake in a moderate oven (180°–200°C) for 45 minutes. Serve with cream or custard.

APPLE HOT DISH

4–6 cooking apples
1 tablespoon lemon juice
½ cup brown sugar
¼ teaspoon salt
½ teaspoon cinnamon

Put peeled and sliced apples into greased ovenproof dish. Mix all ingredients together and put over apples. Bake in a moderate oven (180°–200°C) for 1 hour. Serve with ice cream.

PEACH MELBA

½ cup sugar
2 cups water
1 vanilla bean
4 fresh peaches
500 g fresh or frozen raspberries
½ cup icing sugar
2 cups Ice Cream (see page 79)

Place sugar, water and vanilla bean in a saucepan over medium heat. Stir until sugar dissolves, then bring to the boil and simmer for 5 minutes. Place peeled peaches in syrup, cover and poach gently for 5–10 minutes until just tender. Remove from syrup, drain and chill, covered. Puree raspberries in a food processor or blender. Gradually add sifted icing sugar until sauce thickens. Pile Ice Cream into individual glass dishes, top with peaches and spoon over raspberry sauce.

PASSIONFRUIT DELICIOUS

If you are worried about milk boiling over, stand a spoon in the saucepan of milk.

1 tablespoon butter
½ cup sugar
2 eggs, separated
2 tablespoons plain flour
2½ cups milk
1 teaspoon vanilla essence
4 passionfruit

Cream butter and sugar. Add egg yolks. Beat well. Add flour and stir until smooth. Add boiling milk, vanilla, stiffly beaten egg whites and passionfruit pulp. Pour into greased pie dish. Stand in a dish of water. Bake in a slow oven (150°C) for ¾ hour.

LADY FLO'S FRUIT SALAD

Queensland is famous for its fruits and this is one way I like to use them. I sweeten the fruit with sugar, because I do not like a sour fruit salad. (Honey is also a lovely sweetener for fruit salad and in addition will prevent apples and bananas from going brown.) My grandchildren love this served with ice cream — and so do I!

pawpaws
bananas
passionfruit
oranges
strawberries
rockmelon
1 tablespoon sugar
juice of 1 orange

Cut up fruit into bite sized pieces. Sweeten with sugar sprinkled over fruit and pour orange juice over.

PEAR PUFF

Another delicious dessert that can be served hot or cold.

1 egg
½ cup sugar
⅓ cup self-raising flour
¼ teaspoon ground ginger
pinch salt
2 medium sized pears
½ teaspoon grated lemon
   rind

Beat egg and sugar together until thick. Sift together flour, ginger and salt and fold into mixture. Add peeled and chopped pears and lemon rind. Turn into a shallow, greased ovenproof dish and bake in a moderate oven (180°–200°C) for 45 minutes. Serve hot or cold with cream or custard.

PINEAPPLE RICE

A beautiful dessert served hot or cold with cream.

1 cup rice
1 level teaspoon salt
1 x 440g tin crushed
   pineapple
1 cup brown sugar
2 eggs, lightly beaten

Bring rice, salt and 1½ cups water to boil in saucepan. Cover lightly and cook over low heat, without boiling, until rice is tender and water is absorbed. Combine rice with rest of ingredients and put into a greased ovenproof dish. Bake in a moderate oven (180°–200°C) approximately 30 minutes.

RICE IMPERIAL

Always presoak gelatine in cold water before using. This softens the grains and helps the gelatine dissolve.

½ cup rice
2¼ cups milk
2 eggs
½ cup sugar
½ teaspoon vanilla essence
1 cup cream
1 tablespoon gelatine

Cook rice in 2 cups water, stirring every now and again, for 30 minutes or until water is almost absorbed. Strain. Add 1¼ cups of milk. Simmer for another 20 minutes or until milk is almost absorbed. Let cool. Soak gelatine in ¼ cup cold water. Beat eggs, sugar, vanilla and rest of milk. Add to rice mix. Boil until it starts to coat the back of a spoon. Add soaked gelatine. Cool in fridge, stirring from time to time. When cold, add whipped cream. Set in fridge.

TROPICAL PARFAIT

2 cups cooked rice
1 x 425 g tin fruit salad
grated rind and juice of
   2 oranges
1 tablespoon sugar or
   honey
1 tablespoon butter
1 cup cream
2 sliced bananas

Combine rice with fruit salad liquid, juice of oranges, rind, sugar and butter in saucepan and heat until liquid is absorbed. When cool, add fruit salad pieces, half the cream and half the bananas. Spoon into parfait glasses. Top with remaining whipped cream and bananas.

TRIFLE

1 Sponge Cake
    (see page 194)
raspberry or apricot jam
½ cup fruit juice
2½ cups milk
2 tablespoons sugar
2 tablespoons custard
    powder
cream
almonds or walnuts
glacé cherries or jelly

Line a serving bowl with slices of sponge. Spread with apricot or raspberry jam. Moisten cake with fruit juice. Make up custard with milk, sugar and custard powder. Pour into bowl, decorate with whipped cream, chopped almonds or walnuts, glacé cherries or chopped jelly.

GOLDEN SYRUP DUMPLINGS

Warm lemons before squeezing and you will get more juice.

2 tablespoons butter
1 cup self-raising flour
½ cup milk approximately
1 tablespoon golden syrup
½ cup sugar
juice 1 lemon

Rub butter into flour. Mix to stiff dough with a little milk. Form into balls. Bring 1 cup water, syrup, sugar and juice to the boil. Drop dumplings into boiling syrup. Cook 20 minutes.

MERINGUES

1 egg white
1 cup castor sugar
½ teaspoon vanilla
1 teaspoon vinegar
1 teaspoon baking powder

Beat egg white until stiff. Add sugar and beat until dissolved. Add 2 tablespoons boiling water and beat until mixture stands in peaks. Add vanilla and vinegar. Fold in baking powder. Drop dessertspoons of mixture onto well-greased paper. Bake in a slow oven (120°C) until dry and firm. Serve with fruit salad and cream.

PAVLOVA

1 teaspoon cornflour
1½ cups sugar
1 teaspoon vinegar
1 teaspoon vanilla
2 egg whites
cream

Mix cornflour with sugar, place in basin with vinegar, vanilla and egg whites, lastly adding 4 tablespoons boiling water. Beat until mixture is very thick and white (about 10 minutes). Cover scone tray with foil, shiny side up, and spread mixture, pushing sides up with knife. Bake in a moderately slow oven (160°–180°C) for 1¼ hours. When pavlova shell is cool, cover with whipped cream and topping of your choice (strawberries, kiwi fruit, chocolate shavings etc).

WALNUT PAVLOVA

3 egg whites
1 cup castor sugar
22 Jatz biscuits
1 packet walnuts

Beat egg whites until stiff. Add castor sugar gradually and beat till dissolved. Fold in crushed Jatz biscuits and chopped nuts (reserve some nuts for decoration). Pour mixture into greased 23 cm pie dish and bake in a moderate oven (180°–200°C) for 30 minutes. Top with whipped cream and decorate with walnuts.

SPANISH CREAM

2 tablespoons butter
½ cup sugar
2 egg yolks
2 cups milk
3 teaspoons gelatine
1 teaspoon vanilla

Beat butter, sugar and egg yolks. Add milk and beat. Put mixture into saucepan and bring just to the boil. Stir to prevent curdling. Allow to cool. Gently mix in gelatine dissolved in a little hot water and add vanilla. Allow to set. This may be served in a bowl or parfait glass with cream or custard.

SAGO

This was a recipe my mother gave me when I married Joh.

3 dessertspoons sago
1¾ cups milk
2 dessertspoons sugar
pinch salt
1 egg
½ teaspoon vanilla

Soak sago in 2 cups water for at least 2 hours. Drain and add milk, sugar, salt, and boil for 5 minutes, stirring well. Beat egg and stir through mixture well. Stand off stove and add vanilla to taste. Serve with fruit.

LEMON SAGO

¾ cup sago
½ cup lemon juice
2 tablespoons sugar
1 tablespoon honey or
  golden syrup

Bring 2 cups water to the boil, add sago and stir until the mixture boils then simmer until cooked (15–20 minutes). Add lemon juice, sugar and honey or golden syrup, cook for 2 more minutes. Put into serving dish and allow to cool. Serve with cream or custard.

ANGEL'S FOOD

1 egg, separated
1 cup milk
2 tablespoons sugar
3 teaspoons gelatine
5 drops vanilla essence

Heat milk and sugar, pour onto egg yolk, and mix well. Return to saucepan, heat gently, stirring well without boiling, until mixture coats the spoon. Cool. Dissolve gelatine in 2 tablespoons hot water. Add to cool custard mixture with vanilla. Beat egg white stiffly and fold lightly into mixture. Pour into wet mould and set. Turn out onto serving dish.

BLANCMANGE

This recipe always brings to mind dinners at my family home at New Farm. It seemed to be the standard dish for a sweet on Sunday. I must admit though, there were other sweets that I liked better in those days — perhaps as you grow up your tastes change.

6 level tablespoons
**　　cornflour**
2 tablespoons sugar
2½ cups milk
½ teaspoon vanilla

Blend cornflour with a little milk. Place remaining milk and sugar in saucepan, bring to the boil. Add blended cornflour, stir until it boils and thickens. Add vanilla and pour into a wet dish or mould to set. Turn out onto serving dish.

JUNKET

1 junket tablet
1½ cups milk
2 teaspoons sugar
nutmeg

Dissolve tablet in 1 teaspoon of water. Warm milk to blood heat. Stir dissolved tablet into milk, pour into glass dish, grate nutmeg on top, and stand in a warm place to set. Allow to become quite cold before serving.

JELLY DELICIOUS

1 packet of your favourite
    jelly crystals
1 egg
½ cup sugar
1 cup milk
2 bananas
2 passionfruit

Dissolve jelly crystals in 1 cup hot water. Stand until cool but not set. Add 1 cup cold water. Beat egg with sugar, add milk. Cut up fruit and add to jelly mixture, then add beaten ingredients, mixing well. Put jelly into fridge and allow to set.

COCONUT JELLY

In warm weather a pinch of bicarbonate of soda in a jelly will help it to set quicker.

1 packet of your favourite
    jelly crystals
1 tablespoon sugar
1 egg, separated
1 tablespoon desiccated
    coconut
2½ cups milk
extra coconut

Put jelly crystals into bowl. Add sugar, yolk of egg, and coconut. Mix well. Boil milk and stir into mixture. Stiffly beat egg white. Add to mixture. Sprinkle coconut on top. Set in refrigerator. Serve with fruit and cream.

CHERRY WHIP

1 packet cherry jelly
5 marshmallows
cream
cherries or nuts

Dissolve jelly in 1 cup boiling water. Add 1 cup cold water. Cool until jelly begins to thicken. Add marshmallows chopped finely. Beat mixture until frothy. Spoon into dishes. Decorate with whipped cream. Top with a cherry or nuts.

WAFFLES

1½ cups self-raising flour
1 egg
1 cup milk
1 tablespoon butter

Sift flour. Beat egg, add milk and melted butter. Make a well in the flour, pour in liquid, mix well, leave to stand for about an hour. Pour into well-heated waffle iron and cook till golden brown.

FRITTER BATTER

For crisp fritters, add a little vinegar to the batter.

1 cup self-raising flour
pinch salt
1 tablespoon butter
1 egg white

Sift flour and salt into bowl. Pour in melted butter. Stir gently. Add ⅔ cup warm water gradually, stirring all the time. Beat into a smooth batter. Beat egg white stiffly. Stir in lightly just before using batter. For a sweet batter add 1 tablespoon castor sugar.

BANANA FRITTERS

If you are short of eggs, use 1 teaspoon of custard powder and a dash of vinegar as a substitute in fritter batter.

4 bananas
Fritter Batter (see page 78)
oil for frying
icing sugar

Peel bananas and cut into 4 pieces. Add bananas to Fritter Batter. Heat oil in pan and fry bananas until golden brown. Drain on absorbent paper. Serve with icing sugar sprinkled on top.

ICE CREAM

When I asked my daughter-in-law, Karyn, for John's favourite recipe she said, 'ice cream, ice cream, ice cream'.

1¼ L milk
1 cup sugar
¼ teaspoon vanilla essence
8 heaped tablespoons
  powdered milk
2 level tablespoons
  gelatine

Place milk in bowl and add sugar and vanilla. Sprinkle powdered milk on top and beat with a rotary beater. Dissolve gelatine in ½ cup boiling water and add to mixture. Pour into freezing trays and place in freezer. When just beginning to freeze, return mixture to bowl. Beat until thick and foamy. Pour back into trays and freeze.

HARD SAUCE

½ cup butter
½ cup icing sugar
1 tablespoon brandy

Cream butter and icing sugar. Add brandy. Blend well and serve with pudding.

CAKES, BISCUITS, SCONES AND PASTRY

My Pumpkin Scones

My pumpkin scone recipe has been responsible for raising a lot of money for charity. I write it out by hand, on my Senate headed paper, the charity has it framed and it is auctioned. It raised $1,000 for Spinacare in Sydney.

George Negus when interviewing me on one occasion at Darwin told me he had a framed pumpkin scone recipe in his kitchen, and he had paid $450 for it at a school auction. But it was once auctioned at a school in my home town of Kingaroy where it only raised $25. I guess a prophet has no honour in her own country!

RICH CHRISTMAS CAKE

Can be made without spirits and keeps very well. I have made it many times during my married life.

625 g plain flour
½ teaspoon salt
500 g seedless raisins, cut in half
500 g sultanas
500 g mixed dried fruit
125 g crystallised cherries, cut into quarters
250 g mixed peel, cut small
125 g almonds, blanched and cut small
1 dessertspoon mixed spice
1 dessertspoon nutmeg
500 g butter
500 g castor sugar
10 eggs
2 tablespoons rum or brandy
grated rind of 1 orange
juice of 1 orange
grated rind of 1 lemon

Prepare 2 deep 20 cm cake tins by lining base and sides with three layers of ungreased brown paper. Allow paper around sides to rise 3½ cm above rim of tin.

Sift flour onto large sheet of paper. Add salt, raisins, sultanas, dried fruit, cherries, peel, almonds, spice and nutmeg. In a bowl, cream butter and sugar until quite white and creamy. Add eggs 1 at a time, beating well after each addition. Add rum or brandy slowly. Then add orange and lemon rind and orange juice. Add dry ingredients and mix thoroughly with a wooden spoon. Put mixture into prepared tins and stab well with a knife. Dip hand in cold water and pat over surface of cakes. This will keep the cakes flat while baking and give a finish. Bake very slowly at 150°C for 1¾ hours. Test by inserting skewer after 1½ hours; if it comes out clean the cake is cooked.

BOILED FRUIT CAKE

This boiled fruit cake is a real favourite of both Joh and myself.

125 g butter
375 g mixed fruit
pinch salt
1 teaspoon cinnamon
1 teaspoon nutmeg
1 teaspoon mixed spice
1 cup sugar
1 teaspoon bicarbonate of
 soda
2 eggs
1 cup plain flour
1 cup self-raising flour
½ cup nuts, either pecan
 or walnuts, optional
2 tablespoons rum,
 optional

Place butter, 1 cup water, mixed fruit, salt, spices, sugar and bicarbonate of soda in saucepan. Boil for 5 minutes. Remove from heat. Add well-beaten eggs, stirring constantly. Sift flours together, fold into mixture and stir well. Mix in nuts and rum. Pour mixture into a 20 cm cake tin which has been lined with buttered greaseproof paper. Cook in a moderate oven (180°–200°C) for approximately 60 minutes. Test by inserting a skewer. If it comes out clean the cake is cooked.

BUNDABERG CHRISTMAS CAKE

This recipe was presented to me by the National Party at Bundaberg on 27 September 1986.

3 cups soft brown sugar
3 cups water
3 teaspoons mixed spice
280 g butter
3 teaspoons baking soda
375 g raisins
375 g sultanas
375 g currants or dates
2 x 375 g packets of mixed
 fruit
4–6 eggs
3 cups plain flour
3 cups self-raising flour
½ cup Bundaberg rum

Place sugar, water, spice, butter, baking soda and all fruit into big saucepan and bring to the boil. Simmer for 20 minutes. Remove from heat and cool until mixture is nearly cold. Add eggs, sifted flour, rum and mix together. Grease and line a large cake tin, at least 25 cm in depth. Cook for 3 hours on low shelf, 1 hour at 150°C and 2 hours at 130°C. Test by inserting a skewer into centre of cake. If it comes out clean the cake is cooked.

LIGHT SPONGE

This is Barbara's sponge recipe. She lives next door to my son, John, at the '10 Mile' and this was a most delicious cake she made for our lunch when I stayed up there.

4 eggs, separated
1 cup castor sugar
¼ teaspoon salt
1 teaspoon baking powder
1¼ cups cornflour
125 g butter

Beat egg whites until white and fluffy. Add castor sugar, salt and egg yolks. Sift baking powder and flour, fold into mixture. Add melted butter and stir gently. Pour mixture into 2 well-greased 18 cm round sandwich tins. Bake in a moderate oven (180°–200°C) for 10–15 minutes, or until cake leaves side of tin. When cool, join together with fresh cream and jam and dust top of cake with icing sugar.

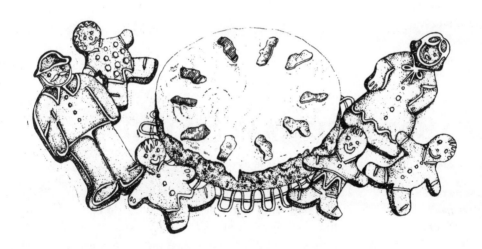

GINGER FLUFF SPONGE

The cake my daughter Ruth uses when she is making birthday cakes for the family — and that includes me.
She puts whipped cream in the centre and on top and decorates it with grated chocolate —
bad for the figure but lovely to eat.

¾ cup cornflour
¼ cup plain flour
pinch salt
½ teaspoon baking soda
1 teaspoon cream of tartar
1 teaspoon ground ginger
1 teaspoon cinnamon
1 teaspoon cocoa
4 eggs, separated
½ teaspoon vanilla essence
1 level cup sugar
1 teaspoon butter
2 tablespoons milk
1 teaspoon syrup

Sift dry ingredients together. Beat egg whites until stiff. Add sugar, yolks and vanilla. Fold dry ingredients into egg mixture gently. Boil milk, add butter and syrup then blend with mixture. Pour mixture into two well-greased 20 cm cake tins. Cook in a moderate oven (180°–200°C) for 15–20 minutes, until cake leaves side of tins. A strip of greased paper on the bottom of the tins makes sure the cake comes out easily.

CINNAMON MELTAWAY SPONGE

To stop a new cake tin from rusting, grease and place in a hot oven for 15 minutes.

4 eggs, separated
¼ teaspoon salt
1 cup castor sugar
½ teaspoon vanilla essence
1 cup plain flour
1 teaspoon baking powder
2 teaspoons cinnamon
2 teaspoons cocoa
4 tablespoons milk
2 level tablespoons butter

Filling:
2 tablespoons butter
1 cup icing sugar
2 teaspoons coffee essence
2 tablespoons walnuts
1 teaspoon warm water

Beat egg whites with salt until thick. Gradually add sugar and beat until sugar has dissolved. Add egg yolks 1 at a time, stirring in well. Add vanilla essence. Sift flour, baking powder, cinnamon and cocoa together thoroughly. Fold lightly into mixture. Heat milk and melt butter in it. Add to mixture and blend well. Pour mixture into 2 greased and floured 20 cm sandwich tins. Bake in a moderate oven (180°–200°C) for 15–20 minutes.

Filling:
Cream butter with sifted icing sugar and coffee essence. If too stiff, stir in 1 teaspoon warm water. Beat well. Add chopped walnuts. When cake is cool, sandwich together with filling. If desired, the cake can be topped with coffee flavoured icing.

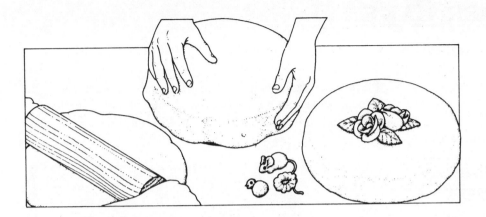

BASIC BUTTER CAKE

A very easy recipe to follow and delicious with your favourite icing.

2 eggs
125 g butter
185 g sugar
250 g self-raising flour
½ cup milk
pinch salt
¼ teaspoon vanilla essence

Beat all ingredients in a bowl for 4 minutes. Pour into a well-greased 18 cm cake tin and bake in a moderate oven (180°–200°C) for 30 minutes.

ORANGE CAKE

I sometimes use this as a recipe for small cakes.

1 cup castor sugar
½ cup milk
125 g butter
pinch salt
2 eggs
1½ cups self-raising flour
rind of 1 large orange

Put sugar and milk into bowl and leave for ½ hour. Add remaining ingredients to bowl and beat for 6 minutes on high speed. Cook in a well-greased 20 cm cake tin in a moderate oven (180°–200°C) for 60 minutes.

VANILLA CAKE

Make up Orange Cake, substituting 1 teaspoon vanilla for orange rind.

WONDER CAKE

My Auntie Dolly's Wonder Cake.

1 cup sugar
125 g butter
2 eggs
6 tablespoons milk
2 cups self-raising flour
1 teaspoon mixed spice
1 teaspoon cinnamon
1 pinch salt
1 x 375 g packet mixed
   fruit

Place all ingredients in bowl and mix well for 4 minutes. Pour mixture into a greased, round cake tin and cook in a moderate oven (180°–200°C) for 45 minutes.

FRANGIPANI CAKE

This is a nice simple cake.

2 tablespoons butter
½ cup sugar
2 eggs, separated
½ cup milk
½ teaspoon vanilla
1 cup self-raising flour
extra ½ cup sugar
1 cup desiccated coconut

Put butter, ½ cup sugar, egg yolks, milk, vanilla and flour in bowl. Beat well for 3 minutes. Place in greased ring cake tin. Beat egg whites until stiff. Add extra sugar. Fold in coconut. Spread on top of cake mixture before baking. Bake in a moderate oven (180°–200°C) for 35 minutes.

EASY CHOCOLATE CAKE

1 cup self-raising flour
1 cup castor sugar
1 teaspoon vanilla
3 tablespoons cocoa
3 tablespoons butter
½ cup milk
2 eggs

Mix all ingredients in a bowl for 4 minutes. Pour mixture into a well-greased 20 cm cake tin. Bake in a moderate oven (180°–200°C) for 45 minutes.

KENTISH CAKE

Before creaming butter and sugar add 1 teaspoon boiling water. It creams much quicker.

125 g butter
125 g sugar
2 eggs
¼ cup milk
1 heaped tablespoon cocoa
185 g self-raising flour
1 heaped tablespoon
    desiccated coconut
1 heaped tablespoon
    chopped peanuts
2 tablespoons sultanas

Icing:
125 g icing sugar
1 dessertspoon butter
1 heaped tablespoon cocoa
few drops vanilla essence
1 teaspoon coffee essence

Cream butter and sugar together. Add beaten eggs, mixing well. Add milk slowly. Blend cocoa with 2 tablespoons boiling water and stir into mixture. Sift flour on top of mixture. Add coconut, peanuts and sultanas and mix in lightly. Put into a greased 25 cm square cake tin and bake in a moderate oven (180°–200°C) for 30–45 minutes. Can also be baked in 2 greased sandwich tins for 20 minutes.

Icing:
Mix icing sugar and butter until smooth. Blend cocoa with 2 tablespoons boiling water and add to mixture. Add coffee and vanilla essence and beat well. Spread icing on cake when cool.

FAMILY SULTANA CAKE

A delicious, moist cake, which keeps well.

500 g sultanas
60 mL orange juice
250 g plain flour
15 g self-raising flour
pinch salt
185 g butter
185 g sugar
1 teaspoon vanilla essence
4 small eggs
90 g blanched almonds

Place sultanas in bowl and sprinkle orange juice over them. Sift together flours and salt. Cream butter and sugar with vanilla essence, until mixture is light and fluffy. Add eggs 1 at a time, beating well after each addition. A little flour may be added with eggs to prevent mixture from curdling. Add sifted flour alternately with sultanas. Lastly, stir in a few chopped almonds, putting remainder aside for decoration. Place mixture in a greased and lined 18 cm deep cake tin with almonds arranged on top. Bake in moderately slow oven (160°C) for approximately 1½–1¾ hours. Cake is baked when a skewer or fork inserted into centre comes out clean.

LEMON CHEESE CAKE

Crust:
125 g butter
2 cups crushed sweet
   biscuits

Crust:
Melt butter, add to crushed biscuits. Press into springform pan.

Filling:
250 g cream cheese
1 x 400 g tin condensed
   milk
½ cup lemon juice

Filling:
Beat cream cheese, gradually add condensed milk, then lemon juice. Pour into biscuit shell and chill.

MADEIRA CAKE

Originally from a friend but I have altered it over the years.

1½ cups castor sugar
2¼ cups self-raising flour
185 g butter
3 eggs
½ teaspoon vanilla

Beat all ingredients plus 1 cup water in large bowl with electric mixer for 4 minutes. Pour into greased 20 cm square cake tin (deep) and bake in a moderate oven (180°–200°C) for 40–45 minutes.

BANANA CAKE

Another of my son John's favourite recipes.

60 g butter
90 g sugar
1 egg
2 mashed bananas
¼ teaspoon bicarbonate of
    soda
2 tablespoons warm milk
125 g self-raising flour

Cream butter and sugar. Add egg, mashed bananas and bicarbonate of soda. Gradually mix in milk and flour alternately. Pour mixture into a well-greased cake tin. Cook in moderate oven (180°–200°C) for 30 minutes.

BRAN CAKE

1 cup Allbran
1 cup sugar
1 cup mixed fruit
1 cup milk
1 cup self-raising flour
125 g butter
2 eggs

Soak Allbran, sugar and mixed fruit in milk overnight. The following morning, add flour, melted butter and eggs. Mix ingredients well and pour into a well-greased loaf tin. Cook in a moderate oven (180°–200°C) for 30–45 minutes or until cooked.

CARROT CAKE

I can recommend this cake, it is a delicious moist one.

2 eggs
1 cup castor sugar
½ teaspoon vanilla
¾ cup vegetable oil
1 cup plain flour
1 teaspoon bicarbonate of
    soda
½ teaspoon mixed spice
½ teaspoon salt
1½ cups finely grated
    carrot
½ cup chopped walnuts

Frosting:
30 g butter
60 g cream cheese
1 teaspoon grated lemon
    rind
1½ cups icing sugar

Combine eggs, sugar, vanilla, oil and beat well. Sift dry ingredients and add to mixture. Add grated carrot and walnuts. Mix well. Pour mixture into a well-greased 20 cm cake tin. Bake in a moderate oven (180°–200°C) for 45–50 minutes.

Frosting:
Melt butter. Add cheese and beat well. Add lemon rind and sifted icing sugar. Continue to beat until icing is nice and smooth.

CINNAMON TEA CAKE

60 g butter
60 g sugar
few drops of vanilla
    essence
1 egg
155 g self-raising flour
pinch salt
½ cup milk

Topping:
1 teaspoon butter
2 dessertspoons sugar
2 dessertspoons desiccated
    coconut
1 teaspoon cinnamon

Beat butter and sugar until creamy. Add vanilla, then add egg and beat well. Sift flour and salt together. Add to mixture alternately with milk. Mix into a soft dough. Pour into a greased and floured 18 cm sandwich tin. Bake in a moderate oven (180°–200°C) for 20 minutes.

Topping:
When cool, brush top with melted butter and sprinkle with a mixture of cinnamon, sugar and coconut.

Coconut Chocolate Cake

2 cups self-raising flour
1 teaspoon baking powder
½ small teaspoon
   bicarbonate of soda
½ cup butter
1 cup sugar
¼ teaspoon salt
½ teaspoon vanilla essence
2 eggs, separated
3 teaspoons cocoa
½ cup desiccated coconut
1 cup milk

Coconut Butter Frosting:
2 tablespoons butter
2 cups icing sugar
3 tablespoons milk
½ teaspoon vanilla essence
desiccated coconut for
   sprinkling

Sift flour, baking powder and bicarbonate of soda together. Blend butter and sugar. Add salt and vanilla. Add egg yolks and beat well. Mix cocoa to a smooth paste with a little warm water. Add to egg mixture and then mix in coconut. Blend in flour alternately with milk, a small amount at a time. Beat until smooth. Beat egg whites until stiff and fold into mixture. Bake in 2 greased 20 cm sandwich tins in a moderate oven (180°–200°C) for 25–30 minutes.

Coconut Butter Frosting:
Cream butter. Gradually work in sifted icing sugar. Add milk and vanilla. Beat well. When cake is cool sandwich together with frosting and also spread frosting on top. Sprinkle top with desiccated coconut.

Coconut Cake

1¾ cups self-raising flour
½ teaspoon salt
125 g butter
1 cup castor sugar
2 eggs
½ cup milk
2 tablespoons desiccated
   coconut

Place all ingredients in bowl. Beat for 5 minutes. Pour mixture into a well-greased deep round or bar tin. Bake in a moderate oven (180°–200°C) for 25–30 minutes.

BELGIAN TEA CAKE

60 g butter
60 g sugar
¼ teaspoon vanilla
1 egg
155 g self-raising flour
pinch salt
½ cup milk
1 apple
1 teaspoon cinnamon
1 extra dessertspoon sugar
1 dessertspoon desiccated
  coconut

Beat butter and sugar together until creamy. Add vanilla, then add egg and beat well. Sift flour and salt together. Add to mixture alternately with milk. Mix into a soft dough. Pour into a greased and floured 18 cm sponge sandwich tin. Peel, core and cut apple into thin slices. Arrange apple slices on top and sprinkle with some of the cinnamon, sugar and coconut. Bake in a moderate oven (180°–200°C) for 20 minutes. When cool, sprinkle with remainder of cinnamon, sugar and coconut.

TEA CAKE

1 tablespoon butter
½ cup sugar
1 egg
½ cup milk
¾ cup mixed fruit
1 cup self-raising flour
extra butter
2 teaspoons castor sugar
1 teaspoon cinnamon

Mix all ingredients well together. Bake in a greased sandwich tin in a moderate oven (180°–200°C) for 30 minutes or until cooked. While cake is still hot rub top with butter. Mix sugar and cinnamon together and spread over cake.

DATE ROLL

¾ cup sugar
1 cup milk
1 tablespoon butter
1 cup dates
1 teaspoon baking powder
¼ cup chopped walnuts
1¾ cups self-raising flour

Put sugar, milk, butter, dates and baking powder in saucepan and bring to the boil. Allow to cool. Add chopped nuts and flour. Pour mixture into a greased slab tin. Bake in a moderate oven (180°–200°C) for 1 hour.

PUMPKIN TEA CAKE

I thought perhaps because I was famous for pumpkin scones, a pumpkin tea cake recipe might be of interest.

250 g butter
¾ cup castor sugar
1 teaspoon grated orange
  rind
2 eggs
½ cup mashed pumpkin
½ cup desiccated coconut
2 cups self-raising flour
¾ cup milk

Icing:
60 g butter
1 cup icing sugar
1 tablespoon milk
¼ teaspoon cinnamon

Beat butter and sugar together. Add grated orange. Add eggs 1 at a time. Add mashed pumpkin and coconut. Stir in sifted flour alternately with milk. Grease a deep 20 cm round cake tin, use greased paper on bottom of tin. Pour mixture into cake tin and cook in a moderate oven (180°–200°C) for 1¼ hours.

Icing:
Mix all the ingredients together in saucepan on stove. Ice cake and sprinkle with coconut.

MUESLI LOAF

90 g butter
½ cup sugar
2 eggs
1 cup muesli (toasted or plain)
1 cup wholemeal self-raising flour
1¼ cups milk
2 teaspoons lemon juice

Beat butter and sugar. Add eggs and beat. Mix in muesli, flour and milk alternately. Add lemon juice. Pour mixture into an 18 cm deep-sided well-greased tin. Bake in a moderate oven (180°–200°C) for 1 hour or until cooked.

DATE AND WALNUT LOAF

1 cup self-raising flour
½ cup sugar
½ teaspoon baking soda
1 teaspoon cinnamon
1 teaspoon mixed spice
½ cup chopped dates
½ cup chopped walnuts
30 g butter

Sift flour, sugar, baking soda, cinnamon and spice into basin. Add dates and walnuts and mix well. Bring butter and ⅔ cup water to the boil in a saucepan. Add hot liquid to mixture, mix thoroughly. Spoon into a greased 25 cm x 8 cm bar tin. Bake in moderate oven (180°–200°C) for 40 minutes.

APRICOT HEALTH LOAF

This healthy loaf is ideal for children's school lunch.

1 cup chopped walnuts or almonds
1 cup dried apricots
1 cup sultanas
¾ cup raw sugar
1 cup Allbran
1½ cups milk
1½ cups wholemeal self-raising flour or 1½ cups wholemeal plain flour
1½ teaspoons baking powder (if using plain flour)

Combine nuts, chopped apricots and sultanas, sugar, Allbran with milk and allow to stand for 2 hours. Then add flour (and baking powder, if using plain flour). Mix well. Bake in a greased loaf tin in a moderate oven (180°–200°C) for 1 hour.

FRUIT LOAF

1 cup mixed dried fruit
¼ cup chopped walnuts
½ cup sugar
1 tablespoon butter
1 level teaspoon baking
   soda
pinch salt
1 egg
1½ cups self-raising flour

Place fruit, walnuts, sugar, butter, baking soda and salt in bowl. Pour ¾ cup boiling water over and mix until butter is melted. Add beaten egg and flour and mix well. Pour into a greased baking tin or loaf tin and bake in a moderate to slow oven (150°–180°C) for 40 minutes.

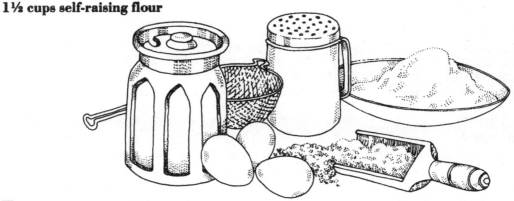

LAMINGTONS

The late Lang Hancock's favourite.

125 g butter
125 g sugar
¼ teaspoon vanilla essence
2 eggs
250 g self-raising flour
pinch salt
½ cup milk

Chocolate Icing:
250 g icing sugar
6–8 level teaspoons cocoa
1 teaspoon butter
few drops of vanilla
   essence
desiccated coconut for
   coating

Beat butter and sugar until creamy. Add vanilla. Add eggs 1 at a time and beat well. Sift flour and salt together. Add flour alternately with milk to the mixture. Turn into a greased and floured lamington tin. Bake in a moderate oven (180°–200°C) for 30 minutes. Allow to cool. Cut cake into squares.

Icing:
Sift icing sugar into a bowl. Blend in cocoa with a little boiling water, add a few drops of vanilla essence. Add butter, mix well, adding a little more boiling water if necessary, until icing is smooth. Dip each cake into icing and then roll in coconut. Set aside until firm.

PATTY CAKES

¾ cup castor sugar
pinch salt
2 cups self-raising flour
125 g butter
½ cup milk
½ teaspoon vanilla essence
2 eggs

Sift all dry ingredients into bowl. Add remaining ingredients and beat for 3 minutes. Spoon mixture into paper patty cups, which have been placed in patty cake tins. Bake in a moderate oven (180°–200°C) for 12–15 minutes.

COCONUT PATTY CAKES

125 g butter
½ cup sugar
1 teaspoon grated orange
   rind
2 eggs
½ cup milk
1½ cups self-raising flour
pinch salt
2 tablespoons desiccated
   coconut

Cream butter and sugar. Add rind, eggs and milk, beat well. Sift flour and salt into mixture and fold in. Add coconut. Spoon into well-greased patty cake containers. Bake in moderate oven (180°–200°C) for 15–20 minutes.

KISS CAKES

¼ cup butter
¼ cup sugar
1 egg
½ cup plain flour
½ cup cornflour
1 teaspoon baking powder
jam
icing sugar

Cream butter and sugar. Beat egg and add to mixture. Add sifted flour, cornflour and baking powder. Stir lightly to make a stiff dough. Put teaspoonfuls of mixture on greased oven slide. Bake in a slow oven (160°–180°C) for about 8 minutes. When cool, sandwich a teaspoon of jam between pairs of cakes and sprinkle with icing sugar.

ROCK CAKES

2 cups self-raising flour
⅓ cup butter
½ cup sugar
½ teaspoon ground ginger
2 tablespoons currants,
**   sultanas, or mixed fruit**
1 egg
3 tablespoons milk

Sift flour. Rub in butter. Add sugar and ginger. Add fruit. Beat egg and add to milk. Add egg and milk to mixture and make into a stiff dough. Place spoonfuls of mixture onto a greased slide. Bake in a hot oven 220°C, for 10–15 minutes. Cool.

BASIC BISCUIT MIXTURE

Should biscuits become soft while stored, place in a moderate oven (200°C) for 5 minutes.

125 g butter
90 g castor sugar
1 egg
250 g self-raising flour

Cream butter and sugar. Add egg and beat well. Add sifted flour to mixture and turn onto a floured board. Knead lightly. Roll out and cut, or alternatively roll into balls, or place in dessertspoonfuls onto a greased tray. Bake in moderate oven (180°–200°C) for 10–12 minutes.

VARIATIONS

Any of the following ingredients can be added to the basic biscuit mixture:

- 2 level tablespoons desiccated coconut
- 90 g sultanas, currants, chopped cherries or chopped peel
- 2 level tablespoons grated lemon or orange rind
- 90 g chopped nuts
- 2 level tablespoons cocoa, as a substitute for the 2 level tablespoons of flour.
- Before cooking, biscuits can be rolled in sugar, rolled into balls and topped with jam or rolled in cereal flakes. After cooking they may be joined together with mock cream or iced with chocolate or lemon icing.

PEANUT CRISP BISCUITS

1 cup sugar
125 g butter
1 egg
¾ cup plain flour
¼ cup self-raising flour
pinch salt
½ teaspoon bicarbonate of
   soda
1 cup rolled oats
¾ cup chopped peanuts
1 cup cornflakes, crushed

Cream butter and sugar, beating well. Add egg. Sift both flours, salt and soda. Add to mixture. Add rolled oats, peanuts and cornflakes and mix well. Place teaspoons of mixture on a greased tray. Press with a fork to flatten slightly. Bake in a moderate oven (180°–200°C) until golden and crisp.

ANZAC BISCUITS

Lovely biscuits made all the better by the addition of Kingaroy peanuts!

125 g butter
1 dessertspoon golden
   syrup
1 heaped teaspoon baking
   soda
1½ cups rolled oats
1 cup self-raising flour
1 cup sugar
1 cup desiccated coconut
½ cup chopped nuts
pinch salt
1 egg

Melt together butter, syrup and baking soda. Add melted ingredients to dry ingredients and mix well. Finally mix in unbeaten egg. Knead mixture for about 5 minutes. Roll into small balls and place on a greased biscuit tray, or alternately, press all of mixture into a large biscuit tray. Bake in a moderate oven (180°–200°C) for 10–15 minutes.

FRUIT CORNFLAKE BISCUITS

A really lovely biscuit.

125 g butter
½ cup sugar
1 egg
1 cup self-raising flour
pinch salt
1 cup mixed fruit
1 cup cornflakes

Cream butter and sugar. Add egg, flour, salt and mixed fruit and mix well. Roll teaspoonsful of mixture into cornflakes. Place onto greased tray and bake in moderate oven (180°–200°C) for 10–20 minutes or until golden brown.

ORANGE CRUNCH BISCUITS

A lump of sugar in your biscuit tin will help to keep biscuits fresh.

125 g butter
125 g brown sugar
½ teaspoon vanilla
grated rind of
   1 large orange
1 egg
185 g self-raising flour
1 cup desiccated coconut
pinch salt

Combine ingredients in a bowl. Beat until blended. Form into 2 long rolls and wrap in greaseproof paper. Chill for 1 hour. Unwrap and cut into 5 mm slices and place on an ungreased tray. Flatten slightly with a fork dipped in flour and bake in a moderate oven (180°–200°C) for 10–15 minutes or until golden brown.

ROLLED OAT BISCUITS

The addition of peanuts gives a lovely nutty flavour.

1 cup desiccated coconut
1 cup rolled oats
½ cup sugar
pinch salt
1 dessertspoon plain flour
½ teaspoon baking powder
½ cup peanuts, optional
125 g butter

Mix together all dry ingredients. Add melted butter and mix well. Press mixture into a well-greased 18 cm sandwich tin. Bake in a moderate oven (180°–200°C) for 25–30 minutes or until golden brown. Cut into slices and cool before removing from tin.

LINCOLN CRISP BISCUITS

Best made with Kingaroy peanuts, of course!

1 cup chopped peanuts
1 cup desiccated coconut
4 cups cornflakes, crushed
pinch salt
2 egg whites
1 cup sugar
1 teaspoon vanilla essence
2 tablespoons butter

Place peanuts, coconut, cornflakes and salt in bowl. Whisk egg whites to a stiff froth and gradually beat in sugar. Flavour with vanilla. Add dry mixture and melted butter. Mix well and place in small heaps on a well-greased tray. Bake in a moderate oven (180°–200°C) until lightly browned.

DATE AND COCONUT SLICE

125 g butter
½ cup sugar
1 cup dates
1 cup desiccated coconut
1 cup self-raising flour
2 tablespoons milk
¼ teaspoon vanilla essence

Cream butter and sugar. Add rest of ingredients and mix well. Press out into greased Swiss roll tin. Bake in moderate oven (180°–200°C) for 20–30 minutes. While still warm, ice with Lemon Icing (see page 249). Allow to set and then cut into slices.

COCONUT SLICE

1 cup self-raising flour
1 tablespoon cocoa
pinch salt
1 cup cornflakes, crushed
½ cup sugar
1 cup desiccated coconut
155 g butter
1 dessertspoon golden
   syrup
½ teaspoon vanilla

Sift flour, cocoa and salt into basin. Add cornflakes, sugar and coconut. Melt butter and syrup together, add vanilla and mix into dry ingredients. Press mixture into greased lamington tray. Bake in moderate oven (180°–200°C) for 35 minutes. When slice is almost cold sprinkle with coconut and cut.

COCONUT BISCUITS

2 tablespoons butter
¾ cup sugar
1 egg
vanilla to taste
1 cup self-raising flour
pinch salt
2 cups desiccated coconut

Cream butter and sugar. Add egg, vanilla, sifted flour, salt and coconut. Mix well. Spoon mixture onto greased trays. Flatten mixture with a fork. Cook in a moderate oven (180°–200°C) until golden brown, approximately 10–15 minutes.

COCONUT MACAROONS

2 cups desiccated coconut
1 cup sugar
2 tablespoons cornflour
pinch salt
2 eggs

Combine dry ingredients in a bowl. Beat eggs and add to ingredients. Mix well. Grease biscuit trays well and use Glad Bake as these biscuits tend to stick. Spoon small quantities onto tray and cook in a slow oven (150°C) for approximately 20 minutes.

COCONUT DROPS

90 g butter
125 g castor sugar
1 egg
1 cup self-raising flour
60 g desiccated coconut
¼ teaspoon lemon essence
glacé cherries

Beat butter and sugar until creamy. Add egg and mix in well. Add sifted flour, coconut and lemon essence. Place teaspoonsful of mixture on a greased tray. Bake in moderate oven (180°–200°C) for approximately 10 minutes. Top with glacé cherries.

APRICOT BALLS

1 cup chopped apricots
½ cup orange juice
4 tablespoons honey
1 cup milk powder
¾ cup chopped almonds or
    peanuts
½ cup desiccated coconut

Simmer apricots, juice and honey for 10 minutes. Add milk powder and nuts to mixture. Stir and cool. Roll into balls and coat with coconut. Store in fridge. Alternatively, roll into logs, coat with coconut and refrigerate. When firm slice.

MONTE CARLO BISCUITS

125 g butter
½ cup sugar
1 egg
2 teaspoons golden syrup
½ teaspoon vanilla
½ cup desiccated coconut
2 cups self-raising flour
pinch salt

Filling:
1 dessertspoon butter
**3 dessertspoons icing
   sugar**
**1 dessertspoon raspberry
   jam**

Cream butter and sugar. Add egg, syrup and vanilla. Beat well. Add coconut, flour and salt. Mix well. Roll teaspoons of mixture into balls. Put onto greased trays. Press down with fork and bake in a moderate oven (180°–200°C) for 10–15 minutes or until golden brown.

Filling:
Cream butter, sugar and jam and sandwich a teaspoon of filling between pairs of biscuits.

MUESLI BISCUITS

**1 cup muesli (toasted or
   natural)**
1 cup sugar
1 cup plain flour
pinch salt
125 g butter
1 tablespoon golden syrup
**1½ teaspoons bicarbonate
   of soda**

Combine muesli, sugar, sifted flour and salt in bowl. Melt butter with syrup over a very low heat. Mix 3 tablespoons boiling water with bicarbonate of soda and combine with butter mixture. Stir into dry ingredients in bowl. Place teaspoons of mixture on a greased tray. Bake in a slow oven (150°C) for 20 minutes or until golden brown.

APRICOT FINGERS

250 g copha
250 g dried apricots
125 g walnuts
3 cups cornflakes
1¼ cups desiccated
   coconut
¾ cup raw sugar
¼ cup full cream milk
   powder

Melt copha over low heat, stirring until just melted. Remove from heat, stir in finely chopped apricots and walnuts. Add the remaining ingredients. Mix well. Press mixture into a greased, paper-lined 28 cm x 18 cm lamington tin. Refrigerate for 2 hours. Remove from tin and cut into fingers.

SHORTBREAD

I have been making this shortbread all my married life. The recipe was given to me by my mother. It is very easy to make, but be sure you don't let it burn.

125 g butter
60 g icing sugar
60 g cornflour
125 g plain flour
good pinch salt

Soften butter. Place in mixing bowl with remainder of ingredients and knead well. Place in a greased 18 cm biscuit tray. Press out and prick with a fork and cook in a moderate oven (180°–200°C) for 30–40 minutes or until golden brown.

CORNFLAKE SHORTBREAD

Shortbread with a difference.

1 cup self-raising flour
1 cup cornflakes, crushed
1 cup desiccated coconut
¾ cup sugar
pinch salt
5 tablespoons butter

Mix all dry ingredients. Melt butter and add to dry ingredients and mix well. Place mixture onto greased Swiss roll tray and press down with a fork. Cook in a slow oven (150°C) for 15–20 minutes. Cut into slices and remove from tray when cool.

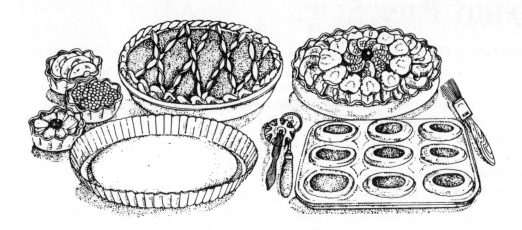

CHERRY MACAROON SLICE

1 x 400 g tin condensed
   milk
250 g desiccated coconut
vanilla to taste
90 g chopped cherries
90 g melted copha
cochineal
packet plain sweet biscuits
30 g extra copha
90 g cooking chocolate

Mix condensed milk, coconut, a few drops of vanilla and the chopped cherries in a bowl. Pour melted copha over mixture with a few drops of cochineal to colour mixture a light pink. Line greased tin with crushed plain sweet biscuits. Press mixture on top of biscuits. Melt remaining copha and chocolate pieces in small saucepan, pour over mixture and spread evenly. Put in fridge to set then cut into slices.

CHERRY NUT SLICE

125 g butter
½ cup sugar
1 egg
vanilla to taste
pinch salt
¼ cup chopped pecan nuts
12 glacé cherries
¾ cup self-raising flour

Melt butter and sugar in pan. When cold add beaten egg, vanilla, salt, nuts, cherries and flour. Spread in a greased biscuit tin and bake in a hot oven (230°C) for 20 minutes. When cold, ice with Lemon Icing (see page 249). Cut in squares.

CHERRY RIPE SLICE

½ packet milk coffee
    biscuits
125 g copha
1 tin condensed milk
1 cup desiccated coconut
100 g cherries
cochineal
½ cup drinking chocolate
90 g extra copha

Cover bottom of 26 cm x 16 cm greased tray with crushed biscuits. Mix melted copha with condensed milk, coconut, chopped cherries, and cochineal. Spread on top of biscuits. Melt extra copha with chocolate, stir a few minutes. Pour over mixture. Set in refrigerator. Cut into squares.

FRUIT OR NUT SLICE

2 cups brown sugar
2 cups self-raising flour
130 g butter
2 eggs
pinch nutmeg
1 cup milk
1 cup peanuts or
    1 cup sultanas

Put sifted flour and sugar into bowl. Rub in butter. Add 1 beaten egg. Press half mixture into a greased 26 cm x 16 cm tin. To the remaining mixture add 1 beaten egg, nutmeg, milk, peanuts or sultanas. Stir and pour over base. Bake in a moderate oven (180°–200°C) for 30 minutes. When cool cut into squares.

HEALTH SLICE

A good recipe for people who like to eat healthily.

¾ cup raw sugar
¾ cup desiccated coconut
1½ cups sultanas
1 cup wholemeal self-
    raising flour
4 tablespoons butter
2 eggs
nutmeg or cinnamon

Mix all dry ingredients (except nutmeg or cinnamon) well. Add melted butter and eggs and mix thoroughly. Spread on a greased tray and sprinkle with cinnamon or nutmeg. Bake for 20 minutes in a moderate oven (180°–200°C) and cut into squares while still hot.

Jelly Slice

Base:
225 g plain biscuit
185 g butter

Filling:
1 x 400 g tin condensed milk
juice of 2 lemons
2 teaspoons gelatine

Topping:
1 packet red jelly

Base:
Mix melted butter into crushed biscuits. Press into base of a 25 cm x 15 cm greased tray.

Filling:
Dissolve gelatine in ¾ cup boiling water. Blend condensed milk with lemon juice and dissolved gelatine. Spread over base and refrigerate until set.

Topping:
Make up jelly according to directions on packet. Cool before pouring over slice. Chill until set. Cut into squares.

Neenish Tarts

20 tart cases (use Shortcrust Pastry see page 117)
2 tablespoons butter
2 tablespoons icing sugar
2 tablespoons condensed milk
2 teaspoons lemon juice

Cream butter and gradually add icing sugar. Beat until fluffy, then slowly add condensed milk and lastly lemon juice. Fill case, ice in 2 colours.

Caramel Slice

125 g butter
125 g sugar
1 teaspoon vanilla
1 egg
125 g self-raising flour
½ cup chopped dates or walnuts

Melt butter, sugar and vanilla. Cool. Add egg and beat well. Add flour and dates and fold in. Pour mixture into well-greased slab tin and bake in a moderate oven (180°–200°C) 20–25 minutes. Cut into slices while still warm and then leave in tin to cool.

CHOCOLATE SQUARES

1 cup self-raising flour
1 cup desiccated coconut
1 cup cornflakes
½ cup brown sugar
1 dessertspoon cocoa
¼ teaspoon vanilla
155 g butter
pinch salt

Mix all dry ingredients. Melt butter and pour over dry ingredients. Add vanilla. Mix well. Press into a greased Swiss roll tin and bake in a moderate oven (180°–200°C) for 20 minutes. While hot, ice with Chocolate Icing (see page 247) and cut into squares. Allow to cool before removing from tin.

CHOCOLATE CRACKLES

250 g copha
1 cup sifted icing sugar
3 heaped tablespoons
    cocoa
1 cup desiccated coconut
4 cups rice bubbles

Melt copha. Combine dry ingredients in good size bowl. Pour copha onto dry ingredients, mix well. Place heaped teaspoons of mixture into paper cups and allow to set.

CHOCOLATE SPIDERS

1 large block dark cooking chocolate
2 tablespoons peanut butter
2 packets crunchy ready cooked egg noodles
½ cup finely chopped crystallised ginger, crystallised cherries or sultanas

Melt chocolate. Stir in peanut butter. Add noodles and fruit. Stir well until chocolate covers everything. Put spoonfuls of mixture on a tray. Set in refrigerator.

FUDGE

½ cup milk
2½ cups sugar
½ cup butter
2 teaspoons cocoa
1 teaspoon vanilla
¼ cup nuts (optional)

Boil milk and sugar until sugar dissolves. Add butter and cocoa and boil for about 20 minutes. Add vanilla and chopped nuts, if used. Remove from heat and beat until quite thick. Pour onto buttered plates and, when set, cut into squares.

PLAIN TOFFEE

2 cups sugar
1 tablespoon vinegar

Place ingredients in saucepan with ¾ cup cold water. Stir over heat until sugar is dissolved. Bring to boil, do not stir. Cook until syrup is golden brown. Remove from heat, allow bubbles to settle. Pour into small paper containers or into a flat greased pan and mark into squares.

HONEYCOMB TOFFEE

**2 tablespoons golden
  syrup
2 tablespoons sugar
1 teaspoon bicarbonate of
  soda**

Boil syrup and sugar for 10 minutes, remove from heat, and stir in soda quickly. While still bubbling, pour onto a greased baking dish.

MARSHMALLOWS

**3 tablespoons gelatine
4 cups sugar
vanilla or lemon essence
icing sugar
cornflour**

Soak gelatine in 1 cup cold water. Bring sugar and 1½ cups hot water to boiling point. Add soaked gelatine. Boil gently 20 minutes. Pour into large mixing bowl, cool and add essence. Beat until thick. Pour into wetted 28 cm x 18 cm slab cake tin. When cold, cut into squares and toss in a mixture of icing sugar and cornflour.

PLAIN SCONES

**2 cups self-raising flour
½ teaspoon salt
2 level tablespoons butter
extra flour for rolling
1 cup milk**

Sift flour and salt into a bowl. Melt butter and pour into flour. Add milk, gradually stirring with a knife until you have a moist dough. Turn onto a floured board. Knead lightly and then press out. Cut to size and place on floured tray. Bake in a hot oven (220°C) for 10–15 minutes.

SWEET SCONES

You can turn these scones into sultana scones by adding 2 tablespoons sultanas to the mixture. There is nothing Joh loves better than a sultana scone.

2 tablespoons butter
½ cup sugar
1 cup milk
1 egg
3 cups self-raising flour
pinch salt

Cream butter and sugar. Add milk, egg, sifted flour and salt. Mix well to a nice soft dough. Cut into squares. Put on a floured and greased tray and bake in a hot oven (230°C) for 10–15 minutes.

PUMPKIN SCONES

Prince Charles has visited Queensland on many occasions and, on his last visit (with the Princess of Wales), the Government gave a State Reception at the Queensland Art Gallery. In his speech Prince Charles said that every time he came to Queensland he found Sir Joh was still the Premier. He wondered whether this was due to the pumpkin scones that his mother had told him about!

1 tablespoon butter
½ cup sugar
¼ teaspoon salt
1 egg
1 cup mashed pumpkin (cold)
2–2¼ cups self-raising flour

Beat together butter, sugar and salt using an electric mixer. Add egg, then pumpkin. Finally stir in, by hand, sifted flour. Turn onto a floured board and cut. Place on a heated floured tray and cook on the top shelf of a very hot oven (225°– 250°C) for 15–20 minutes.

LEMON BUNS

I made this recipe many times when my family was growing up. They loved them!

6 dessertspoon butter
4 tablespoons sugar
2 cups self-raising flour
pinch salt
2 eggs
4 tablespoons milk
2 teaspoons lemon essence
extra sugar

Rub butter into sugar, flour and salt. Add remaining ingredients and mix well. Place in small quantities on two greased trays and sprinkle tops with sugar. Bake in hot oven (220°C) for 10 minutes.

BRAN AND DATE MUFFINS

1 ¼ cups plain flour
1 teaspoon bicarbonate of
    soda
1 teaspoon cinnamon
½ cup sugar
1 ¾ cups unprocessed bran
125 g dates
½ cup oil
1 ½ cups milk
1 egg

Sift flour, soda, cinnamon and sugar. Stir in bran and chopped dates. Make a well in the centre. Add oil, milk and lightly beaten egg. Mix only until combined. Cover and refrigerate overnight. Next day drop spoonfuls of mixture into well-greased muffin tins. Bake in a moderately hot oven (200°–220°C) for 20 minutes. This makes approximately 20 muffins and they are delicious.

BINGA BREAD

My eldest granddaughter, Anna, aged fifteen, gave me this recipe and here she explains its origins:

The school that I go to, Immanuel College, runs an outdoor education centre at a place called Mt Binga in the Blackbutt ranges. Grade ten classes stay there for a month at a time and receive education in survival skills including doing all our own cooking, even the bread. This bread is fondly referred to as 'Binga Bread' by all who know Mt Binga. It's wholemeal, healthy and so delicious that I continued to make it after I came home from Binga.

38 mL dry yeast (a
    medicine glass full)
2 teaspoons sugar
1 kg plain flour
500 g fine wholemeal flour
500 g coarse wholemeal
    flour

Combine yeast, ¾ cup warm water and 2 teaspoons of sugar. Mix and let stand until light and bubbly. Add to flour, then add 4 ¼ cups warm water and knead well. Cover with a cloth and place in a warm place to prove. When risen to double its original size, knead and shape into about 3 loaves. Cover with a cloth and prove again. Place in a pre-warmed, moderately hot oven (200°–230°C) for 25–30 minutes until golden brown.

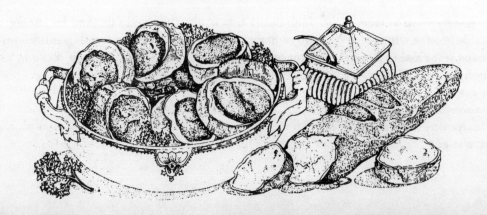

ABLESKEEVER

Joh's favourite Danish recipe.

1 cup plain flour
½ teaspoon salt
2 teaspoons sugar
1 packet yeast
3 eggs
2 cups milk

Place flour, salt, sugar, yeast, beaten eggs and lukewarm milk into a large casserole dish. Allow mixture to stand for 1 hour during which time mixture will rise. Pour into heated greased gem irons. Bake in a hot oven (230°C) for 7–10 minutes.

PIKELETS

A recipe given to me by my twelve-year-old granddaughter, Rachel Folker.

1 cup milk
½ cup sugar
1 egg
½ teaspoon vanilla
1 cup self-raising flour
½ teaspoon baking soda
1 tablespoon butter
extra butter

Beat milk, sugar, egg and vanilla in a bowl. Add sifted flour and baking soda, fold in. Then add melted butter. Mixture should be fairly liquid. Heat pan, grease with a spoonful of butter. Spoon mixture into pan and brown each side of pikelet. Lovely served with butter and homemade jam.

SIMPLE SHORTCRUST PASTRY

A yellow tinted pastry, with a smooth appearance, ideal for savoury pie shells.

1 cup plain flour
⅔ cup butter

Put soft butter with 2 tablespoons of flour and 2 tablespoons water in a deep mixing bowl. Cream these ingredients. Work in remainder of flour to form a manageable dough. Turn onto floured surface and knead lightly until smooth. Chill for 30 minutes. Pastry is cooked in a well-greased pie dish in the centre of a hot oven (220°C) for 15–20 minutes.

SWEET PASTRY

This pastry keeps very well if wrapped in greaseproof paper and stored in the refrigerator. It is ideal for fruit pies.

125 g butter
½ cup sugar
1 egg
few drops vanilla essence
pinch salt
1½ cups self-raising flour
½ cup cornflour

Cream butter and sugar together. Add beaten egg, vanilla and salt and mix well. Sift flour and cornflour and fold into mixture. Turn onto a floured board and knead. Roll out desired quantity. Cook in a moderate oven (180°–200°C) for 15–20 minutes. This recipe makes enough pastry for 4 small or 1 large tart shell. Remainder can be stored.

CHOUX PASTRY

Light shells used for profiteroles, cream puffs and chocolate eclairs.

¼ cup butter
1¼ cups water
1 cup plain flour
3 eggs

Boil butter and water in a saucepan. Remove from stove. Stir in sifted flour all at once and beat until smooth. Return mixture to stove stirring vigorously over low heat until mixture leaves the sides of the saucepan. Allow to cool slightly. Whisk eggs well. Beat into mixture. Force pastry mixture through bag and plain pipe in 5 cm lengths, or put spoonfuls onto greased tray. Bake in a moderately hot oven (200°–230°C) for ½ hour. Pastries may then be dried out for 10 minutes in the turned-off oven.

ROUGH PUFF PASTRY

Rough puff pastry is suitable for all meat pies, sausage rolls and patties.

1 cup plain flour
1 cup self-raising flour
1 egg yolk
few drops lemon juice
¼ cup lard
¼ cup butter

Beat egg, add lemon juice and ½ cup water to egg. Break lard and butter into pieces the size of a walnut and add to sifted flours. Mix into a dough with egg and water. Turn onto a lightly floured board and knead slightly. Roll out square and fold in 3, then in 2. Roll out to size and shape required. Bake in a hot oven (230°–260°C) for approximately 20 minutes. Do not open oven door until pastry has been in 10 minutes.

SHORTCRUST PASTRY

1 cup plain flour
½ teaspoon baking powder
¼ teaspoon salt
1 teaspoon sugar (if used
  for fruit pies)
¼ cup butter

Sift flour, baking powder, salt and sugar. Rub in butter with the tips of fingers till mixture looks like breadcrumbs, lifting it well out of the basin during the process to admit air. Add up to 2 tablespoons water gradually, making into a very dry dough (do not add all water unless necessary). Turn onto a slightly floured board. Roll to shape and size required. Cook in a moderate oven (180°–200°C) for 20 minutes or until golden brown.

FLAKY PASTRY

1 cup plain flour
1 cup self-raising flour
½ cup butter
pinch salt

Sift flour and add salt. Divide butter into 4 equal parts, and rub 1 part lightly into flour with tips of fingers. Mix into an elastic dough with ½ cup water, turn onto a slightly floured board, knead well but quickly. Roll as square as possible and spread on ⅓ of remaining butter, leaving a margin of 5 cm all round. Sprinkle lightly with flour, fold into 3 even folds. Turning pastry so that the open ends are towards you, roll 1 way only — away from you — with light, even pressure. Use remaining 2 parts of butter in the same way. When butter is all rolled in, give the dough 1 extra roll to whatever shape is required. Bake in a hot oven (230°–250°C) for approximately 20 minutes.

ROYAL ICING

500 g icing sugar
2 egg whites
¼ teaspoon lemon juice
1 teaspoon glucose

Sift icing sugar. Place egg whites in basin with lemon juice and glucose. Work icing sugar gradually into the other ingredients until the desired consistency.

MOCK CREAM

Ideal as a substitute for fresh cream.

2 tablespoons butter
4 tablespoons castor sugar
2 tablespoons milk
¼ teaspoon vanilla essence

Beat butter and sugar until light and creamy. Gradually add milk, beating all the time. Add 2 tablespoons water in a steady trickle. Add vanilla essence. Beat until a creamy consistency.

JAMS AND PICKLES

FLO THE DIPLOMAT

During the 1983 State election period miners in a coal mine outside Ipswich were on strike. There appeared to be an impasse. The miners were underground and wanted Joh, who was then Premier, to go down the mine and talk to them. Joh wouldn't agree to this. He suggested they come up and talk to him.

At the time I was listed to campaign for our National Party candidate in Ipswich. He put out a press release that I was to go and talk to the miners, so the commitment having been made, I went.

I made some pumpkin scones in the morning, wrapped them in a Flo pumpkin scone tea towel and away I went, down the mine. I told them Joh wouldn't come down but I suggested they go to the mine face and I would try to get Joh to talk to them there.

Perhaps the scones helped, the miners agreed to my suggestion and I used some wifely persuasion on Joh and the meeting was arranged. Joh then went back down with the miners and the strike was soon over. I call it Pumpkin Scone Diplomacy!

MARMALADE

To ensure success when making jam, the fruit should be firm, sound, and slightly under-ripe. Early fruits are best for jam-making. Generally, 1½ cups of sugar are used to each 500 g of fruit. To test if cooked: place a small quantity on a saucer and let cool. If cooked it will gel and wrinkle when moved.

2 medium oranges
1 lemon
1 kg sugar

Wash and slice fruit thinly; remove seeds. Place in a container, cover with 2 L water, and let stand overnight. Boil fruit and water until rind is soft, about 1 hour. Add sugar all at once, stir until dissolved. Boil until it will gel when tested. Bottle in warm jars and seal.

PLUM JAM

Peaches, apricots or nectarines may be used instead of plums.

2 kg plums
1½ kg sugar

Wash plums, remove stones if possible. Cook with a little of the sugar until fruit is tender. Add remaining sugar. When sugar is dissolved, cook rapidly until jam gels when tested. Pour into warmed jars and seal.

RASPBERRY JAM

Strawberries or blackberries may be used instead of raspberries.

500 g raspberries
1½ cups sugar

Remove stalks from berries and place in saucepan. Cover with sugar and allow to stand about 1 hour. Place over low heat, stir occasionally until sugar is dissolved. Boil till jam gels when tested. Bottle in warm jars and seal.

DRIED APRICOT JAM

2 cups dried apricots
1½ kg sugar

Wash apricots. Cover with 2 L water and allow to soak overnight or until soft. Bring to the boil, cook gently until tender. Add sugar. Stir carefully until sugar is dissolved. Cook quickly until mixture gels when tested. Pour into warmed jars. Seal and label.

BLACK CURRANT JAM

1 kg black currants
3 cups sugar

Boil black currants and 2 cups water for 30 minutes, or until soft. Add sugar, and boil until jam gels, approximately 30 minutes. Bottle in warm jars and seal.

RHUBARB AND PINEAPPLE JAM

1 large bunch rhubarb
1 x 440 g can pineapple
6 cups sugar

Cut rhubarb into short pieces but do not strip unless very stringy. Cut up pineapple finely and add to rhubarb. Boil together for 10 minutes, add sugar, and boil until mixture gels when tested. Bottle in warm jars and seal.

LEMON CURD

3 eggs
90 g butter
1 cup sugar
rind and juice of 2 lemons

Whisk eggs and put into a basin with butter, sugar, finely grated lemon rind and juice. Place basin over a pan of boiling water, stir until mixture is thick and smooth. Pour into clean, warm jars and cover.

CHOKO CHUTNEY

We grow chokoes on 'Bethany'.

1 kg chokoes
½ tablespoon salt
2 cups vinegar
30 g chillies
4 cloves garlic
30 g whole ginger
50 g brown sugar
⅔ cup sultanas

Peel chokoes and cut into long strips. Sprinkle with salt and let stand overnight. Boil vinegar, add chokoes, and simmer till soft. Cut chillies, garlic and ginger into small pieces. Add, with sugar and sultanas, to chokoes and vinegar. Simmer gently until rich brown in colour — about 2 hours. Bottle in warm jars and seal when cool.

TOMATO RELISH

12 large ripe tomatoes
4 large onions
1 tablespoon salt
2 cups sugar
vinegar
1 tablespoon curry powder
½ tablespoon mustard
5 chillies
cayenne to taste

Cut tomatoes and onions to size of walnuts, sprinkle with salt and stand overnight. In the morning, drain off liquid, boil for 5 minutes with sugar and sufficient vinegar to cover. Add other ingredients and boil for 1 hour. When cool, bottle and seal.

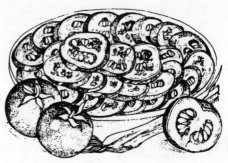

PICCALILLI

1 kg mixed vegetables, e.g.
   cauliflower, cucumber,
   shallots and young
   kidney beans
60 g cooking salt
2½ cups vinegar
15 chillies
1 cup granulated sugar
60 g mustard
15 g turmeric
2 level tablespoons
   cornflour

Cut vegetables into small pieces. Place in large bowl and sprinkle with cooking salt. Leave to stand for 24 hours and then drain well. Boil vinegar and chillies for 2 minutes, allow to stand for ½ hour and then strain vinegar. Mix together sugar, mustard, turmeric and cornflour and blend with a little cooled vinegar. Bring remainder of vinegar back to the boil, pour over the blend, return to saucepan and boil for 3 minutes. Remove from heat and fold in the strained vegetables. Pack into prepared jars and cover at once with vinegar-proof covers.

PICKLED ONIONS

4 kg pickling onions
sugar
vinegar, brown and white

Wash jars thoroughly. Put 1 teaspoon sugar in bottom of every jar. Place peeled onions in jars and fill with half brown vinegar and half white vinegar. Seal jars and store for approximately 4 weeks before eating.

BEVERAGES

Motto On My Wall

'Home where each lives for the other
And all live for God'

LEMONADE

juice of 6 large lemons
4 cups sugar
grated rind of 3 lemons
1 tablespoon citric acid
2 teaspoons epsom salts

Strain lemon juice, add to other ingredients. Pour 900 mL water over, stir till dissolved. Cool and bottle. Dilute with water for drinking. Keeps indefinitely.

GINGER BEER

2 lemons
2½ cups sugar
25 g bruised whole ginger
1 teaspoon cream of tartar
1 tablespoon brewers yeast

Pare lemons as thinly as possible, strip off every particle of white pith. Cut lemons into thin slices, removing pips. Put sliced lemons into bowl with sugar, ginger and cream of tartar and pour in 6 L boiling water. Allow to stand till lukewarm, then stir in yeast, and leave in moderately warm place for 24 hours. Skim yeast off top, strain carefully and bottle, tying corks down securely. Leave for 2 days before drinking. Ginger Beer may be stored for up to 1 year in a cool place.

ICED COFFEE

3 teaspoons instant coffee
1 tablespoon sugar
2 cups milk
ice cubes
vanilla ice cream
½ cup cream, whipped
1 tablespoon grated
   chocolate

Place coffee powder and sugar in a jug, add 2 tablespoons hot water, stir until coffee is dissolved. Pour in milk, add a few ice cubes. Place a dessertspoon of vanilla ice cream in bottom of each glass. Pour in milk mixture. Place a tablespoon of whipped cream on top of each glass. Sprinkle a teaspoon of grated chocolate over cream.

ICED TEA

**6 teaspoons tea or
    6 teacup bags
½ cup sugar
¾ cup lemon fruit juice or
    juice of 3 lemons
ice cubes
mint sprigs
lemon wedges**

Infuse tea with 3 cups boiling water, add sugar. When cold add 3 cups cold water, fruit juice or lemon juice. Keep in fridge. Serve over ice cubes, decorate with sprigs of mint and lemon wedges.

EGG FLIP

**1 egg, separated
1 teaspoon sugar
flavouring
⅔ cup warmed milk**

Mix egg yolk and sugar thoroughly. Beat white until quite stiff. Add yolk and sugar, then flavouring and milk. Mix well. Pour into a tumbler and serve.

Classic Country Baking

Contents

PASTRIES

Of all the pies in the world I like to make
Apple Pie (see p. 146) best of all. However, any fruit
can be used to make a delicious fruit pie. The key
to making a successful pie is the pastry,
which has to be made from a good
shortcrust recipe.

Biscuit or Champagne Pastry

Use as required for sweet dishes, particularly fruit pies and slices.

1¼ cups self-raising flour
1 tablespoon cornflour
pinch of salt
⅓ cup butter
1 egg
¼ cup sugar

Sift flours and salt. Rub in butter. Mix into a dry dough with beaten egg and sugar. Turn onto a floured board and roll out lightly. Use as required.

Cream Cheese Pastry

2 cups plain flour
pinch of salt
cayenne pepper
125 g butter
90 g cream cheese
1 egg yolk
squeeze of lemon juice
1 tablespoon water

Sift flour, salt and pepper into bowl. Cut butter and cream cheese into small pieces, rub into flour. Mix lightly beaten egg yolk, lemon juice and water together. Add to flour and butter mixture to form a dough. Knead lightly to smooth dough. Chill, then use as required.

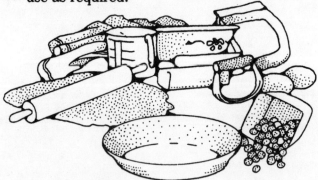

Quick Shortcrust Pastry

2 tablespoons butter
¾ cup cream
¾ cup self-raising flour
¾ cup plain flour
pinch of salt

Melt butter, combine with cream. Add to sifted flours and salt. Mix well and roll out.

Australian Meat Pies

One recipe I just had to include! Makes 8 individual pies.

Filling
750 g minced steak
2 beef stock cubes
2 cups water
salt and pepper
pinch of nutmeg
2 tablespoons plain flour
1¾ cups extra water
1 teaspoon soy sauce

Base
2 cups plain flour
½ teaspoon salt
⅔ cup water
60 g beef dripping

Top
double quantity
  Rough Puff Pastry
  (see p. 116)
1 egg yolk
1 teaspoon water

Filling   Place meat into pan, stir over low heat until well browned. Drain off surplus fat. Add crumbled stock cubes, water, salt, pepper and nutmeg. Stir until boiling. Reduce heat, cover, simmer gently for 20 minutes. Remove from heat. Combine flour and extra water, stirring until smooth. Add flour mixture to meat, stir until combined. Return to heat, stir until meat boils and thickens. Add soy sauce (for brown colour), stir until combined. Simmer, uncovered, for 5 to 10 minutes, remove from heat, allow to become cold.

Base   Sift flour and salt into basin. Place water and dripping into saucepan, stir until dripping melts. Remove from heat. Make a well in centre of dry ingredients, add liquid, and stir until combined. Turn out onto lightly floured surface, knead lightly. Roll out pastry to line 8 greased pie tins. Cut excess pastry from sides. Fill centres with cold meat filling.

Top   Roll out puff pastry on lightly floured board, cut out rounds for pie tops. Use filling as a guide. Wet edges of base pastry, and gently press tops into place. Trim around edges with sharp knife. Pierce centre with pointed knife. Brush top with combined egg yolk and water. Bake in a hot oven (200°–230°C) for 5 minutes or until golden brown. Reduce heat to moderate (180°–200°C) and cook for a further 10 minutes.

Cornish Pasties

250 g minced steak
1 potato, peeled and diced
1 onion, peeled and diced
1 tablespoon chopped
parsley
1 teaspoon salt
pinch of pepper
double quantity Rough Puff
Pastry (see p. 116)
milk for glazing

Mix together steak, potato, onion, parsley, salt and pepper. Divide into 6 or 8 equal parts. Knead pastry until smooth. Cut into 6 or 8 pieces, and roll each piece into a circle. Place mixture onto each pastry piece. Wet edges of pastry halfway round with water. Turn into a half-moon shape, and join pastry edges together by pinching into a small frill. Place onto a greased flat tin. Glaze with milk. Bake in a hot oven (220°C) for 10 minutes, then reduce heat (100°–120°C) for 20 minutes.

Sausage Rolls

Always handy if you have a crowd.

1 onion, finely chopped
500 g sausage mince
salt and pepper to taste
Rough Puff Pastry
(see p. 116)
1 egg, beaten

Mix onion, meat, salt and pepper. Roll pastry out thinly and divide into 2 strips about 10 cm wide. Trim edges. Form mixture into 2 neat rolls and place each roll on a strip of pastry. Brush edges lightly with egg, fold pastry over sausage mince and seal it to opposite edge. Cut each roll into 12 sections. Place sausage rolls on a greased baking tray and make 2 diagonal slashes on top of each roll. Brush tops with remaining egg. Chill for 20 minutes. Bake in a preheated, very hot oven (230°C) for 10 minutes, then reduce heat to moderate (180°C) and cook for a further 10 minutes.

Savoury Cheese Pie

3 bacon rashers
2 large onions
1 tablespoon water
2 teaspoons butter
Cream Cheese Pastry
(see p. 132)
3 eggs
1 cup cream
1 cup tasty cheese
salt, pepper and nutmeg

Remove bacon rind and grill until crisp. Drain and crumble. Peel and slice onions finely, place in saucepan with 1 tablespoon water and butter and cook until transparent. Cool. Roll pastry and line 23 cm pie plate. Sprinkle bacon on bottom of pie shell. Lightly beat eggs, add cream, cooled onions and three-quarters of the grated cheese. Season to taste with salt and pepper and remaining cheese. Bake in a hot oven (200°–230°C) for 10 minutes. Reduce heat to moderate (180°–200°C) for a further 35 minutes.

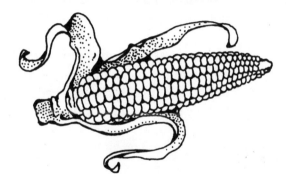

Sweetcorn and Potato Pie

half quantity
Quick Shortcrust Pastry
(see p. 132)
3 medium potatoes
1 onion
1 cup diced ham
1 x 310 g tin sweetcorn
kernels
salt and pepper
2 eggs
¾ cup milk
chopped parsley

Line a 23 cm pie plate with pastry. Peel and slice potatoes and onion. Sauté ham and onion, add sweetcorn and season with salt and pepper. Place in unbaked pie crust. Arrange potatoes on top in overlapping slices. Beat eggs with milk and pour over the potatoes. Add chopped parsley. Bake in a moderate oven (180°–200°C) for about 40 minutes or until set.

Beefsteak Pie

500 g lean beefsteak
seasoned plain flour
2 onions, peeled and finely
    chopped
stock or water
Flaky, Rough Puff or
    Shortcrust Pastry
    (see pp. 116–117)
egg or milk

Trim all gristle and fat from meat, cut into small cubes and roll in seasoned flour. Mix chopped onion and meat, place into a saucepan, adding enough water to cover. Cover and cook gently for 1½–2 hours or until tender. Cool completely. Roll pastry thinly and cut three-quarters of it into shape to line greased tin. Fill pie dish to about three-quarters with meat. Cut lid from remaining pastry, dampen edges and press into place. Cut a vent in the top to allow steam to escape. Chill for 15 minutes, then brush with beaten egg. Bake in a preheated hot oven (200°C) for 25 minutes or until pastry is puffed and golden.

Variations   1 cup diced, peeled potato can be added to the meat and onions halfway through the initial cooking. Half a cup peeled and diced sheep's kidney can be added to the meat/onion mixture.

Seafood Pie

Serves 4 to 6

125 g mushrooms
2 tablespoons butter
1 small finely chopped
    onion
1 clove crushed garlic
½ teaspoon dried oregano
2 tablespoons plain flour
1½ cups milk
2 tablespoons lemon juice
salt and pepper
425 g tin of tuna or salmon
    or 500 g fish fillets
Rough Puff Pastry (see p. 116)

Prepare and slice mushrooms. Heat butter and sauté mushrooms, onion, garlic and oregano. Add flour and cook for 1 minute. Gradually add milk, stirring until thick. Add lemon juice and seasonings, fold in fish. Roll out half of pastry and line greased pie dish (20–23 cm). Add filling and top with remaining pastry. Trim edges and flute. Make pastry leaves for top, brush with milk and bake in hot oven (220°C) for 20 minutes or until pastry is golden brown.

Melton Mowbray Pie

An English pork pie to be served with a salad and eaten cold.

Hot Water Pastry
3 cups plain flour
½ teaspoon salt
2 egg yolks
125 g lard
⅔ cup water

Filling
1 veal knuckle
4 cups water
1 large onion
salt and pepper
2 kg large lean pork chops
1 egg yolk
1 tablespoon water

Hot Water Pastry   Sift flour and salt into bowl. Make a well in centre, add yolks, cover with some of the flour. Place lard and water into pan, stir over low heat until lard melts, bring to boil. Pour boiling liquid into flour all at once, then mix to a firm pastry. Turn out onto lightly floured board, knead lightly. Cover pastry, let stand for 10 minutes. Knead again lightly. Roll out two-thirds of pastry to line base and sides to top edge of a deep, greased 20 cm cake tin.

Filling   Cut veal into pieces, and place with veal bones, water, chopped onion, salt and pepper into pan. Bring to boil. Reduce heat and simmer, covered, for 2 hours. Strain stock, skimming off any fat. Set aside. The stock makes the jellied filling for the pie. Remove bones and fat from pork, cut meat into 1 cm cubes. Season with salt and pepper. Pack meat evenly into pastry-lined tin. Spoon over 3 tablespoons of stock. Brush edges of pastry with combined egg yolk and extra water. Roll out remaining pastry to cover pie. Place over meat, press edges of pastry together. Pinch edges to give decorative edge. Cut a circle out of top of pie, approximately 2.5 cm wide. Brush pastry with egg yolk mixture. Bake in a hot oven (230°C) for 30 minutes or until pastry is golden brown. Reduce heat to moderately slow (160°C) for a further 1½ hours. If necessary cover with sheet of brown paper to stop pastry becoming too brown. As juices appear in hole in pastry top, carefully spoon out to stop pastry softening. When baked, remove from oven. Allow pie to cool a little in tin. Heat jellied stock to make a liquid, cool. Using a funnel, pour stock slowly into the hole in pie top so that stock settles to the bottom. Refrigerate.

Hunza Pie

A high-fibre vegetarian dish with a crisp wholemeal pastry.

Wholemeal Pastry
2 cups wholemeal plain
flour
1 teaspoon vegetable salt
1 cup wheatgerm
250 g butter
¼ cup water

Filling
1.25 kg potatoes
vegetable salt to taste
2 tablespoons oil
1 small bunch spinach

Base   Sift flour and salt into bowl, add husks in sifter to flour. Add wheatgerm, lightly mix into flour. Rub in butter until mixture resembles fine breadcrumbs. Add water, mix to a firm dough. A tablespoon or two more of water may be needed. Turn out onto lightly floured surface, knead lightly. Divide pastry in half. Roll out one half to fit 23 cm pie plate.

Filling   Peel potatoes, cut into quarters. Boil until tender, drain. Place cooked potatoes into bowl, mash very lightly. Add salt, oil and washed and shredded spinach. Mix well. Leave until cold. Spoon filling into pastry case, packing down well. Roll out remaining pastry to cover pie dish. Trim and decorate edges. Brush with water, make a few slits in top of pastry. Bake in a hot oven (200°–230°C) for 15 minutes or until pastry is golden brown. Reduce heat to moderate (180°–200°C), cook for a further 15 minutes. Serve hot or cold.

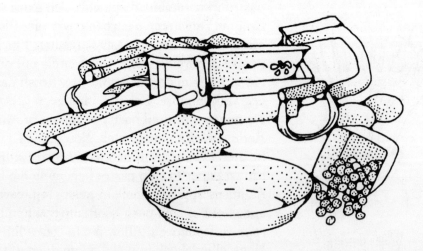

Speedy Spinach Flan

1 sheet ready-rolled
  wholemeal pastry
250 g packet frozen
  spinach, thawed and
  drained
1 cup cream
1 cup grated tasty cheese
3 eggs
1 chopped onion
salt and pepper
1 tablespoon parmesan
  cheese

Thaw pastry and cut to line a 20 cm pie or flan dish. Combine spinach, cream, grated cheese, beaten eggs and onion. Season and mix well. Pour into pastry base. Sprinkle with parmesan cheese. Bake in a moderately hot oven (190°C) for 35 to 40 minutes or until firm.

Quick Quiche

My daughter Helen makes wonderful quiches like this one.

3 eggs
1½ cups milk
1½ cups grated cheese
1 medium onion, chopped
3 rashers rindless bacon,
  chopped
¾ cup Robur pastry mix
salt and pepper to taste
parsley flakes

Place all ingredients in bowl and mix well. Pour into buttered pie dish and bake in hot oven (230°–250°C) for 40 minutes or until lightly browned on top, and knife comes out clean when inserted into centre. (This mixture forms its own light crust when baked.) Sliced tomatoes can be placed on top before baking.

Variations   Any or all of the following can be added:

> 1 small can corn kernels
> ½ cup finely chopped red and/or green
>   capsicums
> 1 can drained shredded tuna instead of bacon
> 1 small can champignons, chopped

Salmon Quiche

Nice for a luncheon.

Base
1 cup plain flour
pinch of salt
90 g butter
1 egg yolk
1 tablespoon lemon juice
*a few teaspoonfuls of water
   if needed*

Filling
250 g can red salmon
4 rashers bacon
1½ cups cream
3 eggs
salt and pepper
½ teaspoon paprika
*2 tablespoons chopped
   parsley*
*1 tablespoon grated
   parmesan cheese*

Base   Sift flour and salt into bowl. Rub in butter until mixture resembles fine breadcrumbs. Mix to firm dough with lightly beaten egg yolk and lemon juice. Add one or two teaspoonfuls of water if necessary. Turn pastry onto lightly floured board, knead lightly. Roll pastry to a circle large enough to fit base and sides of 23 cm flan tin. Gently place in flan tin, easing into grooves, being careful not to break pastry. Trim around top with sharp knife and refrigerate pastry case for one hour. Put flan tin on oven tray.

Filling   Drain salmon, reserving liquid. Flake salmon lightly, remove bones. Dice bacon, fry gently until crisp, remove from pan, drain well. Beat together cream, eggs, salt, pepper, paprika, parsley, parmesan cheese, and reserved salmon liquid. Arrange salmon evenly over base of pastry shell, sprinkle bacon on top. Carefully pour egg mixture over back of spoon to cover salmon and bacon. Bake in a moderately hot oven (190°–220°C) for 10 minutes, then reduce heat to moderately slow (160°–170°C) and cook for a further 30 to 35 minutes, or until filling has set. Cut into wedges to serve.

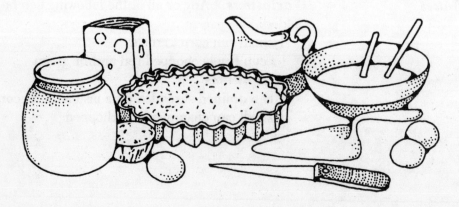

Beef Wellington

For a very special dinner.

1.25 kg fillet of beef
freshly ground black pepper
60 g butter
250 g pâté de foie gras
125 g small mushrooms
salt
double quantity Rough Puff
  Pastry (see p. 116)
1 egg yolk
2 teaspoons water

Madeira Sauce
pan drippings
2 tablespoons plain flour
3 cups water
3 beef stock cubes
¼ cup Madeira
salt and pepper

Remove all fat and gristle from meat. Tie securely with string (to hold fillet in shape). Grind black pepper over meat, pressing in firmly. Heat butter in baking dish. Add meat, sear on all sides until dark golden brown; do this over high heat. Put meat in a moderate oven (180°–200°C) for 10 minutes. Remove meat from pan, allow to become cold. Reserve pan drippings for Madeira sauce. Remove string from meat. Beat pâté de foie gras until it is soft enough to spread. Spread a thin layer of pâté over entire surface of meat. Sprinkle a little salt over. Press thinly sliced mushrooms on top of meat. Roll out pastry to approximately 35 x 25 cm; pastry size needed will depend on length and thickness of meat. Turn meat over and put it top side down in centre of pastry. Fold two outside edges of pastry over meat. Seal with combined beaten egg yolk and water. Press ends together so it's not too thick or pastry will not cook through. Trim ends, brush with egg yolk mixture then fold ends towards the centre join. Press down firmly. Brush with egg yolk mixture. Bake in a very hot oven (230°–250°C) for 5 minutes. Reduce heat to moderate (180°–200°C) and bake for a further 15 to 25 minutes.

Madeira Sauce   Put baking dish with pan drippings over very high heat until drippings are very dark golden brown; do not allow to burn. Reduce heat, add flour, stir until flour is golden brown, remove pan from heat. Add water, stir until combined. Return pan to heat, stir until sauce boils and thickens. Add crumbled stock cubes and Madeira. Season with salt and pepper. Simmer, uncovered for 10 minutes. Strain. Serve over Wellington slices.

Pizza

This recipe makes two great pizzas — one for now, and you can freeze one for later.

Base
30 g compressed yeast
1 teaspoon sugar
1 cup lukewarm water
3 cups plain flour
½ teaspoon salt
4 tablespoons oil

Filling
1 tablespoon oil
1 onion
2 cloves garlic
470 g can whole tomatoes
3 tablespoons tomato paste
1 teaspoon oregano
1 teaspoon basil
2 teaspoons sugar
salt and pepper

Topping
250 g mozzarella cheese
4 tablespoons grated
  parmesan cheese
2 x 60 g cans anchovy
  fillets (optional)
1 small green pepper
60 g mushrooms
125 g black olives
4 tablespoons oil

Filling   Make filling first. Heat oil in pan, add finely chopped onion. Sauté until transparent. Add crushed garlic, stir for 1 minute. Stir in undrained tomatoes and remaining ingredients. Bring sauce to boil, reduce heat. Simmer uncovered, stirring occasionally for 20 to 25 minutes, or until sauce is thick and smooth. Cool.

Base   Cream yeast with sugar, add water, let stand for 10 minutes or until bubbles appear on surface. Sift flour and salt into bowl, make well in centre, add oil and yeast mixture. Mix to firm dough with hand. Turn onto floured surface, knead for 15 minutes or until dough is smooth and elastic. Place in lightly oiled bowl, cover, stand in warm place for 30 minutes or until dough has doubled in bulk. Knock dough down, divide in half, knead each half into a ball. Flatten dough into circle about 2.5 cm thick. Roll out from centre to edge to fit 25 cm pizza pan or 30 x 25 cm Swiss roll tin. Repeat with remaining dough. Spread filling evenly over each pizza base with back of spoon. Combine grated cheeses, sprinkle over pizzas. Top with well-drained anchovy fillets, finely chopped pepper and finely sliced mushrooms. Sprinkle with halved olives. Spoon 2 tablespoons of oil over each pizza to prevent drying out in cooking. Bake in a hot oven (200°–230°C) for 10 to 15 minutes until crust is golden brown.

Topping   Apart from topping ingredients listed, variations could include: finely chopped ham; drained diced pineapple; finely diced red and green capsicums; finely sliced onion.

Almond and Peach Pie

Serves 6

Almond Base
185 g blanched almonds
1 cup coconut
¼ cup sugar
60 g butter

Filling
1 cup sour cream
pinch of salt
¾ cup icing sugar
1 teaspoon orange juice
1 teaspoon grated orange rind
1 teaspoon vanilla essence
825 g can sliced peaches
¾ cup cream

Almond Base Chop almonds finely. Stir in coconut and sugar. Rub butter into mixture. Reserve 3 tablespoons of crumb mixture for topping. Press remaining crumbs onto base and sides of greased 23 cm flan tin. Bake in a moderately hot oven (190°–220°C) for 12 to 15 minutes or until golden brown. Cool. Place reserved crumbs into small pan, stir over low heat until golden, approximately 4 minutes.

Filling Combine sour cream, salt, ½ cup sifted icing sugar, orange juice and rind, and vanilla. Pour into prepared pie shell. Arrange well-drained peach slices over top of filling. Lightly whip cream and remaining sifted icing sugar. Spoon or pipe around pie edge. Sprinkle with the toasted crumbs. Refrigerate before serving.

Lemon Meringue Pie

I think most people like this dessert.

Base
2 cups plain flour
pinch of salt
1 tablespoon icing sugar
185 g butter
1 tablespoon lemon juice
1 to 2 tablespoons water

Filling
4 tablespoons plain flour
4 tablespoons cornflour
2 teaspoons grated lemon
    rind
¾ cup lemon juice
1 cup sugar
1¼ cups water
90 g butter
4 egg yolks

Meringue
4 egg whites
2 tablespoons water
pinch of salt
¾ cup castor sugar

Base   Sift flour, salt and sugar into basin. Chop butter roughly, rub into mixture until it resembles coarse breadcrumbs. Add lemon juice and enough water to mix to firm dough. Refrigerate for 30 minutes. Roll pastry on lightly floured surface to fit 23 cm pie plate. Use rolling pin to lift pastry onto pie plate. Trim and decorate edges. Prick base and sides of pastry with fork. Bake in a moderately hot oven (190°–220°C) for 10 to 15 minutes or until lightly browned. Allow to cool.

Filling   Combine sifted flours, lemon rind, lemon juice and sugar in saucepan. Add water, blend until smooth, stir over heat until mixture boils and thickens. Reduce heat, stir for a further two minutes. Remove from heat, stir in butter and lightly beaten egg yolks until butter has melted. Cool. Spread cold lemon filling evenly over base.

Meringue   Combine egg whites, water and salt in small electric mixer bowl. Beat on high speed until soft peaks form. Gradually add sugar, beating well until dissolved. Spoon meringue on top of lemon filling, spreading decoratively with knife. Bake in a moderate oven (180°–200°C) for 5 to 10 minutes or until lightly browned. Cool, then refrigerate.

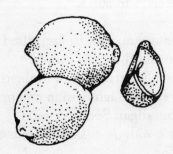

Crumb Crust Lemon Pie

A Crumb Crust base is a nice alternative to the conventional pie pastry base.

Base
1 cup plain sweet biscuits
½ cup butter

Base Melt butter, add to crushed biscuits, press firmly into a pie dish. Bake in a moderately slow oven (150°–160°C) for 5 minutes. Allow to cool.

Filling
400 mL condensed milk
⅓ cup lemon juice
⅔ cup cream
cinnamon or nutmeg

Filling Place condensed milk into a bowl, gradually add lemon juice and allow to stand for a few minutes. Beat the cream, fold through mixture. Pour onto biscuit base and refrigerate. Sprinkle lightly with cinnamon or nutmeg before serving.

Southern Pecan Pie

I prefer to make sweet pies.

3 eggs
⅔ cup sugar
pinch of salt
1 cup dark corn syrup
⅓ cup butter
1 cup pecan halves
Biscuit or Champagne
*   Pastry (see p. 132)*

Beat eggs thoroughly with sugar, salt, corn syrup and melted butter. Add pecans. Pour into pastry shell. Bake in a moderate oven (180°–200°C) for 50 minutes or until knife, inserted halfway between outside and centre of filling, comes out clean. The crust will turn very dark, but this is how it should be. In testing, the knife must come out truly *clean*. You must use corn syrup as no other syrup will be successful.

Butterscotch Pie

Biscuit or Champagne
Pastry (see p. 132)
2 tablespoons butter
¾ cup brown sugar
3 tablespoons cornflour
¾ cup milk
2 eggs, separated
¼ teaspoon vanilla essence
4 tablespoons white sugar

Line greased tart plate with pastry. Melt butter and brown sugar. Blend cornflour with a little milk. Heat but do not boil remaining milk, then add slowly to butter and sugar. Stir over low heat until combined. Combine egg yolks with blended cornflour and milk. Add to saucepan, stirring all the time. Add vanilla. Pour into pastry-lined tart plate. Bake in a hot oven (200°–220°C) for about 20 minutes until set. Beat egg whites until stiff, then gradually add white sugar and beat until thick. Pile roughly on top of pie and brown lightly in the oven.

Apple Pie

Rhubarb, blackberries, peaches or apricots can be used instead of apples. This pie is especially delicious when served with hot Stirred Custard (see p. 244)

4 cooking apples
4 tablespoons sugar
2 cloves
½ teaspoon grated lemon
rind
sweet Shortcrust Pastry
(see p. 117)
egg white or water and
sugar for glazing
icing sugar

Peel, quarter and core apples. Slice into a pie dish, adding sugar, cloves and lemon in layers. Heap up towards the centre. Roll out pastry in pie dish shape, but 2.5 cm larger. Cut a strip off all round. Wet the edge of the dish and attach the strip, with the cut edge outward. Brush with water, place remaining pastry on top. Trim edges and flute. Make a small cut in the top of pastry to allow steam to escape. Glaze by brushing with egg white or with water and sugar. Bake in a hot oven (220°C) for about 20 minutes until brown. If raw apples have been used, reduce temperature to 180°C after 20 minutes and cook until they are soft. Sprinkle with icing sugar and serve.

Banana Cream Pie

*Shortcrust Pastry
(see p. 117)*
3–4 sliced bananas
2 eggs, separated
¹/₂ cup castor sugar
¹/₂ cup sugar
1 cup cream
lemon or orange flavouring

Line pie dish with pastry. Slightly bake pastry then fill with sliced bananas. Beat yolks with castor sugar and cream, pour over the bananas and bake for ½ hour in a moderate oven (180°–200°C). Whip egg whites, 3 tablespoons sugar and flavouring until stiff. Pile on top of pie and bake for a further 10 minutes in a moderate oven until meringue is slightly golden.

Lime and Kiwifruit Pie

*sweet Shortcrust Pastry
(see p. 117)*
2 cups milk
1 heaped cup sugar
4 tablespoons cornflour
3 egg yolks
juice of 3 limes
grated zest of 2 limes
1 teaspoon vanilla essence
1 cup marmalade
*3 kiwifruit, cut into thin
rounds*

Line a deep 23 cm greased pie dish with pastry. In a saucepan whisk the milk, sugar, cornflour, lightly beaten egg yolks, lime juice and zest and vanilla. Bring to the boil, constantly stirring until the custard thickens. Pour into pastry casing and bake at 200°C for 25 minutes. Reduce the temperature to 160°C for 20 to 25 minutes or until the custard sets. Remove the pie from the oven. Warm the marmalade and brush over the custard. Decorate with the kiwifruit and brush with more marmalade. Allow to cool slightly before serving.

Coconut Fruit Pie

Flaky or Shortcrust Pastry
  (see p. 117)
2–3 tablespoons raspberry,
  strawberry or apricot jam
60 g sultanas or currants
125 g margarine
1 cup sugar
2 eggs
2 cups coconut
¼ teaspoon vanilla or
  almond essence

Roll pastry out thinly to fit 23 cm square tin or pie plate. Spread jam evenly over the pastry. Sprinkle fruit over jam. Soften margarine in a mixing bowl. Add sugar and eggs and beat for 30 seconds with a wooden spoon. Add coconut and flavouring. Mix well, pour over the fruit, spreading the mixture evenly. Bake in a hot oven (200°–230°C) for 10 minutes. Reduce temperature to moderate (180°–200°C) and bake for a further 15 to 25 minutes until the coconut topping is evenly browned and the centre feels firm. Do not overcook.

Mince Tart

1 cup sultanas
1 cup currants
½ cup nuts
½ cup grated apple
sprinkling of sugar
grated rind of 1 lemon
Shortcrust Pastry
  (see p. 117)
icing sugar

Mince fruit and nuts together finely, sprinkle with sugar. Spread onto thinly rolled pastry and cover with same. Cut into squares. Bake on a greased oven slide in a moderate oven (180°–200°C) for 10 to 15 minutes. When cold, sprinkle the tart with icing sugar.

Glazed Strawberry Tarts

Base
60 g margarine
1 cup plain flour
pinch of salt
1 teaspoon iced water
2 egg yolks
3 tablespoons sugar
½ teaspoon vanilla

Filling
250 g cream cheese
1 tablespoon orange juice
3 tablespoons sugar
1 tablespoon cream
*1 teaspoon grated lemon
   rind*
1 punnet strawberries

Glaze
½ cup redcurrant jelly
1 tablespoon water
2 tablespoons orange juice

Base Rub margarine into sifted flour until mixture resembles breadcrumbs. Combine remaining ingredients, blend into flour with knife. Turn onto well-floured board, knead lightly, wrap in greaseproof paper and chill for at least 30 minutes. Roll pastry out on lightly-floured board. Fit into a 20–23 cm flan ring. Prick well. Chill until firm. Bake in moderately hot oven (200°–230°C) for about 20 minutes. Allow to cool. Fill with cream cheese filling. Top with hulled whole strawberries. Spoon glaze over and chill.

Filling Cream all ingredients except strawberries. Chill.

Glaze Place ingredients into a small saucepan, heat gently until smooth. Cool slightly, stirring occasionally.

Butterscotch Tart

Base
1 tablespoon butter
1 tablespoon sugar
1 egg
1 cup self-raising flour

Filling
1 egg yolk
½ cup sugar
3 tablespoons plain flour
1 tablespoon honey
1 cup milk
3 tablespoons water
2 tablespoons butter
pinch of salt
2 drops vanilla essence

Meringue Topping
1 egg white
1 tablespoon castor sugar

Base   Cream butter and sugar, add beaten egg and flour. Mix well. Roll out to fit pie plate. Bake in a moderate oven (180°–200°C) for 10 minutes.

Filling   Put all ingredients into saucepan and stir over medium heat until mixture thickens. Pour into baked tart shell. Top with meringue mixture and bake in a moderate oven (180°–200°C) for 10 minutes or until lightly browned. Serve with whipped cream.

Meringue Topping   Beat egg white and castor sugar until stiff. Spread on pie.

Pineapple Tart

Shortcrust Pastry
  (see p. 117)
2 tablespoons plain flour
1 egg, separated
1 tablespoon milk
2 drops vanilla essence
1 x 400 g tin crushed
  pineapple or 500 g
  fresh pineapple
1 tablespoon butter
2 tablespoons sugar

Line a pie plate with thin layer of pastry. Combine flour, egg yolk, milk and vanilla with pineapple. Put in saucepan, stir until it boils and thickens, then pour into pastry case. Beat egg white with sugar until stiff. Put on top of tart and bake in a moderate oven (180°–200°C) for 10 minutes. Reduce heat (160°–170°C) and bake for a further 20 minutes.

Lemon (Cream Cheese) Tart

Base
250 g plain sweet biscuits
125 g butter

Filling
125 g cream cheese
1 x 400 mL tin condensed milk
2 eggs, separated
rind and juice of 2 lemons
½ cup castor sugar

Base   Melt butter and stir into crumbed biscuits. Press into base and halfway up side of greased pie tin.

Filling   Beat cheese with milk, rind and juice, and egg yolks. Pour into crumb crust base. Whip whites, gradually beat in half the sugar, beat until stiff, fold in remainder of sugar and spread evenly over filling. Bake in a hot oven (200°–230°C) for 10 minutes to brown. Remove from tin. Serve.

Brandied Tart

A very good party sweet which can be made up to four days ahead.

125 g chocolate
2 tablespoons black coffee
4 eggs
½ cup sugar
½ cup plain flour
brandy

Melt chocolate in coffee, place over hot water while doing so. Whip eggs and sugar until thick and foamy. Fold in sifted flour then chocolate mixture. Turn into greased tins. Bake in a moderate oven (180°–200°C) for 30 to 35 minutes. Leave for 5 minutes before turning out. Sprinkle with brandy when cold, then place in a covered container. Refrigerate overnight. Coat top and sides with whipped cream and grated chocolate.

Custard Tart

A very pleasant tart.

2 eggs
2 tablespoons sugar
1¼ cups milk
3 drops vanilla essence
Shortcrust Pastry
  (see p. 117)
1 tablespoon jam
nutmeg

Beat eggs and sugar. Add milk and vanilla. Roll out pastry and line a greased pie dish. Spread pastry base with jam. Add mix, pouring in slowly. Grate nutmeg on top. Bake in moderate oven (180°–200°C) for about 20 to 30 minutes until set.

Orange Cream Tart

First layer
1 cup milk
1 dessertspoon cornflour
1 dessertspoon custard
  powder
¼ cup water
60 g butter
90 g castor sugar
Shortcrust Pastry
  (see p. 117)
Second layer
1 cup water
1 cup orange juice
1 cup sugar
1 tablespoon cornflour
1 tablespoon custard
  powder
¼ cup extra water
30 g butter

First layer   Heat milk in saucepan. Blend cornflour and custard powder with water. Add to milk. Stir over heat until mixture boils and thickens. Allow to cool. Cream butter with castor sugar until smooth. Beat in cooled custard and quickly spread over cooked pastry case. Chill.

Second layer   Combine water, juice and sugar and stir over heat until sugar dissolves. Blend cornflour and custard powder with extra water, stir into mixture and bring to boil, stirring constantly. Add butter, allow to melt. Cool slightly, then spoon onto custard mixture. Return to refrigerator and chill well. Just before serving, spoon whipped cream on top.

Small Tarts

Use my Shortcrust Pastry recipe (see p. 117) for small pastry cases.

Lemon Cream   Cook pastry cases. Cool. Fill with Lemon Filling (see p. 144) and top with whipped cream or meringue

Coconut   Place 1 teaspoon of jam in bottom of uncooked pastry cases. Mix 1 cup coconut and ½ cup sugar. Beat 1 egg and add to mixture. Place spoonfuls into cases on top of jam and bake in a moderate oven (180°–200°C) for about 20 minutes until golden brown.

Butterscotch   Fill uncooked pastry cases with mixture for Butterscotch Pie (see p. 20). Bake in moderate oven (180°C) for about 20 minutes until set. Top with Meringue Topping (see p. 144)

Swiss Apple Flan

Shortcrust Pastry
  (see p. 117)
500 g sweetened stewed
  apples
3 large peeled, cored and
  thinly sliced cooking
  apples
1 egg
1 dessertspoon sugar
1 cup milk
1 teaspoon vanilla essence
whipped cream

Roll pastry thinly and line a Swiss roll tin. Trim surplus pastry. Cover with apple purée. Arrange apple slices on top of purée. Make an egg custard by lightly beating the egg and sugar, then add the milk and vanilla. Pour custard over apples. Bake in a moderately hot oven (190°–200°C) for 30 to 35 minutes. Serve hot or cold with whipped cream.

French Fruit Flan

Base
1 cup plain flour
1 tablespoon icing sugar
¼ teaspoon baking powder
pinch of salt
90 g butter
1 egg yolk
1 teaspoon lemon juice
1 teaspoon water

Custard
3 tablespoons custard
   powder
2 tablespoons sugar
1 cup milk
½ teaspoon vanilla
½ cup cream

Fruit topping
470 g can black cherries
470 g can apricot halves
1 punnet strawberries

Glaze
2 tablespoons apricot jam
1 tablespoon brandy

Base Sift dry ingredients into bowl, rub in butter until mixture resembles coarse breadcrumbs. Mix to firm dough with lightly beaten egg yolk, lemon juice and water, adding a little more water if necessary. Knead lightly on floured board. Wrap in plastic food wrap, refrigerate for 30 minutes. Roll pastry on lightly floured surface to a circle large enough to fit base and sides of 20 cm flan tin. Lift pastry gently over rolling pin, lift into flan tin. Ease pastry into sides of tin with fingers, press lightly into grooves. Roll rolling pin over top of tin firmly, to cut off excess pastry and neaten edges. Prick base with fork. Bake in a moderately hot oven (190°–220°C) for 10 to 15 minutes or until pale brown. Allow pastry to cool in tin. When completely cold, fill base with cold custard. Arrange well-drained fruit and strawberries over custard. Brush glaze over fruits.

Custard Combine custard powder and sugar in saucepan, gradually add milk, stir until blended and smooth. Bring to boil, stirring constantly. Add vanilla, cool. When cold, fold in lightly whipped cream.

Glaze Gently heat jam and brandy until boiling. Push through sieve to give a smooth glaze.

Cream Puffs

Made from Choux Pastry (see p. 116), cream puffs are a beautifully light, cream-filled special treat.

Choux Pastry (see p. 116)
300 mL whipping cream
icing sugar

Make up a quantity of Choux Pastry into puffs. When cold, carefully cut puffs in half and remove any soft filling. Fill with whipped cream and sprinkle tops with sifted icing sugar.

DESSERTS

Nowadays many diet-conscious families
don't bother with puddings. However, I have
made puddings nearly every week of
my married life.
When I was married, I was given a lot of
my Mum's recipes, including Golden Syrup
Pudding (see p. 166). Since then I've added
Jamaican Apples (see p. 170) and many others.
I hope you enjoy making them
as much as I do.

Basic Pudding

1 cup self-raising flour
pinch of salt
½ cup sugar
1 tablespoon butter
1 egg
½ cup milk

Sift flour and salt into basin. Add sugar. Melt butter and add to flour with egg and milk. Beat at a slow speed until smooth. You can use this basic mixture for any of the following pudding recipes if desired.

Chocolate Sauce Pudding

Serves 6

Pudding
¾ cup self-raising flour
2 tablespoons cocoa
1½ teaspoons instant coffee powder
pinch of salt
125 g butter
⅔ cup castor sugar
2 eggs
½ teaspoon vanilla essence
1–2 tablespoons milk
1 tablespoon chopped walnuts
walnut halves
whipped cream

Sauce
⅔ cup brown sugar, firmly packed
1 tablespoon cocoa
1 cup hot water

Pudding   Sift flour, cocoa, instant coffee and salt. Cream butter and sugar until light, then gradually beat in slightly beaten eggs and vanilla. Add a little flour mixture with last few additions of egg, then fold in remaining flour and enough milk to achieve a fairly soft consistency. Spoon mixture into well-greased oven dish and spread evenly.

Sauce   In a small bowl, mix together cocoa and sugar, stir in hot water and mix until sugar is dissolved and sauce is smooth. Sprinkle pudding mixture with walnuts, pour sauce over and bake in a moderately hot oven (190°–220°C) for 40 minutes. Decorate with walnut halves and serve warm with whipped cream.

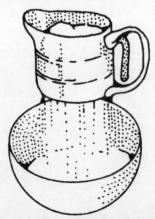

Banana Batter Pudding

Batter
½ cup plain flour
½ cup self-raising flour
3 tablespoons melted butter
pinch of salt
1 egg
3 tablespoons milk
2 sliced bananas
extra melted butter

Topping
1 tablespoon sugar
1 teaspoon cinnamon
1 teaspoon grated orange
   rind

Batter   Mix all ingredients except for the bananas to make a smooth batter. Pour into greased 20 cm sandwich cake tin. Top with sliced bananas, then brush with some melted butter.

Topping   Mix ingredients and sprinkle mixture over top of pudding. Bake in a moderate oven (180°–200°C) for 30 to 40 minutes.

Butterscotch Self-saucing Pudding

Pudding
1 cup self-raising flour
¾ cup sugar
½ teaspoon salt
60 g butter
½ cup milk

Sauce
2 tablespoons golden syrup
1½ cups hot water
30 g butter

Pudding   Sift flour, sugar and salt into bowl. Add melted butter and milk. Combine thoroughly. Pour into greased dish.

Sauce   Combine ingredients in saucepan, stir over low heat until butter melts. Pour mixture on top. Bake in a moderate oven (180°–200°C) for 30 to 40 minutes.

Spiced Apricot Pudding

1 ½ cups self-raising flour
pinch of salt
½ teaspoon nutmeg
½ teaspoon cinnamon
60 g butter
2 tablespoons sugar
½ teaspoon grated lemon
   rind
1 egg
½ cup milk
apricot halves, canned or
   cooked, dried apricots
2 tablespoons brown sugar
1 extra teaspoon cinnamon

Sift flour, salt, nutmeg and cinnamon. Rub in butter. Add sugar and lemon rind. Mix to a soft dough with beaten egg and milk. Turn into a well-greased 20 cm sandwich tin. Arrange apricot halves on top. Sprinkle with brown sugar and cinnamon. Bake in a hot oven (200°–230°C) for 35 to 40 minutes. Serve hot with Stirred Custard (see p. 244)

Pineapple Pudding

2 tablespoons butter
2 tablespoons plain flour
½ cup pineapple juice
½ cup milk
2 eggs, separated
4 tablespoons sugar
400 g pineapple pieces,
   fresh or canned

Melt butter in a saucepan, stir in flour smoothly, cook for one minute. Add juice and milk. Continue to cook until mixture boils and thickens. Stir in egg yolks and half of sugar. Put pineapple pieces in pie dish and cover with mixture. Whisk egg whites to a stiff froth, stir in sugar. Pile meringue over pineapple mixture. Bake in a moderate oven (180°–200°C) until firmly set and light golden brown. Serve hot or cold with Stirred Custard (see p. 244) or cream.

Lemon Soufflé Pudding

2 tablespoons butter
½ cup sugar
3 eggs
¼ teaspoon salt
2 lemons
2 tablespoons plain flour
2 cups milk

Cream butter and sugar, add beaten egg yolks with half the salt, then add juice of 2 lemons and rind of 1 lemon. Add flour and milk. Mix well. Lastly add stiffly beaten egg whites with remainder of salt. Mix well. Pour into greased pie dish, stand in water and bake in a moderate oven (180°–200°C) for 30 minutes.

Baked Sultana Pudding

A very successful variation of the traditional steamed pudding recipe.

Pudding
2 tablespoons butter
¾ cup sugar
1 egg
1 ½ cups self-raising flour
¼ teaspoon salt
½ cup sultanas
½ cup milk

Syrup
2 cups brown sugar
2 cups boiling water

Pudding　Cream butter and sugar; add beaten egg. Sift in flour and salt. Add sultanas and milk to mix. Pour into a buttered dish and cover with syrup.

Syrup　Mix ingredients. Pour over batter and bake in a moderate oven (180°–200°C) for 30 to 40 minutes. Serve with Stirred Custard (see p. 244), Brandy Sauce (see p. 250) or cream.

Apple Dapple Pudding

Sultanas and apples are always a good combination. Serves 6

Pudding
½ cup self-raising flour
½ cup sugar
1 teaspoon cinnamon
¾ cup water
1 egg, slightly beaten
1 tablespoon lemon juice
1 teaspoon almond essence
   (optional)
4 cups sliced apple
½ cup slivered or chopped
   almonds
½ cup raisins, currants or
   sultanas
cream for serving

Topping
½ cup self-raising flour
¼ cup brown sugar, firmly
   packed
1 teaspoon cinnamon
¼ teaspoon salt
1 teaspoon grated lemon
   rind
60 g butter

Pudding   Sift flour, sugar and cinnamon. Combine water, egg, lemon juice and almond essence. Add apples, almonds and dried fruit. Add dry ingredients and mix well. Turn into a well-buttered 20 x 20 x 5 cm ovenproof dish.

Topping   Combine flour, sugar, cinnamon, salt and lemon rind. Rub in butter until mixture resembles coarse breadcrumbs. Sprinkle topping over and bake in a moderate oven (180°–200°C) for about 1 hour. Serve warm with cream.

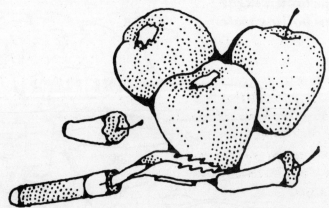

Apple Sponge

Other fruits may be used.

750 g apples
¼ cup sugar
2 tablespoons water
3 cloves
¼ cup butter or margarine
¼ cup castor sugar
1 egg
¼ cup self-raising flour
3 tablespoons milk

Cook apples, sugar, water and cloves until tender. Place in a greased casserole and keep hot. Cream butter and castor sugar, add the egg. Sift in flour and milk alternately. Pour over hot apples. Bake in a moderate oven (180°–200°C) for 30 to 45 minutes.

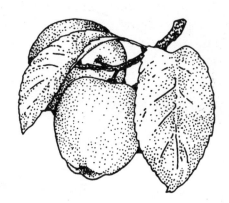

Orange Ginger Pudding

A touch of ginger is just right.

1 cup self-raising flour
¼ teaspoon salt
2 level teaspoons ginger
¾ cup brown sugar
⅓ cup milk
1 teaspoon vanilla
2 tablespoons melted butter
¼ cup chopped walnuts
sprinkling of brown sugar
grated rind and juice of 1
**   orange**
1 tablespoon golden syrup
¾ cup water

Sift flour, salt and ginger. Add sugar, milk, vanilla and butter. Mix until smooth. Pour into greased dish. Top with walnuts, brown sugar and rind. Melt golden syrup, add orange juice and water. Mix together and pour over the pudding. Bake in a moderate oven (180°–200°C) for 50 to 55 minutes. Serve hot.

Coconut Pudding

1 cup coconut
1 cup milk
3 tablespoons breadcrumbs
3 tablespoons sugar
1 cup raisins
1 egg

Add all ingredients together. Mix well. Pour into a buttered pie dish and bake in a slow oven (150°C) for one hour. Serve hot, with stewed fruit or Wine Sauce (see p. 250).

Betsy Pudding

Just like my mother used to make.

2½ cups milk
1½ cups fresh breadcrumbs
1 egg
1 tablespoon sugar
*apricot jam (or jam of your
   choice)*
nutmeg

Heat milk until nearly boiling. Pour onto breadcrumbs. When cool, stir in well beaten egg and sugar. Spread a good layer of jam in the bottom of pie dish. Pour mixture gently on top of jam. Sprinkle nutmeg on mixture. Bake in a hot oven (230°C) for 30 minutes.

Lemon Delicious Pudding

It is *delicious too!*

1 tablespoon butter
1 cup sugar
2 tablespoons self-raising flour
juice and grated rind of 1 lemon
1 cup milk
2 eggs

Cream butter and sugar, add flour, lemon juice and rind, milk and well beaten egg yolks. Beat all together well. Beat the whites stiffly and fold into the mixture. Pour into greased pie dish, set it in a dish of water in the oven, and bake slowly (150°C) for 45 to 60 minutes, until set and golden brown.

Caramel Lemon Delicious Pudding

Caramel
½ cup sugar
¼ cup water

Pudding
⅓ cup plain flour
½ cup sugar
60 g butter
1 teaspoon grated lemon rind
3 tablespoons lemon juice
4 eggs, separated

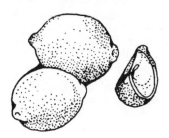

Caramel   Put sugar and water in saucepan, stir over low heat until sugar has dissolved, brushing down sides of saucepan with a brush dipped in hot water to dissolve any sugar grains. Increase heat, boil gently. Pour caramel evenly into base of four individual heatproof dishes (small soufflé dishes are ideal). Swirl dishes to coat base and a little of the sides.

Pudding   Sift flour into bowl, add sugar. Rub in butter until mixture resembles coarse breadcrumbs. Add lemon rind and juice and egg yolks. Beat well. Beat egg whites until firm peaks form, fold into lemon mixture. Spoon lemon mixture evenly into dishes, stand dishes in baking dish filled with enough water to come halfway up the dishes' sides. Bake in moderately slow oven (160°–170°C) for 50 minutes or until golden brown on top. Loosen edges of pudding with knife, turn out, top with whipped cream.

Sultana Caramel Pudding

Sauce
¾ cup brown sugar
1½ cups water
60 g butter

Pudding
60 g butter
¼ cup brown sugar
1 egg
1 teaspoon vanilla
1¼ cups self-raising flour
½ cup sultanas

Sauce Combine all ingredients in a saucepan. Bring gently to boil, boil steadily for 5 minutes.

Pudding Cream butter and sugar, add egg and vanilla. Beat well. Sift flour. Stir into creamed mixture with sultanas. Pour hot caramel sauce into lightly greased casserole dish. Spoon pudding mixture on top. Bake in a moderate oven (180°–200°C) for approximately 35 minutes. Serve warm with a spoonful of whipped cream on top of each serving.

Golden Syrup Pudding

Serves 4 to 6

Pudding
1 cup self-raising flour
½ cup brown sugar
60 g butter
½ cup milk
few drops of vanilla essence

Sauce
1 tablespoon golden syrup
1½ cups boiling water
¼ cup brown sugar
30 g butter

Pudding Mix all ingredients. Put into a 6-cup casserole dish. Pour sauce over. Bake in a moderate oven (180°–200°C) for 40 minutes.

Sauce Mix all ingredients and pour over batter.

Baked Golden Syrup Dumplings

An old favourite.

Dumplings
1 cup self-raising flour
¼ teaspoon salt
1 egg
2–3 tablespoons milk
1 tablespoon butter

Syrup
1 ¼ cups boiling water
¼ cup sugar
1 tablespoon butter
1 tablespoon golden syrup

Dumplings Sift together flour and salt, beat egg and add milk. Rub butter into flour, add liquid and mix to a soft dough.

Syrup Place ingredients for syrup into a saucepan, stir until sugar is dissolved and bring to the boil.

Place dessertspoons of dough into a greased pie dish or casserole. Pour syrup over dumplings and bake in a moderately hot oven (190°–220°C) for 20 to 30 minutes. Serve with Stirred Custard (see p. 244), cream or ice-cream.

Cornflake Crumble

4 large green apples
1 cup water
1 tablespoon sugar
1 ½ cups cornflakes
½ cup coconut
½ cup brown sugar finely packed
½ cup condensed milk

Peel and core apples, slice thinly. Put in saucepan with water and sugar, stir over low heat until sugar dissolves. Cook until tender. Remove from heat, spoon into greased dish. Combine cornflakes, coconut, sugar, condensed milk. Mix well and spread over apple. Bake in a moderate oven (180°–200°C) for approximately 20 minutes until topping is firm and golden.

Apple Hot Pie Dish

4–6 cooking apples
1 tablespoon lemon juice
½ cup brown sugar
¼ teaspoon salt
½ teaspoon cinnamon

Put peeled and sliced apples into greased ovenproof dish. Mix all ingredients together and put over apples. Bake in a moderate oven (180°–200°C) for 1 hour. Serve with ice-cream.

Apple and Banana Crumble

A variation to my Apple Crumble which is very moist and delicious.

Fruit
4–6 stewed apples, drained
** of juice**
2–3 bananas, sliced
** lengthways**

Crumble
1 ½ cups plain flour
¾ cup sugar
60 g butter

Fruit   Place stewed apples and bananas in layers into greased dish until dish is full. Put crumble on top. Bake in a moderate oven (180°–200°C) for 30 to 40 minutes or until golden brown on top.

Crumble   Place flour and sugar into bowl. Rub in butter to resemble breadcrumbs, sprinkle on top of apple and banana layers.

Apple Strudel

An apple dessert with a difference! Serves 6

Filling
4 *large apples*
½ *cup castor sugar*
1 *teaspoon vanilla*
30 *g butter*
1 *cup white breadcrumbs*
½ *cup brown sugar, lightly
   packed*
¼ *teaspoon nutmeg*
1 *teaspoon cinnamon*
1 *teaspoon grated lemon
   rind*
¾ *cup sultanas*

Pastry
1½ *cups plain flour*
1 *egg*
1 *tablespoon oil*
⅓ *cup warm water*
125 *g butter*
60 *g extra butter*

Filling Peel, core and slice apples thinly. Place slices into bowl with sugar and vanilla; mix well. Cover bowl and allow to stand for 1 hour. Melt 30 g butter in pan, add breadcrumbs, stir over low heat until breadcrumbs are golden brown. Cool. Mix breadcrumbs and sugar together. Drain off excess liquid from apples. Combine apples, nutmeg, cinnamon, lemon rind and sultanas in bowl. Mix lightly.

Pastry Sift flour into bowl, make a well in centre of dry ingredients, add egg and oil. Gradually add water, mixing to a soft dough with hands. Turn out onto lightly floured surface, knead into a ball. Pick up dough and throw down. Repeat this about 100 times. Knead again for 5 minutes. The more the dough is thrown down and kneaded, the lighter it becomes. Make dough into ball and place in lightly oiled bowl. Cover and stand in warm place for 45 minutes. Cover large table with clean cloth, rub flour over surface. Roll out dough as far as possible. Flour hands, slip them under dough, then start pulling from centre with back of hands, rather than fingers. Continue stretching dough until it is paper-thin and approximately 87 cm square. Brush with melted butter. Sprinkle combined breadcrumbs and brown sugar over half the pastry. Spoon apple mixture along one end of pastry about 5 cm in. Fold in sides of pastry to edge of apple filling. Gather cloth in hands and carefully roll up apple strudel, pulling cloth to you as you roll. Place on large greased tray, curling gently into horseshoe shape. Brush with 60 g extra melted butter. Bake in a moderately hot oven (190°–220°C) for 35 to 40 minutes. When cold, dust with sifted icing sugar.

Jamaican Apples

6 medium-sized apples
1 cup brown sugar, tightly
    packed
¾ cup apricot jam
3 tablespoons rum
few chopped almonds

Peel and core apples, leaving whole. Place in buttered heatproof dish. Mix sugar, jam and rum together, fill centre of apples with mixture. Pour enough water into dish to come 2.5 cm up the sides. Bake in a moderate oven (180°–200°C) for 30 minutes or until apples are cooked, basting with liquid while cooking. Brush apples with remaining sugar and jam mixture. Just before end of cooking time, top apples with chopped almonds, allowing them to brown.

Banana Caribbean

Serves 6

6 medium-sized bananas
¼ cup brown sugar
½ cup orange juice
grated rind of 1 orange
¼ teaspoon each ground
    cinnamon and nutmeg
½ cup sherry
30 g butter
4 tablespoons rum
vanilla ice-cream or
    whipped cream

Peel the bananas, place in a flat buttered baking dish. Combine sugar with juice, rind, spices and sherry. Heat and pour over the bananas. Dot with butter. Bake in a moderate oven (180°–200°C) for 10 to 15 minutes, remove from oven. Heat rum, ignite and pour over the bananas. Serve with ice-cream or whipped cream.

Caramelised Peach Dessert

It's just as effective a dessert without meringue.

Cake
2 tablespoons butter
½ cup sugar
1 egg
½ cup milk
1 cup self-raising flour

Caramel
2 tablespoons butter
2 tablespoons brown sugar
1 can sliced, or fresh sliced
  peaches

Meringue
2 egg whites
½ cup sugar

Cake   Cream butter and sugar, then add egg and milk. Set aside to stand while making caramel.

Caramel   Cream butter and sugar and place in bottom of greased and floured tin. Place ring of peaches around tin on top of caramel mixture. Beat cake mixture until creamy, then add flour. Pour mixture over peaches. Bake in a moderate oven (180°–200°C) for approximately 25 minutes. Turn out after leaving to stand for 5 minutes.

Meringue   Beat egg whites until stiff, then add ½ cup sugar, beat again. Cover mixture with meringue, then set in a moderate oven (180°–200°) for about 10 minutes. Serve with cream.

Passionfruit Delight

1 tablespoon butter
1 small cup sugar
2 tablespoons plain flour
2 eggs, separated
pulp of 6 passionfruit
1 cup milk

Cream butter and sugar. Add flour, egg yolks and passionfruit pulp. Beat well, then add milk slowly, stirring all the time. Lastly add stiffly beaten egg whites. Pour into buttered pie dish, stand in a dish of water and bake in moderate oven (180°–200°C) for approximately 30 minutes or until set.

Fruit Dumplings

A fruity change.

Dumplings
2 tablespoons butter
2 cups plain flour
2 teaspoons baking powder
milk
drained peaches, pears,
   apricots or similar
   (reserve juice for sauce)

Sauce
water and reserved juice
   from fruit to make 3 cups
   liquid
1½ cups sugar
1½ tablespoons plain flour
1½ tablespoons butter

Dumplings   Rub in butter to sifted dry ingredients, add enough milk to make a stiff dough. Roll out into oblong shape and cut into approximately 10 to 12 squares. Put a half piece or several slices of fruit on each pastry square and fold over ends to centre. Place each dumpling into greased large dish with folded ends underneath.

Sauce   Place ingredients into a saucepan. Stir while bringing to boil, then pour over dumplings. Bake in a moderately hot oven (190°–200°C) for approximately 40 minutes until golden brown.

Crème Caramel

A lovely light dessert.

Caramel
¾ *cup sugar*
1 cup water

Custard
4 eggs
3 extra egg yolks
1 teaspoon vanilla essence
½ *cup castor sugar*
2 cups milk
300 mL cream

Toffee Strawberries
1 punnet strawberries
2 cups sugar
1 cup water

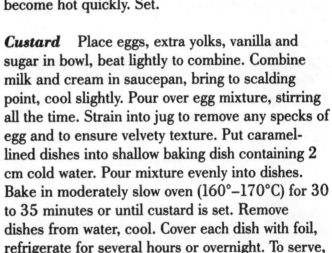

Caramel   Place sugar and water in saucepan, stir over low heat until sugar dissolves. Stop stirring, increase heat, bring to boil, boil until mixture turns deep golden brown. Do not stir. Pour into six individual soufflé dishes. Caramel will set almost immediately, like toffee, so work quickly. Rotate dishes so that caramel coats base and sides of dishes. Use a cloth to protect hands, as dishes become hot quickly. Set.

Custard   Place eggs, extra yolks, vanilla and sugar in bowl, beat lightly to combine. Combine milk and cream in saucepan, bring to scalding point, cool slightly. Pour over egg mixture, stirring all the time. Strain into jug to remove any specks of egg and to ensure velvety texture. Put caramel-lined dishes into shallow baking dish containing 2 cm cold water. Pour mixture evenly into dishes. Bake in moderately slow oven (160°–170°C) for 30 to 35 minutes or until custard is set. Remove dishes from water, cool. Cover each dish with foil, refrigerate for several hours or overnight. To serve, ease custards away from sides of dishes with fingers. Turn out onto plates.

Toffee Strawberries   Wash strawberries, spread on absorbent paper to dry. Put sugar and water in saucepan, stir over low heat until sugar has dissolved. Increase heat and bring to boil. Boil syrup until it becomes very pale gold. Remove from heat immediately. Using tongs, dip strawberries by stems into syrup, coating entire fruit except the stems. Put on lightly greased baking trays and leave until toffee has hardened. Serve before the juice makes the toffee sticky.

Profiteroles with Brandy Alexander Sauce

Always popular for formal dinners. Makes around 30 puffs.

Profiteroles
Choux Pastry
  (see p. 116)
300 mL thickened cream

Brandy Alexander Sauce
125 g dark chocolate
1 egg yolk
¼ cup water
2 tablespoons Crème de Cacao
1 tablespoon brandy
1 tablespoon cornflour
½ cup milk
½ cup thickened cream

Profiteroles   Make up a quantity of Choux Pastry into puffs. When cold, cut puffs in half horizontally. Whip cream until firm peaks form. Place a heaped teaspoonful of cream into bottom of each puff, place other puff half on top.

Brandy Alexander Sauce   Put chopped chocolate, egg yolk and water in top of double saucepan. Stir over simmering water until chocolate has melted and mixture thickens slightly. Remove from heat, add Crème de Cacao and brandy; allow to cool. Mix cornflour to a smooth paste with the milk, add to chocolate mixture, stir until smooth. Stir over medium heat until sauce boils and thickens. Reduce heat and simmer for 2 minutes. Add cream, reheat without boiling. Drizzle Brandy Alexander Sauce over each puff.

Baked Caramel Custard

½ cup sugar
2 tablespoons water
3 eggs
1 tablespoon sugar
2 cups milk
½ teaspoon vanilla essence

Put sugar and water in a small pan, stirring until sugar is dissolved. Boil without stirring until it turns a pale amber colour. Pour quickly into pie dish, coating sides. Beat eggs and sugar lightly, warm milk, add to eggs and sugar and vanilla. Pour into pie dish, standing in larger dish containing water. Bake in a moderate oven (180°–200°C) for 45 minutes or until set.

Baked Rice Custard

My children loved this dessert.

2 cups water
pinch of salt
2–3 tablespoons short-
   grain rice
3 eggs
⅓ cup sugar
1 teaspoon vanilla
¼ cup sultanas
2½ cups milk

Bring water and salt to the boil. Gradually add rice. Boil rapidly, uncovered for 10 minutes. Drain well. Beat eggs, sugar and vanilla, add rice and sultanas. Add milk gradually, stir to combine. Pour into ovenproof dish. Stand in baking dish of water to come halfway up sides of dish. Bake in a moderate oven (180°–200°C) for 35 minutes. Slip a long fork under the skin on top, and stir gently to evenly distribute rice. Reduce heat to moderately low (160°–170°C) and bake for a further 15 minutes, then stir with fork again. Cook for a further 15 to 20 minutes, or until set.

Cream Cheese Cobbler

Pudding
185 g cream cheese
2 tablespoons sugar
juice of ½ lemon
1 egg yolk
60 g butter
30 g sultanas
30 g raisins
1 small can sliced peaches
   or 2 fresh ones

Batter
90 g butter
½ cup sugar
1 egg, separated
½ teaspoon vanilla
1 tablespoon milk
1 cup self-raising flour
1 egg white

Pudding Beat cream cheese until smooth, gradually beat in sugar, lemon juice, egg yolk, and softened butter. Lastly fold in sultanas and raisins. Arrange drained sliced peaches in greased tart plate. Spread cream cheese mixture over.

Batter Cream butter and sugar. Add egg yolk, vanilla, mix well. Fold in sifted flour alternately with milk, then lastly the stiffly beaten egg whites. Pour over fruit and cream cheese layer. Bake in a moderate oven (180°–200°C) for approximately 30 to 40 minutes.

Liqueur Soufflé

90 g butter
3 tablespoons plain flour
½ cup milk
½ cup orange juice
¼ cup sugar
¼ cup Grand Marnier or
  Cointreau
4 eggs, separated

Melt butter in top of double saucepan over simmering water, remove from heat. Stir in sifted flour, continue stirring until mixture is smooth and free of lumps. Stir in milk and orange juice until mixture is smooth. Return to heat, stir over simmering water until smooth and thick. Remove from heat, stir in sugar and Grand Marnier while still hot; cool slightly. Scrape mixture into large bowl. Beat egg yolks until fluffy, gradually stir into sauce. Using clean bowl and beaters, beat egg whites until short, moist peaks form. Don't overbeat or finished soufflé will be dry. With metal spoon, lightly fold half the egg whites into sauce, then fold in remaining egg whites. (Adding whites in two parts makes it easier to fold them in lightly yet thoroughly. Air beaten in is not released, so there will be no white streaks.) Pour mixture over back of metal spoon into four greased individual soufflé dishes. Fill dishes to within 1 cm of top. Bake on oven tray in a moderately hot oven (190°–220°C) for 25 to 30 minutes.

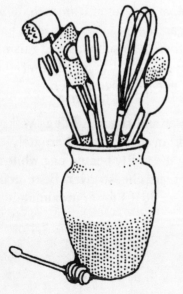

Variations

Chocolate   Substitute 1 cup milk for the ½ cup milk and ½ cup orange juice in original recipe. Sift 1 tablespoon cocoa with the flour. Stir in 125 g grated dark chocolate to the hot sauce, before adding egg yolks and whites. Stir until chocolate has melted. Grand Marnier can be omitted.

Strawberry   Omit orange juice from original recipe. Add 1 punnet of washed, hulled and mashed strawberries to the hot sauce, before adding egg yolks and whites.

CAKES

When birthdays come around in our
family, my daughter Ruth usually makes
her renowned Ginger Fluff Sponge
(see p. 86). However, before her
last birthday, Ruth asked me why she was
making the sponge yet again when it was her
own birthday. I replied that it was definitely
my turn to do the baking.
I used my well-worn Sponge Cake recipe
(see p. 194), joined the cakes with whipped
cream, and sprinkled grated chocolate over
as decoration. It turned out well and the
cake disappeared very rapidly!

Spiced Apple Cake

1 cup plain flour
1 teaspoon baking soda
½ cup butter
1 teaspoon cinnamon
1 teaspoon mixed spice
½ teaspoon ground ginger
½ cup brown sugar
1 egg
1–2 cups cold stewed apple

Sift flour and baking soda into basin. Rub butter into flour, add dry ingredients. Add well beaten egg. Divide into equal parts. Roll out half and place into bottom of sandwich tin. Spread with Apple Filling (see p. 244), then cover with rest of mixture. Bake in moderate oven (180°–200°C) for 45 to 60 minutes.

Cheesecake

Shortcrust Pastry
  (see p. 117)
2 eggs
125 g cream cheese at
  room temperature
¹/₄ cup sugar
1 tablespoon plain flour
¹/₂ teaspoon vanilla essence

Line 18 cm tart plate with pastry and bake in a moderately hot oven (190°–220°C) for 15 to 20 minutes. Separate egg yolks from whites. Add yolks to cream cheese, sugar, flour and vanilla essence. Mix well. Beat whites until stiff. Fold into mixture, place in pastry shell. Bake in a moderate oven (180°–200°C) for about 15 to 20 minutes, until set.

Chocolate Fudge Cake

3 eggs
180 g butter
½ cup cocoa
1 ½ cups castor sugar
1 teaspoon vanilla
1 ½ cups self-raising flour
¾ cup plain flour
1 cup cold water
whipped cream
icing sugar

Separate eggs. Beat butter and sifted cocoa together. Add sugar gradually and beat until light and fluffy. Add vanilla. Beat in egg yolks one at a time. Stir in sifted flour alternately with water. Fold in stiffly beaten egg whites. Pour into two greased 20 cm sandwich tins. Bake in moderately slow oven (160°–170°C) for 1 hour or until cooked. Cool in tin for 10 minutes then turn out onto wire rack. When cold sandwich together with whipped cream and sprinkle top with icing sugar.

Orange Macaroon Cake

Base
2 tablespoons butter
½ cup sugar
*1 teaspoon grated orange
rind*
2 egg yolks
5 tablespoons milk
1 cup self-raising flour
½ teaspoon salt

Topping
2 egg whites
½ cup sugar
½ cup coconut
½ teaspoon vanilla

Base Cream butter and sugar, add orange rind and egg yolks. Stir in milk with flour and salt alternately. Place mixture in a deep greased and lined cake tin.

Topping Beat egg whites until stiff. Gradually add sugar and beat until thick, then stir in coconut and vanilla. Spread on top of uncooked cake. Bake in a moderate oven (180°–200°C) for 45 minutes.

Pumpkin Fruit Cake

Here's yet another recipe for you to try, using one of my favourite vegetables — pumpkin!

¾ cup butter
2 tablespoons golden syrup
1 cup sugar
500 g mixed fruit
2 eggs, well beaten
*1 cup cooked mashed
pumpkin*
1 cup self-raising flour
1 cup plain flour
1 teaspoon cinnamon
1 teaspoon nutmeg
pinch of salt

Melt butter, add golden syrup, sugar and mixed fruit. Stir until sugar is dissolved. Remove from heat, add beaten eggs and mashed pumpkin. When cool, add flours, spices and salt. Place in greased square cake tin and bake in a moderate oven (180°–200°C) for 90 minutes.

Fruity Teacake

Cake
1 tablespoon melted butter
½ cup sugar
1 egg
½ cup milk
¾ cup mixed fruit
1 cup self-raising flour

Cinnamon topping
extra butter
2 teaspoons castor sugar
1 teaspoon cinnamon

Cake   Mix all ingredients well. Bake in a greased sandwich tin in a moderate oven (180°–200°C) for 30 minutes or until cooked.

Cinnamon Topping   While cake is still hot rub the top with extra butter. Mix sugar and cinnamon and sprinkle over cake.

Peach Blossom Cake

¼ cup butter
1 cup sugar
1¼ cups self-raising flour
½ cup milk
3 egg whites

Cream butter and sugar, add flour and milk and lastly fold in beaten egg whites. Colour half of it pink. Swirl pink and white mixtures together in a well-greased ring tin and bake in moderate oven (180°–200°C) for 30 minutes.

You can use egg yolks for the Egg Yolk Cakes recipe on p. 193.

Date Chocolate Torte

A rich and fruity chocolate sweet.

3 egg whites
½ cup castor sugar
125 g finely chopped almonds
125 g finely chopped dates
125 g grated dark chocolate
whipped cream

Beat egg whites until soft peaks form. Gradually beat in sugar until dissolved. Fold in almonds, dates and chocolate. Pour into greased aluminium foil-lined 23 cm springform pan. Bake in a moderate oven (180°–200°C) for 35 to 40 minutes. Cool in tin. Turn out carefully. Top with whipped cream.

Apricot Fudge Cake

Cake
25 g margarine
6 tablespoons soft brown
   sugar
1 egg
1 tablespoon cocoa
2 cups self-raising flour
¼ teaspoon bicarbonate of
   soda
¾ cup skim milk
½ teaspoon vanilla essence
1 cup dried chopped
   apricots, soaked
   overnight in water to cover
(Reserve 3½ tablespoons of
   apricot liquid)

Apricot Frosting
45 g melted margarine
1½ tablespoons reserved
   apricot liquid
185 g icing sugar

Cake Cream margarine and sugar. Add beaten egg and beat well. Dissolve cocoa in 2 tablespoons of reserved apricot liquid. Add to creamed mixture alternately with flour, soda and skim milk. Lastly, add vanilla essence and soaked apricots. Mix lightly. Pour into greased tin. Bake in a moderate oven (180°–200°C) for 35 to 40 minutes.

Apricot Frosting Combine ingredients. Beat until thick and creamy. Spread over top of cooled cake.

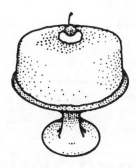

Sand Cake

castor sugar and cornflour
   to coat cake tin
125 g butter
¾ cup castor sugar
grated rind of 1 lemon
2 eggs
1 cup cornflour
1 tablespoon ground rice
pinch of salt
½ teaspoon baking powder

Grease a ring tin or 15 cm cake tin and coat with equal quantities of castor sugar and flour. Cream butter, sugar and lemon rind. Beat eggs and add gradually, beating well after each addition. Sift together cornflour, rice, salt and baking powder. Add lightly to creamed mixture one-third at a time. Pour mixture into prepared tin. Bake in a moderate oven (180°–200°C) for 1 hour.

Spicy Coffee Cake

Cake Base
1 ¾ cups plain flour
1 teaspoon baking powder
½ teaspoon bicarbonate of
   soda
½ teaspoon salt
¼ teaspoon ground
   cinnamon
¼ teaspoon nutmeg
1 teaspoon coffee powder
¾ cup sugar
1 cup whole bran cereal
⅓ cup oil
1 egg
½ cup sour milk
¾ cup raisins

Topping
3 teaspoons cinnamon
¼ cup sugar

Cake   Sift together flour, baking powder, bicarbonate of soda, salt, spices, coffee and sugar into a mixing bowl. Mix with bran cereal. Make a well in dry ingredients, add oil, slightly beaten egg, sour milk and chopped raisins. Stir until well blended and pour into greased 20 cm square cake tin.

Topping   Combine ingredients and sprinkle over the mixture. Bake in a moderate oven (180°–200°C) for about 35 minutes. Cut into squares and serve warm.

Date and Walnut Cake

1 cup dates
3 dessertspoons cold water
1 teaspoon bicarbonate of
   soda
½ cup butter
1 cup of sugar
1 egg
1 cup milk
2 ¼ cups self-raising flour
1 cup walnuts
extra walnuts to decorate

Soak dates in water and bicarbonate of soda for 1 hour. Stand aside. Cream butter and sugar, add egg, mix well. Add dates, milk, flour and walnuts. Mix thoroughly. Pour into greased ring tin. Bake in a moderate oven (180°–200°C) for 40 to 45 minutes. Ice with Chocolate Icing (see p. 247) and decorate with walnuts.

Walnut Cherry Cake

2¼ *cups self-raising flour*
½ *teaspoon salt*
250 g *butter*
1¼ *cups sugar*
1¼ *teaspoons vanilla*
½ *teaspoon cinnamon*
4 *eggs*
¼ *cup milk*
90 g *cherries*
½ *cup sultanas*
90 g *walnuts*

Sift together flour and salt. Cream butter and sugar until light and fluffy. Beat in vanilla and cinnamon. Add eggs one at a time, beating well after each addition. Add sifted dry ingredients alternately with milk. Fold in fruits and chopped walnuts. Pour into greased paper-lined tin. Bake in a slow oven (150°C) for 75 to 90 minutes When cool, sprinkle with icing sugar.

Is the cake baked?
Cakes are baked if:
    Skewer comes out clean when inserted into cake middle.
    Cake shrinks from edge of pan.
    Cake springs back when lightly touched with finger.

Walnut Cake

125 g *butter*
250 g *sugar*
2 *eggs*
250 g *plain flour*
½ *teaspoon bicarbonate of*
   soda
1 *teaspoon cream of tartar*
125 g *chopped walnuts*

Cream butter and sugar, add eggs one at a time. Sift flour, bicarbonate of soda, cream of tartar and add to mixture. Then add the walnuts. Bake in a moderate oven (180°–200°C) for 35 to 40 minutes. It can be iced with the icing of your choice (see Fillings, Icings and Sauces) and decorated with walnuts if desired.

Caraway Seed Cake

250 g butter
1 cup sugar
3 eggs, beaten
lemon essence
¾ cup milk
2 cups plain flour
1 teaspoon bicarbonate of
  soda
2 teaspoons cream of tartar
3 teaspoons caraway seeds

Cream butter and sugar. Add eggs, lemon essence and milk, beating well. Add sifted dry ingredients, then seeds, mixing to a smooth batter. Pour into greased and floured deep pan and bake in a moderate oven (180°–200°C) for 50 to 60 minutes, or until it passes the clean skewer test.

Rainbow (Tricolour) Cake

My grandchildren and their friends love the many different colours in this cake.

1 cup butter
2 cups sugar
4 egg whites
1 cup milk
5 cups plain flour
1 heaped teaspoon baking
  powder
vanilla
cochineal
cocoa powder

Cream butter and sugar. Add egg whites and milk. Fold in flour and baking powder. Divide mixture into three equal quantities, colouring one with vanilla, the second with cochineal, and the third with cocoa powder. Pour into buttered cake tin in alternate layers. Stir only once with knife, bake in a moderate oven (180°–200°C) for 30 to 40 minutes.

Date and Coconut Cake

250 g dates
1 cup water
½ teaspoon bicarbonate of
   soda
125 g butter
¾ cup brown sugar
2 eggs
¾ cup self-raising flour
1 cup plain flour
pinch of salt
½ cup coconut
1 teaspoon vanilla

Simmer dates, water and soda, allow to cool. Cream butter and sugar, add eggs. Fold in sifted flours and salt alternately with date mixture, coconut and vanilla. Bake in a deep, greased 20 cm round tin in a moderate oven (180°–200°C) for 50 to 60 minutes.

Burnt Sugar Cake

1¾ cups sugar
⅓ cup hot water
2½ cups plain flour
¼ teaspoon salt
3 teaspoons baking powder
185 g butter
3 eggs
½ teaspoon vanilla essence
½ cup milk

Caramel Icing
60 g butter
2 cups brown sugar
½ cup milk
½ teaspoon vanilla essence
blanched almonds dipped
   in chocolate

Place ½ cup sugar in a heavy saucepan and stir over a low heat. When dark brown, remove from the heat and add hot water. Stir until sugar dissolves. Cool. Sift flour, salt and baking powder three times. Cream butter and add remaining sugar, beating until light and fluffy. Add the eggs, one at a time, beating thoroughly. Add vanilla and syrup. Stir in flour and milk alternately. Divide between two greased and floured 20 cm sandwich tins. Bake in a moderate oven (180°–200°C) for 25 to 30 minutes.

Caramel Icing Heat butter, sugar and milk slowly to boiling point. Boil for exactly 9 minutes. Remove from heat, stand until bubbles subside, then beat with a wooden spoon until thick. Add vanilla. When cold join the cakes with half the Caramel Icing and quickly frost top with remaining icing. Decorate with almonds.

Devil's Food Cake

1 2/3 cups plain flour
1 1/4 teaspoons bicarbonate
    of soda
1/2 cup cocoa
1 1/2 cups sugar
1 teaspoon salt
1/2 cup butter
1 cup milk
1 teaspoon vanilla essence
3 eggs

Fluffy White Frosting
1 cup sugar
1/3 cup water
1/4 teaspoon cream of tartar
pinch of salt
2 egg whites
1 teaspoon vanilla essence

In a large mixer bowl, stir together dry ingredients, add softened butter, milk and vanilla. Blend thoroughly (about 1 minute). Beat 2 minutes on medium speed on mixer. Add eggs and beat further 2 minutes, scraping sides of bowl frequently. Pour into two greased and floured 20 cm layer tins. Bake in a moderate oven (180°–200°C) for approximately 40 minutes. Cool and frost with Fluffy White Frosting.

Fluffy White Frosting   Combine first four ingredients in a saucepan. Bring to boil, stirring until sugar dissolves. Very slowly add sugar syrup to egg whites in mixing bowl. Beat constantly with electric mixer until stiff peaks form (about seven minutes). Beat in 1 teaspoon of vanilla. This quantity makes enough to completely cover the chocolate cake.

Genoa Cake

250 g butter
1 cup sugar
3 eggs
2 cups plain flour
2 teaspoons baking powder
750 g mixed fruit
1 tablespoon custard
    powder
1 cup boiling water

Beat butter and sugar, add eggs then flour, baking powder and fruit alternately. Mix custard powder with a little milk, add boiling water, allow to cool. When cool add to other mixture. Pour into greased cake tin. Bake in a moderate oven (180°–200°C) for about 2 hours.

Prune Cake

250 g prunes
pinch of bicarbonate of
   soda
sugar to taste
125 g butter
¾ cup sugar
2 eggs
¼ teaspoon cinnamon
little grated nutmeg
2 tablespoons cocoa
1 cup plain flour
½ teaspoon bicarbonate of
   soda
a little prune juice

Egg Yolk Icing
1 egg yolk
1 tablespoon butter
1 tablespoon orange juice
1 dessertspoon orange rind
1½ cups icing sugar

Put prunes on to boil until soft, with a pinch of soda and sugar to taste. Cream butter and sugar, adding eggs one at a time, then add cinnamon and nutmeg. Sift cocoa and flour into mixture. Melt soda with a little prune juice and add to mixture. Lastly add the stoned prunes. Pour into a greased ring tin and bake in moderate oven (180°–200°C) for 45 to 60 minutes.

Egg Yolk Icing Beat egg yolk with butter, add orange juice and rind, then add icing sugar to make a good spreading icing. Decorate with sprinkled nuts.

Streusel Cake

125 g butter
1 cup sugar
3 eggs
1 tablespoon strained,
   cooked apples
lemon essence
2 cups self-raising flour
pinch of salt
1 cup milk

Topping
1 tablespoon butter
2 tablespoons plain flour
3 tablespoons sugar

Cream butter and sugar, add eggs one at a time. Add apples and essence. Mix in flour and salt alternately with the milk. Beat well until evenly blended. Pour into a greased 20 cm deep cake tin and sprinkle with topping before baking in a moderate oven (180°–200°C) for approximately 25 minutes.

Topping Rub ingredients together to resemble breadcrumbs. Sprinkle on top of unbaked cake.

Yoghurt Cake

Joh loves yoghurt, especially in the form of a cake!

1 cup butter
1½ cups sugar
1 cup yoghurt
5 eggs
3 cups self-raising flour
½ cup chopped nuts

Cream butter and sugar. Add yoghurt and mix well. Add eggs and beat for 5 minutes. Gradually mix in sifted flour, at slow speed. Fold in nuts. Pour into greased oven dish 30 x 23 cm. Bake in a moderate oven (180°–200°C) for 50 to 60 minutes. Cool on wire rack. Ice with Chocolate Icing (see p. 247).

Is there peaking and cracking in your cake?
This is due to:
> *The oven being set too high.*
> *The mixture being too stiff.*
> *The cake being placed too close to the top of the oven.*
> *The cake tin being too small for the quantity of mixture.*

Eggless Bran Cake

Ideal if eggs are in short supply!

1 cup self-raising flour
1 cup unprocessed bran
1 cup brown sugar
1 cup milk
¼ teaspoon bicarbonate of soda
1 cup mixed fruit or dates

Mix all ingredients together, adding the fruit last. (Nuts may also be added if desired.) Place in a greased bar tin. Bake in a moderate oven (180°–200°C) for 45 minutes. Chopped nuts may be added on top of cake before baking.

Foundation Cake

185 g butter
185 g sugar
3 eggs, well beaten
6 tablespoons milk
315 g self-raising flour

Optional flavourings
½ cup coconut
2 tablespoons cocoa powder
1 tablespoon grated orange rind
1 teaspoon vanilla essence

Cream butter and sugar, beat in the eggs gradually. Add milk. Lightly fold in sifted flour. Pour into a greased slab tin and bake in a moderate oven (180°–200°C) for 35 minutes. Ice if desired, or use Apple Filling (see p. 244)

Anzac Cake

Cake
½ cup golden syrup
125 g butter
2 cups self-raising flour
¼ cup castor sugar
½ cup shredded coconut
2 eggs, lightly beaten
1 cup milk

Icing
60 g melted butter
1 teaspoon honey
1 teaspoon vanilla essence
1½ cups icing sugar
1 tablespoon hot water

Cake Combine golden syrup and butter in pan, stir over heat until smooth. Combine sifted flour, sugar and coconut in bowl. Add syrup mixture, mixing well. Using an electric mixer, gradually beat in eggs and milk until smooth. Pour mixture into greased tin, bake in a moderate oven (200°C) for about 30 minutes, or until cooked when tested with a skewer. Cool. Spread icing over cake. Cut into squares.

Icing Combine butter, honey and vanilla in bowl. Using an electric mixer, gradually beat in sifted icing sugar and water. Beat until smooth.

Carrot and Nut Ring

This cake freezes well.

90 g butter
½ cup castor sugar
2 eggs
1½ cups self-raising flour
pinch of salt
¼ cup milk
½ cup grated carrot
¼ cup chopped walnuts
¼ cup chopped unblanched almonds
¼ cup chopped glacé cherries

Topping
2 tablespoons chopped walnuts
2 tablespoons unblanched almonds
2 tablespoons chopped glacé cherries
2 tablespoons sugar

Cream butter and sugar. Add eggs, one at a time, beating well. Sift together flour and salt and stir in, alternately with the milk. Add the carrot, walnuts, almonds and cherries with wooden spoon until thoroughly mixed. Spread evenly into a greased 20 cm ring tin, sprinkle topping over and bake in a moderate oven (180°–200°C) for 40 to 50 minutes or until skewer comes out clean when inserted. Leave in tin for 5 minutes and then carefully turn out.

Topping   Put walnuts, almonds and cherries into bowl. Stir in sugar. Sprinkle over cake before baking.

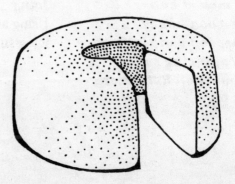

Cherry Rum Cake

A special cake for a special occasion.

Chocolate Sponge
¼ *cup plain flour*
¼ *cup self-raising flour*
¼ *teaspoon salt*
60 g *dark chocolate*
4 *eggs*
½ *cup castor sugar*
1 *teaspoon vanilla*
¼ *teaspoon bicarbonate of*
   soda
2 *tablespoons water*
extra castor sugar

Filling
470 g *can black cherries*
1 *teaspoon vanilla*
2 *tablespoons sugar*
2 *tablespoons rum*
300 mL *thickened cream*

Topping
½ *cup thickened cream*
¼ *teaspoon vanilla*
30 g *dark chocolate*

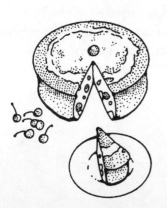

Chocolate Sponge   Sift together flours and salt. Melt roughly-chopped chocolate in top of double saucepan over simmering water. Beat eggs, sugar and vanilla until thick and creamy, making sure all sugar is dissolved. Fold in sifted flour mixture. Add combined bicarbonate of soda and water to chocolate, stir until smooth. Fold quickly and evenly into egg-and-flour mixture. Pour into greased and greasepaper lined 30 x 25 cm Swiss roll tin. Bake in a moderately hot oven (190°–220°C) for 12 to 15 minutes or until roll springs back when centre is pressed. Turn out immediately onto a tea towel lightly dusted with castor sugar. Peel off paper, trim edges with sharp knife. Roll cake up in tea towel like a Swiss roll. Allow to cool. Unroll the cake.

Filling   Drain and pit cherries. Set aside. Place vanilla, sugar, rum and cream into bowl, beat cream until firm peaks form. Place the cherries side by side along the short edge at one side of the cake. Spread the rum cream over the whole cake and roll it up again, starting from the end which has the cherries, so they are in the middle of the cake. Cover cake with plastic food wrap and refrigerate for several hours or overnight.

Topping   Place cream and vanilla into bowl, beat until firm peaks form. Place chopped chocolate in top of double saucepan over simmering water, stir until chocolate has melted. Spoon whipped cream into piping bag fitted with star nozzle. Pipe cream decoratively on top of cake. Drizzle melted chocolate over cream with spoon. Refrigerate cake until serving time.

Cup Cakes

Nice for children's play lunch.

¾ *cup castor sugar*
pinch of salt
2 *cups self-raising flour*
125 *g butter*
½ *cup milk*
2 *eggs*
½ *teaspoon vanilla essence*

Sift dry ingredients. Add remaining ingredients and beat for 3 minutes. Spoon mixture into paper patty pans, placed in cake tins. Bake in moderate oven (180°–200°C) for 12 to 15 minutes.

Variations

Butterfly Cakes   Cut a circle from top of each cooked cake, fill with a spoonful of sweetened, whipped cream and place circle, cut into two, in butterfly-wing fashion on top. Dust with icing sugar.
Cherry   Fold in ½ cup sliced glacé cherries with the flour.
Chocolate   Use 3 eggs and add 4 tablespoons cocoa. Ice with Chocolate Icing (see p. 134).
Sultana   Use 1 teaspoon finely grated lemon rind instead of vanilla. Fold in ½ cup sultanas with the flour.
Jelly Cakes   Use 1 packet red or lime-green jelly crystals and coconut for rolling cakes in. Dissolve jelly crystals in 1 cup boiling water and allow them to almost set. Take each cake and dip into soft jelly, then roll in coconut. Place in refrigerator to set. Cut off top of cake, add a good dollop of whipped cream, and replace the lid.

Cooking note   If cup cakes are to be iced and smooth tops required, bake in a moderately hot oven (190°–220°C). For peaked tops (necessary for butterfly cakes), bake in a hot oven (200°–230°C) and place cakes in hottest part of oven, usually near the top of gas ovens and at the bottom of electric ovens. Check oven guide for your particular stove.

Egg Yolk Cakes

Makes 18

3 egg yolks
¼ cup milk
60 g sugar
60 g butter
1 cup self-raising flour

Mix yolks with a little milk. Cream sugar and butter, add yolk mixture. Fold in flour and remainder of milk to make a smooth batter. Bake in patty tins in a moderate oven (180°–200°C) for 12 to 15 minutes.

Lemon Cakes

2 eggs
1 cup sugar
125 g soft margarine
1½ cups self-raising flour
pinch of salt
¾ cup milk
rind of lemon

Place all ingredients into a basin and beat with electric mixer for 3 minutes at medium speed. Pour into greased 20 cm cake tin and bake in a moderate oven (180°–200°C) for 30 to 40 minutes. When cold, top with favourite icing (see Fillings, Icings and Sauces section).

Nutties

1½ cups plain flour
¼ teaspoon salt
1 teaspoon cinnamon
¾ cup chopped dates and
  sultanas
½ cup roughly chopped
  walnuts
215 g butter
½ cup sugar
2 eggs, beaten
1 level teaspoon
  bicarbonate of soda
  dissolved in 1 tablespoon
  of boiling water

Mix dry ingredients with nuts and fruit. Cream butter and sugar, add eggs. Add dry ingredients and mix well. Stir in soda and boiling water. Put into ungreased patty cake tins. Bake in hot oven (230°C) for 10 to 15 minutes, then in a slow oven (150°C) for a further 10 to 15 minutes.

Sponge Cake

4 eggs, separated
small cup sugar
½ teaspoon vanilla essence
¾ cup cornflour
¼ cup plain flour
½ teaspoon baking soda
1 teaspoon cream of tartar
pinch of salt
2 tablespoons milk
1 teaspoon butter

Beat egg whites until stiff. Add yolks, sugar and vanilla. Sift flours, baking soda, cream of tartar and salt, fold into mixture. Boil milk and butter. Add to mixture then pour into well-greased 20 cm cake tins. Bake in moderate oven (180°–200°C) for 15 minutes or until the cake leaves the side of the tin. Cut in half crossways and fill with fresh cream and/or jam. Dust top with icing sugar.

Quick Mix Sponge Cake

4 tablespoons butter
4 tablespoons sugar
2 large or 3 small eggs
125 g self-raising flour
pinch of salt

Beat butter until soft, add sugar, beat lightly. Add eggs, beat lightly. Add flour and salt and beat mixture for 1 minute. Bake in greased 20 cm round sponge tin in a moderate oven (180°–200°C) for 25 to 30 minutes.

To turn this cake into a real dessert, evenly spread half the mixture into tin. Spread evenly over half a layer of apple pulp, then spread remaining cake batter over apples. Sprinkle with cinnamon. Bake as per instructions above.

Did your cake rise evenly?
Uneven rising may be due to:
  The mixture not being evenly spread in the tin.
  The oven shelf being tilted.
  The tin touching the oven walls or another cooking
    utensil.

Chocolate Fluff Sponge

3 eggs, separated
pinch of salt
½ cup sugar
½ cup self-raising flour
¼ cup cornflour
¼ cup cocoa
1 tablespoon honey
2 tablespoons hot water

Filling
1 cup cream
1 tablespoon brown sugar

Beat egg whites and salt until soft peaks form, add sugar gradually, beating well after each addition. Add egg yolks, beat until combined. Sift dry ingredients several times, fold into egg mixture, mix well. Melt honey in hot water, fold into cake mixture, mix well. Pour mixture evenly into two well-greased 18 cm sandwich tins. Bake in a moderate oven (180°–200°C) for 15 to 20 minutes. Cool.

Filling Whip cream and sugar until soft peaks form. Join two layers of sponge together, dust top with sifted icing sugar.

Variation *3 Minute Chocolate Sponge* Use 2 cups self-raising flour, 1 cup sugar, 60 g cocoa, 2 eggs, 90 g butter, 1 teaspoon vanilla, 1 cup milk. Mix all ingredients until smooth and beat for about 3 minutes. Bake in greased ring tin in a moderate oven (180°–200°C) for 25 to 30 minutes.

Cornflour Sponge

I make this sponge quite a lot.

4 eggs
1 cup sugar
¼ teaspoon salt
¾ cups cornflour
¼ cup plain flour
1 teaspoon cream of tartar
½ teaspoon baking soda
1 tablespoon butter
2 tablespoons boiling milk

Beat egg whites, salt and sugar until thick. Add the egg yolks, then add sifted dry ingredients. Add butter melted in the hot milk. Mix well. Place in greased sponge tins (you will need very large tins as the sponges rise quite high) in a moderate oven (180°–200°C) for 10 to 15 minutes. The sponges are cooked when the mixture leaves the sides of the tins.

Custard Sponge

4 eggs, separated
¾ cup sugar
1 cup custard powder
1 teaspoon cream of tartar
½ teaspoon bicarbonate of
    soda

Beat egg whites till frothy, fold in sugar. Add egg yolks. Sift custard powder, cream of tartar and bicarbonate of soda three times, add to egg and sugar. Pour into greased 20 cm cake tin and bake in a moderate oven (180°–200°C) for 20 minutes.

Baked Jam Roll

Roll
90 g butter
1½ cups self-raising flour
water for mixing to soft
    dough
jam of your choice

Roll Rub butter into flour, add enough water to mix to a soft dough. Roll out and spread with jam. Roll up and put into a buttered dish.

Syrup Mix all ingredients together and pour over roll before baking. Bake in a moderate oven (180°–200°C) for 30 minutes.

Syrup
½ cup hot water
1 dessertspoon butter
½ cup sugar
juice of 1 lemon

Is the cake too dense in volume?
This could be caused by:
    Too slow an oven — the air expanded before the cake
        was set enough to hold its shape after rising.
    Too hot an oven — the outside crust set before the air
        had time to expand and make the mixture rise.

Coffee Sponge Sandwich

4 eggs, separated
1 cup castor sugar
1¼ cups self-raising flour
1 tablespoon cornflour
30 g butter
4 tablespoons water
1 tablespoon coffee essence

Filling and Topping
6 tablespoons sugar
6 tablespoons water
185 g butter
vanilla essence
1 tablespoon coffee essence

Beat egg whites until stiff and dry. Gradually beat in sugar, keeping mixture stiff. Beat well, then add egg yolks and beat again. Add flours, which have been sifted three times. Fold lightly into egg and sugar mixture, then heat butter, water and coffee and fold in gently. Pour into two greased 20 cm sandwich tins and bake in a moderate oven (180°–200°C) for 20 minutes.

Filling and Topping   Heat sugar and water until sugar is dissolved. Allow syrup to cool. Cream butter until light, then add cooled syrup gradually. Continue beating until mixture is light and fluffy. Divide the cream in half; flavour one half with vanilla and use as filling. Top sponge with remaining cream to which the coffee has been added.

Tasmanian Sponge Sandwich

As Joh spends a good deal of time in Tasmania, I thought this to be an appropriate recipe!

4 eggs
1 cup sugar
1 cup plain flour
1 teaspoon cream of tartar
½ teaspoon bicarbonate of
   soda
5 tablespoons boiling milk

Separate eggs. Cream egg yolks and sugar well. Add stiffly beaten egg whites. Add flour, cream of tartar and lastly milk and bicarbonate of soda combined. Pour into lightly greased sandwich tin and bake in a moderate oven (180°–200°C) for 15 to 20 minutes. Cream and/or ice (see Fillings, Icings and Sauces) as desired.

Chocolate Sandwich

90 g butter
1 small cup sugar
2 eggs
1 cup plain flour
2 teaspoons cream of tartar
2 teaspoons cocoa
1 teaspoon bicarbonate of
　soda
2 tablespoons milk

Cream butter and sugar. Add beaten eggs, sifted flour, cream of tartar, cocoa. Dissolve the bicarbonate of soda in the milk and add to mixture. Bake in a hot oven (230°C) for 15 to 18 minutes. Ice with Chocolate Icing (see p. 247) and decorate as required.

Sponge Lilies

3 eggs, separated
1 cup sugar
1 cup self-raising flour

Beat the yolks a little, then add sugar and beat until white and creamy. Whip the whites until stiff, add to yolks and sugar, and mix until well blended. Stir in the sifted flour. Drop teaspoonfuls of mixture onto a greased baking tray, allowing room to spread. Bake in a fairly hot oven (200°–230°C) until pale brown. They must not be allowed to bake until crisp. As each is removed from oven, roll into a round shape. When cold fill with whipped cream and place some Lemon Jelly Filling (see p. 245) in centre of each top.

Sponge Roll

3 eggs
½ cup sugar
¾ cup self-raising flour
1 tablespoon cinnamon
pinch of salt
1 tablespoon hot water
1 tablespoon honey

Beat eggs well. Add sugar a little at a time and beat again until blended. Remove beater and fold in flour sifted with cinnamon and salt. Add water and honey and stir quickly. Pour batter into greased Swiss roll pan. Bake in a moderate oven (180°–200°C) for 10 minutes. Turn out, roll in dry cloth. When cool, unroll and spread with whipped or Mock Cream (see p. 118)

Swiss Roll

¾ cup self-raising flour
pinch of salt
3 eggs
¾ cup castor sugar
1 tablespoon hot water
3–4 tablespoons warm jam
castor sugar for dredging

Grease a 38 x 25 x 2.5 cm Swiss roll tin and line with greased, greaseproof paper. Sift flour with salt three times. Place eggs and sugar in a bowl and stand over a pan of gently steaming but not boiling water. Whisk well until mixture is very thick and creamy, (about 10 minutes) or use an electric mixer. Remove bowl from water and continue whisking until mixture is cool. Fold in flour as lightly as possible with a metal spoon. Lastly, fold in hot water. Pour into prepared tin and shake into corners. Spread evenly using a spatula. Bake in a hot oven (200°–230°C) for 7 to 10 minutes until pale golden and springy. Quickly turn out sponge onto a tea towel well sprinkled with castor sugar. Carefully strip off lining paper. Trim off crisp edges with a sharp knife. Roll in towel, cool, then unroll. Warm jam in saucepan and spread over sponge, almost to the edges. Lifting the edges of the sugared tea towel nearest you, roll the sponge into a neat, firm roll. Stand roll on a cooling rack with join underneath. Leave until cold, away from any draughts. Sprinkle with a little more castor sugar before serving.

Honey Spiced Sponge Roll

Sponge Roll
3 eggs
½ cup castor sugar
½ cup arrowroot
1 tablespoon plain flour
½ teaspoon ground cinnamon
1 teaspoon mixed spice
1 teaspoon cream of tartar
½ teaspoon bicarbonate of soda
1 tablespoon honey (room temperature)

Honey Cream Filling
125 g butter
4 tablespoons honey
1 tablespoon water

Sponge roll   Line a 38 x 25 x 2.5 cm Swiss roll tin with greased, greaseproof paper. Beat eggs until thick and add sugar gradually. Continue beating until mixture is thick and holds its shape, about 10 minutes. Sift together arrowroot, flour, cinnamon, mixed spice, cream of tartar and bicarbonate of soda three times. Lightly fold into egg mixture and add honey, mixing gently until evenly distributed. Pour into prepared tin and gently shake to evenly spread mixture. Bake in a moderately hot oven (190°–220°C) for 15 to 20 minutes. Turn out onto a tea towel which has been lightly dusted with castor sugar and quickly peel off paper and trim edges. Roll up immediately in tea towel, starting with narrow end. Allow to cool and then unroll.

Honey Cream Filling   Beat butter until light and add honey a tablespoon at a time, then add water. Continue beating until mixture is smooth and creamy. Fill roll with Honey Cream Filling and roll again. If serving as dessert, roll cake, starting with wide end, and cut into diagonal slices.

Chocolate Cream Roll

½ cup plain flour
½ teaspoon baking powder
¼ teaspoon salt
60 g cooking chocolate
4 eggs (at room
temperature)
¾ cup sifted castor sugar
1 teaspoon vanilla essence
¼ teaspoon bicarbonate of
soda
2 tablespoons cold water
icing sugar
300 mL whipped cream
¼ teaspoon almond or
vanilla essence

Grease a 38 x 25 x 2.5 cm Swiss roll tin and line with greased, greaseproof paper. Sift together flour, baking powder and salt. Melt chocolate in basin over hot water. Break eggs into large bowl, sift in sugar and beat at high speed until very light and thick. Fold flour mixture and vanilla essence all at once into egg mixture. Add bicarbonate of soda and cold water to chocolate. Stir until smooth and light. Fold quickly and evenly into egg and flour mixture. Pour into prepared tin and bake in a hot oven (200°–230°C) for 15 minutes or until the cake springs back when centre is gently touched. When cake is cooked, loosen edges and turn onto a tea towel thickly sprinkled with icing sugar. Peel off paper and trim edges of cake with a sharp knife. Roll immediately in towel, first folding towel hem over cake edge and rolling towel in the cake to prevent sticking. After cake is rolled, leave to cool on wire rack for at least 1 hour. Before serving, carefully unroll cake and quickly spread with whipped cream, flavoured with almond or vanilla essence. Re-roll cake. Dust with icing sugar.

Strawberry Hazelnut Torte

Base
4 egg whites
pinch of salt
1¼ cups castor sugar
140 g ground hazelnuts
1 teaspoon vinegar
2 tablespoons black coffee
few drops vanilla

Filling
185 g chocolate
3 tablespoons water
600 mL whipped cream
1 punnet strawberries

Base   Beat egg whites with salt until stiff. Gradually add sugar and beat until mixture is of a meringue consistency. Fold in remaining ingredients. Spread into two greased and floured 20 cm sandwich tins. Bake in a moderate oven (180°–200°C) for approximately 35 minutes. Cool.

Filling   Place a layer of meringue onto serving plate. Spread with thin layer of chocolate melted with water. Spread a 2 cm layer of whipped cream over chocolate. Top with layer of sliced strawberries. Place second meringue layer on top of strawberries, spread with remaining chocolate. Cover sides and top with remaining cream. Refrigerate overnight. Decorate with grated chocolate and fresh strawberries.

Strawberry Shortcake

60 g butter
2 tablespoons sugar
2 egg yolks
¾ cup plain flour
1 punnet strawberries
½ cup plum jam or
*   strawberry jam*
2 teaspoons water

Cream butter and sugar until light and fluffy. Add egg yolks, beat well. Work in sifted flour until well combined. Knead dough on lightly floured board. Press dough into greased 20 cm sandwich tin, bake in a moderate oven (180°–200°C) for 15 to 20 minutes. Remove from tin, allow to cool slightly. Hull strawberries, (reserving a few for decoration) cut in halves, arrange over warm shortcake. Combine jam and water, stir over low heat until boiling, push through sieve. Cool slightly, then brush generously over strawberries and shortcake. Refrigerate until set. Decorate with whipped cream and reserved strawberries. You can brush some of the glaze over the strawberries for a pretty effect.

Swiss Fingers

Rough Puff Pastry
(see p. 116)
whipped cream
raspberry, strawberry or
blackberry jam
icing sugar

Preheat oven to 230°C. Dampen an oven slide with cold water. Roll out pastry to ½ cm, cut into oblong pieces approximately 10 x 4 cm. Lift onto tray and bake in oven for 20 minutes, until golden brown. Lift onto cake cooler. When cold, split, fill with a layer of jam and whipped, sweetened cream. Sprinkle tops with sifted icing sugar.

Almond and Chocolate Gateau

Very rich but very nice.

Base
1 x 20 cm plain sponge cake
generous ⅔ cup very strong
coffee
½ tablespoon Tia Maria

Filling
90 g butter
90 g icing sugar
1 egg yolk
60 g ground almonds or
crushed nuts
60 g cocoa
1–2 tablespoons strong
coffee

To serve
⅔ cup cream
30 g icing sugar
1 egg white
1–2 tablespoons Tia Maria
few chopped browned
almonds
a little grated chocolate

Base Line 20 cm cake tin with greaseproof paper. Cut cake into three rounds, put one into the tin. Mix the coffee and Tia Maria, moisten the bottom layer of cake.

Filling Cream ingredients to soft consistency. Spread half over cake. Cover with second layer of cake. Moisten cake with coffee and cover with remaining chocolate almond mixture. Put on third layer of cake, use remainder of coffee to moisten. Cover with plate. Leave for several hours in the refrigerator. Turn out.

To serve Whip the cream, fold in sugar. Whip egg white stiffly, fold into cream with Tia Maria. Spread all over cake and sides. Decorate with nuts and chocolate.

Healthy Loaf

1 cup unprocessed bran
1¼ cups milk
¾ cup raw sugar
½ cup sultanas and
apricots or dates
1½ cups self-raising flour
¼ cup walnuts or blanched
almonds

Combine bran, milk, sugar and fruit and soak for 15 minutes. Add flour and nuts, mixing well. Pour into greased loaf pan and bake in a moderate oven (180°–200°C) for approximately 50 minutes.

Banana and Fruit Loaf

1 cup milk, left to stand for
15 minutes
1 cup wholemeal self-
raising flour
1 teaspoon bicarbonate of
soda
½ cup raw sugar
½ cup chopped apricots
½ cup sultanas
½ cup sesame seeds or 1
cup coconut
½ cup wheatgerm
2 eggs, beaten
3 mashed ripe bananas

Mix all ingredients together. Bake in a greased, lined bar tin in a moderate oven (180°–200°C) for one hour. Butter slices of the loaf before serving, if desired.

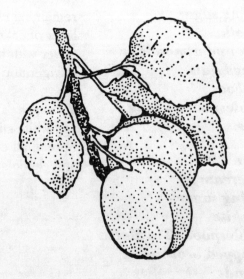

Fruity Health Loaf

It is delicious served sliced and buttered.

1 cup wholemeal self-
raising flour
1 cup chopped dried fruit
1 cup milk
½ cup raw sugar
1 cup coconut
¼ teaspoon salt

Mix all ingredients together. Place mixture in a greased and floured loaf tin. Bake in a moderate oven (180°–200°C) for 50 to 60 minutes.

Spiced Loaf

125 g butter
½ cup brown sugar
2 eggs
3 tablespoons milk
1½ cups plain flour
1 teaspoon baking powder
½ teaspoon allspice
60 g candied peel
250 g currants
250 g sultanas

Cream butter and sugar. Add eggs and milk. Sift flour with baking powder and allspice. Mix flour gradually into mixture. Add the fruit and peel. Pour mixture into greased and double-lined loaf tin. Bake in moderate oven (180°–200°C) for approximately 2 hours.

Nut Loaf

Serve warm or cold with butter.

30 g butter
½ cup honey
1 egg
1 cup plain flour
pinch of salt
1 teaspoon baking powder
¼ cup milk
½ cup chopped walnuts
½ cup sultanas

Cream butter and honey until light. Add egg and beat in well. Sift flour with salt and baking powder three times. Fold into creamed mixture alternately with milk, walnuts and sultanas. Spoon into a greased loaf tin and bake in a moderate oven (180°–200°C) for 50 to 60 minutes or until a fine skewer comes out clean when inserted.

Banana Loaf

125 g butter
¾ cup raw sugar
1 egg, lightly beaten
2 mashed bananas
¼ cup yoghurt
1 cup plain wholemeal
  flour
½ cup wholemeal self-
  raising flour

Cream butter and sugar. Add egg and mix well. Add bananas to yoghurt, then blend with creamed mixture. Add flours, stir until combined. Place in a greased and lined loaf tin. Bake in a moderate oven (180°–200°C) for 50 minutes.

Bran and Sultana Loaf

2 cups plain flour
1 heaped cup bran
2 tablespoons sugar
1 sachet (7 g) dry yeast
350 g sultanas
1 tablespoon peanut oil
1¼ cups warm water

Mix dry ingredients and sultanas in a large bowl. Combine the oil and water and gradually add it to the dry mixture. Mix to a dough and knead for about 10 minutes before putting in a greased bowl. Cover and leave in a warm place for 1 hour to rise.

Knock the dough down and knead again for a few minutes. Put into a lightly oiled 23 x 10 cm loaf tin. Brush top with a little warm water and leave in a warm place for 30 minutes. Bake in a very hot oven (230°C) for 35 minutes. Remove loaf from oven and allow to cool before serving with cheese or other topping. It's also delicious toasted and spread with jam.

Pear and Ginger Loaf

2 pears
juice and grated rind of 1
   lemon
1 egg, lightly beaten
¼ cup vegetable oil
½ teaspoon vanilla essence
½ teaspoon crystallised
   ginger, chopped finely
1 cup self-raising flour
1 cup wholemeal self-
   raising flour
1 teaspoon ground ginger
½ teaspoon baking powder

Mix grated pears, lemon juice and rind, lightly beaten egg, oil, vanilla and chopped ginger. Combine remaining ingredients and fold into wet ingredients, stirring thoroughly. Pour into lightly greased loaf pan. Bake in moderate oven (180°C) for 50 to 60 minutes or until cooked. Turn out on to wire rack to cool.

Golden Fruit Cake

250 g sultanas
125 g mixed peel
60 g slivered almonds
125 g glacé cherries
125 g glacé pineapple
125 g glacé apricots
125 g glacé ginger
250 g butter
1 teaspoon grated lemon
    rind
1 cup castor sugar
4 eggs
1 ½ cups plain flour

Combine sultanas, peel and almonds in bowl, add chopped glacé fruit. Cream butter, lemon rind and sugar; beat in eggs one at a time. Stir into fruit mixture, then stir in sifted flour. Spread mixture evenly in deep 20 cm round cake tin lined with three layers of greaseproof paper, bringing paper 5 cm above edge of tin. Decorate top with almonds if desired. Bake in slow oven (150°C) for 3 hours or until cooked when tested with skewer. Cover and cool in tin.

American Fruit and Nut Cake

A nice variation to the Australian fruit cake.

125 g glacé pineapple
125 g glacé apricots
250 g dates
125 g red glacé cherries
125 g green glacé cherries
125 g whole blanched
    almonds
250 g brazil nuts
2 eggs
½ cup brown sugar, lightly
    packed
½ teaspoon vanilla essence
½ teaspoon rum essence
90 g butter
⅓ cup plain flour
3 tablespoons self-raising
    flour

Roughly chop pineapple and apricots, leave remaining fruit and nuts whole. Mix all together well. Beat eggs until thick and creamy, add sugar, vanilla, rum essence and softened butter, beating until combined. Stir sifted flours into fruit and nut mixture. Divide mixture between 2 greased bar tins (7 x 25 cm), line base with greaseproof paper. Press mixture firmly into tins. Bake in slow oven (150°C) for 1¼ hours or until cake is firm to the touch. Cool in tin for 10 minutes. When cold, wrap in plastic foodwrap and store in airtight container in refrigerator.

Russian Christmas Cake (Mazurka)

125 g currants
125 g sultanas
125 g raisins
125 g dates
125 g figs
125 g blanched almonds
125 g mixed peel
60 g glacé cherries
60 g glacé pineapple
3 eggs
⅓ cup honey
1¼ cups plain flour

Combine currants and sultanas in basin. Chop all other fruit and almonds into small pieces, add to basin with lightly beaten eggs, honey and sifted flour. Mix well until ingredients are thoroughly combined. Press mixture evenly over base of greased and lined Swiss roll tin, then bake in slow oven (150°C) for 1 hour. Cool in tin. Cut when cold. Store in airtight container; it will keep refrigerated for up to 1 month.

Baking Fruit Cakes: Pitfalls

Damp fruit — *If fruit has been washed, it must be spread out on trays to dry for at least 24 hours.*

Sticky glacé cherries — *If wet with syrup, they should first be washed and dried, then lightly floured.*

Too soft a mixture — *Rich fruit cakes should be fairly stiff, so as to support the weight of the fruit.*

Using the wrong flour — *If you use self-raising flour when the recipe states plain, or if you use too much baking powder, the cake will rise but the fruit will not.*

Dry fruit cakes may be due to:
   The mixture being too stiff.
   The oven temperature being too high.

A sinking cake may be due to:
   Too soft a mixture.
   Opening or banging the oven door while cake is cooking.
   Too cool an oven.
   Too hot an oven, making the cake appear done before it is cooked through.
   Too short a baking time.

Wedding Cake

A very dear friend from the Church, Vera Horne, baked all of my daughters' wedding cakes.

1.75 kg mixed fruit
750 g dates
juice and rinds of 2 oranges
and 2 lemons
2 grated apples (skin and
flesh)
2 x 100 g packets almonds
2 tablespoons chopped
ginger
4 tablespoons rum
500 g butter
500 g sugar
8 eggs
1 tablespoon golden syrup
6 tablespoons jam
5 ½ cups plain flour
1 teaspoon salt
1 teaspoon baking soda
2 teaspoons allspice
Parisian essence
vanilla essence

Soak all fruits, dates, juices and rinds, grated apple, almonds, ginger and rum for 12 hours. Stir now and again so that juices and rum can soak into fruits. Cream butter, sugar and eggs until soft and fluffy. Fold in syrup and jam. Sift flour, salt, soda and spice. Add slowly to creamed mixture with fruits. Add vanilla and Parisian essences. Bake in a slow oven (150°C) for about 8 hours in 25 cm tin lined with brown paper.

Note   This quantity makes a 1 x 25 cm round or square cake. For a two-tier cake, make 1½ times the recipe quantity, and use 1 x 25 cm and 1 x 18 cm tins. For a three-tier cake, double the mixture and use 1 x 25 cm, 1 x 20 cm and 1 x 15 cm tins.

Almond Paste
250 g icing sugar
pinch of salt
250 g almond meal
1 egg yolk
3 tablespoons orange juice
½ teaspoon almond essence

Sift icing sugar and salt, mix in almond meal. Beat egg yolk, mix in orange juice and essence. Work all ingredients together and knead well. Use hands for mixing. Turn onto a board, dusted with a little icing sugar and knead well. Roll and use as required.

BISCUITS

You can never have too many biscuit recipes.
I always like to have home-made biscuits on
hand when my grandchildren, Rachel, David
and Mark, arrive home on the school bus,
which only comes as far as 'Bethany'. I give
them one of my baked treats for their
afternoon snack, and then take them home.

Water Biscuits

1 cup plain flour
½ teaspoon baking powder
pinch of salt
30 g butter
water

Sift flour into a bowl with baking powder and salt. With the fingertips, rub butter into ingredients until evenly distributed. Stir in enough water to make a firm dough. Roll out on a lightly floured board to about 1 cm thickness. Cut with a floured biscuit cutter into small rounds. With a lightly floured rolling pin roll each round into very thin rounds or ovals and prick them with a fork. Bake on a baking sheet in a hot oven (200°–230°C) until they are well puffed and golden.

Bran Biscuits

Delicious served with camembert or brie cheese.

50 g butter
25 g sugar
1 large egg
100 g plain flour
1 teaspoon baking powder
pinch of salt
150 g bran

Cream butter and sugar then mix in egg. Sift in the flour, baking powder and salt before folding in the bran. Roll into small balls and bake on a lightly oiled tray in a moderately hot oven (190°–220°C) for 15 to 20 minutes.

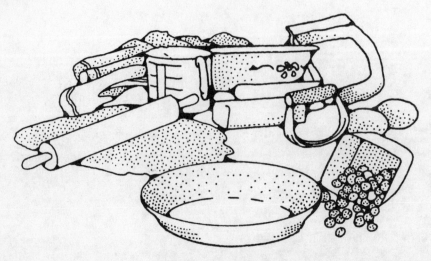

Cheese Daisies

Delicious with pre-dinner drinks.

2 tablespoons sesame seeds
185 g butter
1½ cups finely grated
   cheddar cheese
¼ cup grated parmesan
   cheese
1½ cups plain flour
1 teaspoon paprika
1 teaspoon salt
3 tablespoons poppy seeds

Toast sesame seeds in dry saucepan until golden, set aside. Cream butter, cheddar and parmesan. Sift flour, paprika and salt together. Add to creamed mixture with sesame seeds. Mix well and put dough into biscuit forcer, using flower disc or pastry tube with a large star pipe. Press onto ungreased baking trays. Centre each flower with a tiny ball of dough rolled in poppy seeds. Bake in a moderate oven (180°–200°C) for 12 to 15 minutes.

Cheese Straws

60 g butter
1 cup plain flour
125 g grated cheese
1 teaspoon dry mustard
cayenne to taste
2 eggs

Rub butter into flour. Add cheese, mustard and cayenne. Add beaten eggs and mix to a stiff paste. Roll and fold like pastry. Roll out to 3 cm thickness. Cut into 10 x 2 cm strips. Bake on floured tray in a hot oven (230°C) for about 10 minutes. Serve hot or cold.

Munchies

2 cups rolled oats
1 cup brown sugar
1 cup plain flour
1 cup coconut
1 cup butter
2 tablespoons golden syrup
1 teaspoon bicarbonate of
   soda
3 tablespoons boiling water

Mix all dry ingredients. Melt butter, add syrup, heat to boiling point. Dissolve soda in boiling water and add to butter and syrup. This will rise and foam; add this immediately to dry ingredients. Put small spoonfuls onto greased tray and bake in a hot oven (200°–230°C) for about 30 minutes.

Ginger Crunch Biscuits

Biscuits
125 g butter
¼ cup sugar
1 cup plain flour
1 teaspoon baking powder
1 teaspoon ground ginger

Topping
⅓ cup icing sugar
60 g butter
1 teaspoon ground ginger
3 teaspoons golden syrup

Biscuits   Cream butter and sugar, add sifted dry ingredients, mix well. Spread into greased 28 x 18 cm lamington tin and bake in a moderate oven (180°–200°C) until lightly browned, 15 to 20 minutes.

Topping   Place all ingredients in saucepan, stir over gentle heat until butter is melted and ingredients well mixed. Pour over biscuit layer while both are still warm. Cut into squares when cold.

Sultana Cookies

1 heaped cup self-raising
   flour
¼ level teaspoon
   bicarbonate of soda
1 level teaspoon allspice
¾ cup coconut
¾ cup cornflakes
½ cup sultanas
¾ cup sugar
1 egg
1 tablespoon golden syrup
3 tablespoons butter
few drops lemon essence

Mix dry ingredients together. Combine egg, syrup, melted butter and lemon essence. Stir into dry ingredients. Place in spoonfuls onto greased tray and bake in a moderately slow oven (160°–170°C) for 10 to 15 minutes.

Crunchy Fruit Biscuits

1 small cup butter
1 cup sugar
2 eggs
1 level dessertspoon golden
   syrup
1 small cup mixed fruit
   dates or nuts may be used
2½ cups self-raising flour
pinch of salt
sugar

Cream butter and sugar. Break in eggs and beat well. Add golden syrup and fruit and finally the flour and salt. Beat well together. Drop small teaspoonfuls onto greased tray and sprinkle with sugar. Bake in a moderate oven (180°–200°C) for 15 minutes.

Cereal and Fruit Biscuits

125 g butter
¾ cup sugar
1 cup crushed cornflakes or
  weeties
1 cup rolled oats
1 egg
1 cup mixed fruit
½ cup self-raising flour
½ cup plain flour
1 teaspoon baking soda
1 teaspoon bicarbonate of
  soda
vanilla essence

In a large saucepan gently melt butter, add sugar and stir. Remove saucepan from heat and add the cornflakes and oats. Stir. Add beaten egg. Stir and add fruit, sifted flours and the two sodas. Mix well. Add vanilla to taste. Drop mix in spoonfuls onto a greased baking tray and bake in a moderate oven (180°–200°C) for 20 to 25 minutes or until brown. Separate while warm and leave until cold.

Caramel Biscuits

When the grandchildren visit my biscuits tins are soon empty.

½ cup butter
½ cup sugar
1 egg
2 dessertspoons golden
  syrup
1¼ cups self-raising flour
1 teaspoon cinnamon
½ teaspoon allspice

Beat butter and sugar, add egg and then syrup. Sift flour and spices and add to butter mixture. Mix well. Drop spoonfuls onto greased tray and flatten with fork. Bake in a moderate oven (180°–200°C) for 10 to 15 minutes.

Nutty Jam Squares

90 g butter
½ cup sugar
1 egg yolk
¾ cup grated cheese
2 tablespoons milk
1½ cups plain flour
1 teaspoon baking powder
apricot or raspberry jam
¼ teaspoon cinnamon
½ cup chopped nuts

Cream butter and sugar. Add egg yolk, cheese and milk and mix to a dry dough with sifted flour and baking powder. Chill for 30 minutes. Knead lightly and roll on lightly floured board to an oblong shape about ½ cm thick. Place on a greased baking tray, spread with jam and sprinkle with nuts and cinnamon. Bake in a moderate oven (180°–200°C for 20 to 30 minutes. Cut into small squares while still warm.

Fudge Squares

Makes about 15 squares

1 cup chocolate pieces
125 g softened butter
¾ cup brown sugar, firmly
  packed
1 teaspoon vanilla essence
1½ cups plain flour
1 teaspoon baking powder
½ teaspoon salt
185 g chopped walnuts

Melt chocolate pieces over hot water. Cream butter, sugar and vanilla. Sift flour, baking powder and salt and add to creamed mixture. Add chocolate and half the walnuts. Spread mixture into greased 28 x 18 cm tin, sprinkle with remaining walnuts and press in gently. Bake in a moderate oven (180°–200°C) for 30 to 35 minutes. Remove from oven and cut into squares. Allow to cool in tin.

Almond Butter Balls

250 g butter
3 tablespoons castor sugar
1 teaspoon vanilla essence
2 cups plain flour
½ teaspoon salt
¾ cup chopped, blanched
   almonds
1 cup icing sugar

Cream butter with sugar and vanilla until light and fluffy. Sift flour and salt together and blend into creamed mixture. Stir in almonds. Shape into balls the size of walnuts, or mould into crescent shapes. Bake on ungreased baking tray in a moderate oven (180°–200°C) for about 15 minutes. Remove from tray and roll in icing sugar. Cool on wire rack and roll again in icing sugar.

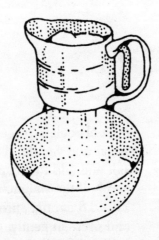

Yo-Yos

Biscuits
185 g butter
⅓ cup icing sugar
1½ cups plain flour
⅓ cup custard powder

Filling
½ cup icing sugar
2 tablespoons butter
2 teaspoons custard powder
½ teaspoon vanilla

Biscuits   Cream butter and icing sugar, add well-sifted flour and custard powder. Mix well. Form into balls, place onto greased oven trays and press with a fork to form biscuits. Bake in moderate oven (180°–200°C) for about 15 minutes.

Filling   Cream ingredients together. Use as required for joining biscuits.

Nutty Gingerbread

60 g blanched almonds
2½ cups plain flour
½ teaspoon bicarbonate of soda
½ teaspoon salt
1½ teaspoons ground cinnamon
1½ teaspoons ground ginger
125 g sultanas
⅔ cup brown sugar
185 g butter
¼ cup treacle
¼ cup golden syrup
1 egg

Chop almonds roughly. Sift flour, soda, salt, cinnamon and ginger into a large bowl. Stir in the sultanas and chopped almonds. Put sugar, butter, treacle and syrup into a large saucepan and heat gently until the butter has melted. Add to flour mixture with beaten egg and beat well until smooth. Pour into well greased lamington tin and bake in a moderate oven (180°–200°C) for 30 minutes. Turn out to cool. Top with Vienna Icing (see p. 247), Creamy Syrup Icing (see p. 247) or Glacé Icing (see p. 247) or cut cake into three portions and spread each with one of the above icings.

Custard Kisses

Base
125 g butter
3 tablespoons sugar
1 egg
5 tablespoons self-raising flour
pinch of salt
3 tablespoons custard powder

Filling
30 g butter
1 tablespoon custard powder
2 tablespoons icing sugar

Base   Cream butter and sugar. Add beaten egg. Then sift in flour, salt and custard powder. Mix well. Place small spoonfuls onto cold greased tray, and bake in a moderate oven (180°–200°C) for 10 to 12 minutes.

Filling   Mix all ingredients. Join pairs together with filling when cold.

Coffee Meringue Kisses

This recipe uses only one egg white and makes about 90 tiny biscuits, although you can make larger ones. They keep well in an airtight container.

¾ cup raw sugar
1 teaspoon instant coffee
   powder
2 tablespoons water
1 egg white
1 teaspoon vinegar
2 teaspoons cornflour

Coffee Cream
60 g butter
⅔ cup icing sugar
1 teaspoon instant coffee
   powder
2 teaspoons hot water
2 teaspoons coffee liqueur
   (Tia Maria or Kahlua)

Combine sugar, coffee and water in saucepan, stir constantly over low heat until sugar is dissolved (this will take about 5 minutes, as raw sugar is more difficult to dissolve than white). It may be necessary to brush sides of saucepan with brush dipped in hot water to make sure all grains are dissolved. Increase heat, bring to boil, remove from heat immediately. Combine egg white, vinegar and cornflour in small electric mixer bowl, beat until foamy. Keep mixer going on medium speed and pour hot coffee syrup in a constant thin stream onto egg white, then beat for 10 minutes or until thick. Lightly grease two oven trays, dust with cornflour, shake off excess cornflour. Spoon meringue into piping bag fitted with fluted star pipe. Pipe small meringues, about 2.5 cm in diameter, onto trays about 2.5 cm apart. Pipe as many small meringues as desired or make larger ones as required. Bake in a very slow oven (120°C) for 30 minutes for small meringues, and 1 hour for larger ones. Meringues should feel dry and crisp to touch when cooked. Allow to cool on trays.

Coffee Cream   Beat butter until creamy, add sugar, beat until combined. Dissolve coffee in hot water, add coffee liqueur. Add liquid to creamed mixture, beat until smooth. Join two small meringues with Coffee Cream.

Variations   Coffee powder could be replaced with cocoa powder, or for small coloured ones, a few drops of your favourite colouring or flavouring could be added.

Chocolate Eclairs

Classic éclairs should be no more than 8 to 10 cm long, and the icing should be a glossy chocolate or coffee icing.

Choux Pastry (see p. 116)
¼ pint cream
a few drops of vanilla essence

Chocolate Glacé Icing
90 g dark cooking chocolate
1 cup icing sugar
1 tablespoon warm water

Put pastry into forcing bag with plain tube, and pipe in 8 to 10 cm lengths onto a greased baking tray. Bake in a hot oven (200°–230°C) for 15 minutes (do not open oven door during this time). Reduce heat to moderately hot (190°–220°C) and bake for a further 10 minutes or until the éclairs are dry inside. Place on a wire rack to cool.

Chocolate Glacé Icing Break chocolate into small pieces and put into a small bowl. Melt over hot but not boiling water. Add sifted icing sugar and water. Stir until well mixed and smooth. Just before serving éclairs, slit open and fill with stiffly whipped cream flavoured with vanilla and sweetened slightly. Spread tops with Chocolate Glacé Icing using a teaspoon.

Bethany Brownies

These brownies have been named after our property.

1 cup mixed fruit
1 cup brown sugar
1 cup hot tea
1 egg
½ teaspoon vanilla
2 cups self-raising flour
½ teaspoon mixed spice or cinnamon
pinch of salt

Place mixed fruit, sugar and hot tea in bowl. Stir to dissolve sugar, cool, then add beaten egg and vanilla. Stir in flour, sifted with salt and spice. Cook in bar tin in a moderate oven for about 45 minutes (180°–200°C). Serve sliced with butter.

Chocolate Brownies

250 g unsalted butter
180 g dark cooking
  chocolate
100 g white cooking
  chocolate
150 g brown sugar
150 g castor sugar
1 ½ tablespoons golden
  syrup
1 ½ tablespoons honey
3 eggs
150 g sifted self-raising
  flour
300 g chopped macadamia
  nuts
90 g desiccated coconut
icing sugar for dusting

Melt butter and both chocolates in a double-boiler. Remove from heat. Stir in sugars, golden syrup and honey. Stir in the eggs one at a time, then the flour, nuts and coconut. Pour into greased and paper-lined 25 x 30 x 3 cm baking tray. Bake in a moderate oven (180°–200°C) for 30 minutes or until firm. Cool in the pan and dust with icing sugar before cutting into squares.

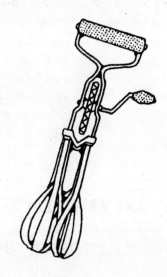

Chocolate Chip Drops

½ cup condensed milk
½ teaspoon baking powder
1 ½ cups coconut
1 cup coarsely chopped
  chocolate

Combine all ingredients and drop in teaspoonfuls onto a well-greased oven tray. Bake in a slow oven (150°C) until the biscuits are tinted brown at the edges.

Chocolate Biscuits

125 g butter
¼ cup castor sugar
¼ teaspoon vanilla essence
1 cup plain flour
3 tablespoons cocoa
pinch of salt
½ cup rolled oats

Cream butter and sugar until light and fluffy. Add vanilla. Fold flour, cocoa and salt into the creamed mixture and combine well. Divide mixture in half, shape into two rolls (4 cm wide, 15 cm long). Cover in rolled oats. Wrap rolls in plastic food wrap or foil and refrigerate until firm. Cut into 3 cm slices, place on greased oven trays, then bake at 190°C for 10 to 15 minutes.

Chocolate Cornets

These should be made on the day they are to be served. They're ideal for a party.

1 egg white
⅓ cup icing sugar
½ teaspoon vanilla
30 g butter
30 g ground almonds
¼ cup plain flour
30 g dark chocolate
1 teaspoon copha
whipped cream

Beat egg white with fork until foamy. Beat in sifted icing sugar and vanilla, then melted butter and almonds. Mix lightly. Fold in sifted flour. Lightly grease two oven trays, mark two 8 cm circles on each tray using a plain cutter. Drop teaspoonfuls of mixture into circles, spread to fill circle. Bake in a moderately hot oven (190°–220°C) for 5 to 6 minutes. Cornets are ready when mixture is very light golden brown around edges. Only bake two cornets at a time as they have to be shaped very quickly. Lift cornets quickly from trays, roll into cone shape, and hold lightly with fingers until crisp. This takes only a few seconds. Continue cooking until all mixture is used. Melt chocolate and copha in top of double saucepan over hot water. Remove from heat, cool. Dip open ends of cornets into melted chocolate. Allow chocolate to set. Fill with whipped cream just before serving.

Chocolate Crunch

Joh and I always enjoy something sweet with our morning tea.
Makes 24 slices

1 cup self-raising flour
1 tablespoon cocoa
1 cup coconut
1 cup cornflakes
½ cup sugar
150 g butter
½ teaspoon vanilla

Sift flour and cocoa, mix in other dry ingredients. Gently melt the butter. Add vanilla and mix all together. Press mixture into greased slab tin, smooth flat with a spatula and bake in a moderate oven (180°–200°C) for 25 to 30 minutes. Cool in tin. Ice with Chocolate Icing (see p. 247). While still warm, cut into finger slices.

Crisp Crunch

Makes about 35

1 cup self-raising flour
¾ cup brown sugar
¾ cup coconut
1 cup crushed cornflakes
130 g butter

Sift flour, add sugar, coconut and cornflakes. Mix lightly. Melt butter and stir into dry ingredients, mixing well. Press evenly into greased slab tin. Bake in a moderate oven (180°–200°C) for 20 to 25 minutes. Cool in tin then cut into finger slices.

Burnt Butter Biscuits

Makes 48 to 50

125 g butter
½ cup sugar
1 egg
1 teaspoon vanilla essence
1½ cups self-raising flour
24 blanched almonds,
   halved

Melt butter in medium-size saucepan, allow to cook gently until light brown in colour. Cool slightly. Add sugar and beat well. Stir in beaten egg and vanilla. Work in flour and mix into a stiff consistency. Roll mixture into small balls, place on greased oven tray, allowing room for mixture to spread. Place an almond on each biscuit. Bake in a moderate oven (180°–200°C) for 10 to 12 minutes or until biscuits are golden. Cool on wire rack.

Fruity Nougat Slice

¾ *cup castor sugar*
1 cup coconut
1 cup self-raising flour
1 cup mixed fruit
1 egg
125 g butter

Mix together sugar, coconut, flour and fruit. Add beaten egg and melted butter. Mix well. Press into greased lamington tin and bake in a moderate oven (180°–200°C) for 25 to 30 minutes. Allow to cool in tin before cutting into fingers.

Cherry and Walnut Slice

125 g butter
¾ *cup brown sugar*
1 egg
1 dessertspoon golden syrup
1 cup chopped dates or
*   mixed fruit*
½ *cup self-raising flour*
1½ cups plain flour
glacé cherries to decorate
⅓ *cup chopped mixed nuts*

Cream butter and sugar. Add egg, syrup, fruit and flours, mixing well. Press into large greased slab tin, sprinkle top with chopped nuts and cherries. Bake in a moderate oven (180°–200°C) for 30 minutes. Cool in tin and cut into squares.

Chocolate Peppermint Slices

Biscuit Layer
1 ½ cups self-raising flour
1 cup coconut
½ cup brown sugar
185 g butter

Peppermint Icing
1 cup icing sugar
30 g copha
3 dessertspoons milk
½ teaspoon peppermint
   essence

Chocolate Icing
90 g copha
½ cup cocoa

Biscuit Layer   Mix all dry ingredients. Melt butter and pour over ingredients. Mix well. Press into greased Swiss roll tin and bake in a moderate oven (180°–200°C) for 20 minutes. Whilst still warm, top with Peppermint Icing.

Peppermint Icing   Sift icing sugar. Add melted copha, milk and peppermint essence. Mix well and spread over biscuit layer. When cold top with Chocolate Icing.

Chocolate Icing   Pour melted copha over cocoa and mix well. Cool slightly, pour on top of Peppermint Icing. When set, cut into slices.

Apple and Oat Slices

1 ¼ cups cooked, strained
   apple
¾ cup rolled oats
1 cup raisins
125 g butter
¾ cup sugar
1 egg
1 ½ cups plain flour
1 teaspoon bicarbonate of
   soda
¾ teaspoon salt
1 teaspoon cinnamon
½ teaspoon ground cloves

Add hot apple to oats and raisins, mix and let stand for 20 minutes. Cream butter and sugar, add egg, beat well. Sift flour, soda, salt and spices, add to creamed butter and sugar, then mix in apple mixture. Place in greased lamington tray. Bake in a slow oven (150°–160°C) for 45 minutes to 1 hour. Ice with Lemon Icing (see p. 249) when cool, and sprinkle with cinnamon. When cold, cut into squares.

Jam Slices

I enjoy cooking and so do my family. Makes 48

Slice
250 g butter
½ cup sugar
1 egg
1 teaspoon vanilla essence
3 cups plain flour
pinch of salt
apricot jam or redcurrant
   jelly

Glaze
½ cup sifted icing sugar
1 tablespoon hot water

Cream butter and sugar. Add egg and vanilla, beating well. Sift flour and salt. Mix dough until smooth. Chill for 30 minutes. Divide into quarters. Roll into long rolls about 1 cm thick. Put on greased baking trays. With end of a knife handle press a hollow down the length of each roll. Bake in a moderately hot oven (190°–220°C) for 10 minutes. Remove from oven and spoon or pipe jam into hollow. Return to oven and bake until edges are pale golden.

Glaze   Mix icing sugar and water. Remove from oven and while still hot brush roll with glaze. Cut into 2.5 cm diagonal slices when quite cool.

Toffee Nut Slice

Pastry
90 g butter
2 tablespoons sugar
½ teaspoon vanilla
¾ cup plain flour

Topping
30 g butter
½ cup sugar
⅓ cup slivered almonds
1½ tablespoons cream
1½ tablespoons plain flour
125 g dark chocolate
30 g copha

Pastry   Line a 28 x 18 cm lamington tin with aluminium foil. Beat butter, sugar and vanilla until light and fluffy. Add sifted flour, mix to a firm dough. Knead lightly into a smooth round shape. Press dough into base of prepared tin, bake in a moderate oven (180°–200°C) for 10 minutes.

Topping   Put butter, sugar, almonds, cream and flour into saucepan, stir over low heat until butter has melted and sugar has dissolved. Spread topping mixture over base, return to moderate oven, bake for a further 30 to 35 minutes until light golden brown. Turn biscuit slice out when cold, cut into 4 cm squares. Put chocolate and copha in top of double saucepan, stand over simmering water until melted. Dip biscuits into chocolate mixture diagonally, so that half the biscuit is coated in chocolate.

Apricot Yoghurt Slice

Base
¼ cup toasted coconut
125 g Granita biscuits
60 g butter

Filling
125 g dried apricots
½ cup boiling water
2 x 200 g cartons plain
   yoghurt
3 tablespoons honey
2 eggs

Base   To toast coconut, place coconut in heavy pan, and stir with wooden spoon over moderate heat until coconut is light golden brown. Remove from pan immediately. Combine in bowl finely-crushed biscuits, coconut and melted butter. Mix well. Line 18 x 28 cm lamington tin with aluminium foil. Press crumb mixture evenly over base of tin, refrigerate while preparing filling.

Filling   Cover apricots with boiling water, stand 30 minutes, put apricots and liquid in blender, blend until smooth again. Add yoghurt, honey and eggs, blend until smooth again. Spread yoghurt mixture over base, bake in a moderate oven (180°–200°C) for 30 to 35 minutes or until set. Cool. Refrigerate for several hours before serving. Sprinkle with a little extra toasted coconut.

Raspberry Coconut Slice

It's nice for children to experiment in the kitchen — here's a perfect recipe for them!

Base
125 g butter
⅔ cup sugar
1 egg yolk
2 tablespoons milk
2 cups self-raising flour
pinch of salt
raspberry jam

Topping
1 egg white
1 cup coconut
¾ cup sugar

Base   Cream butter and sugar. Add egg yolk and mix well. Add milk, flour and salt. Line a greased lamington tin with the pastry. Spread pastry with raspberry jam. Sprinkle topping evenly and bake in a moderate oven (180°–200°C) for 20 minutes.

Topping   Beat egg white slightly and gradually add sugar. Mix in coconut.

Vanilla Slices

double quantity Rough Puff
  Pastry (see p. 116)
1 cup sugar
¾ cup cornflour
½ cup custard powder
4 cups milk
60 g butter
2 egg yolks
2 teaspoons vanilla

Passionfruit Icing
1 cup icing sugar
1 teaspoon butter
1 passionfruit
1 teaspoon water

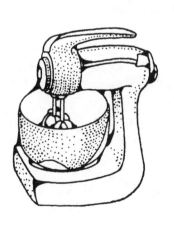

Have pastry at room temperature. Roll out into two pieces, each 32 cm square. Trim with sharp knife to 30 cm square. Place one square of pastry onto large, ungreased oven tray. Bake in a very hot oven (230°–250°C) for 5 to 10 minutes, or until well browned. Trim pastry with a sharp knife to 23 cm square. Bake and trim remaining pastry in the same way. Flatten 'puffy' side of both pieces of pastry with hand.

Vanilla Slices   Line a 23 cm square slab tin with aluminium foil, bringing the foil up over sides (this makes it easy to remove slice when set). Place one piece of pastry into base of tin, flattened side uppermost. Combine sugar, cornflour and custard powder in heavy-based saucepan, mix well to combine. Blend with a little of the milk until smooth, stir in remaining milk; add butter. Stir mixture constantly over heat until custard boils and thickens, reduce heat, simmer 3 minutes. Remove from heat, quickly stir in vanilla, then stir in the beaten egg yolks. Pour hot custard immediately over pastry in tin. Place remaining pastry on top of custard so the flattened side touches the hot custard. Press pastry firmly with hand. Spread evenly with Passionfruit Icing. When cool, refrigerate for several hours or overnight until filling has set.

Passionfruit Icing   Sift icing sugar into a small basin, add softened butter and pulp from passionfruit. Add enough water (approximately 1 teaspoonful) to achieve a thick spreading consistency. Beat well.

Marshmallow Slices

Makes 24 to 28

1¼ cups self-raising flour
½ cup sugar
3 crushed weetbix
1 cup coconut
170 g butter

Mix all dry ingredients together. Gently melt butter. Pour onto dry ingredients and mix well. Press into greased Swiss roll tin, smooth evenly with a spatula. Bake in a moderately hot oven (190°–200°C) for 15 to 20 minutes. Allow to become cold in tin, then pour over Marshmallow Topping (see p. 250). When set, cut into slices.

Apricot and Ginger Slices

Makes about 30

½ cup dried apricots
boiling water to cover
    apricots
1½ cups self-raising flour
pinch of salt
¼ teaspoon cinnamon
1½ tablespoons cocoa
125 g butter
¾ cup castor sugar
½ cup chopped walnuts
2 tablespoons chopped
    glacé ginger
1 egg
½ cup milk

Chop apricots, pour boiling water to cover until just soft. Sift flour, salt, cinnamon and cocoa. Rub in butter, add sugar, walnuts and ginger. Drain apricots and add. Mix well. Stir in beaten egg and milk. Spread in greased Swiss roll tin and bake in a moderate oven (180°–200°C) for 25 to 35 minutes. Cool and top with Chocolate Icing.

Chocolate Icing   Mix all ingredients with enough boiling water to give a good spreading consistency. Spread on top and allow to set. Cut into squares or fingers.

Chocolate Icing
2 cups sifted icing sugar
2 tablespoons cocoa
1 teaspoon coffee essence
very little boiling water
12 chopped marshmallows

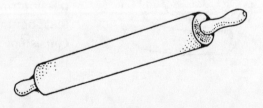

Crunchy Coconut Oat Slice

3 tablespoons golden syrup
150 g butter
1 cup self-raising flour
¾ cup coconut
1 cup rolled oats
1 cup sugar

Melt golden syrup and butter, combine with all other ingredients. Press mixture into a greased 28 x 18 cm tin. Bake in a moderately slow oven (160°–170°C) for 35 to 40 minutes. Cut into fingers while still hot. Remove from tin when cold.

Golden Drops

250 g butter, softened
½ cup golden syrup
2 cups self-raising flour
pinch of salt

Cream butter and syrup. Add salt and flour, mix well. Drop teaspoons of mixture onto greased tray, press with fork. Bake in moderate oven (180°–200°C) for 12 to 15 minutes, until golden brown.

Coconut Fancies

90 g butter or margarine
1 cup self-raising flour
60 g sugar
6 tablespoons coconut
1 egg
1 teaspoon vanilla
few drops of almond essence
a little milk if required

Rub the butter into flour and sugar. Add coconut. Beat the egg slightly, add essences and, if needed, a little milk. Mix into dry ingredients and mix to a soft dough. Roll out to 2 cm thick and cut into shapes. Place on a greased tray. Bake in a moderate oven (180°–200°C) for 15 to 20 minutes.

Coconut Meringues

Makes about 24

2 egg whites
¾ cup icing sugar
1½ cups coconut
6 drops vanilla
pinch of salt

Beat egg whites until stiff, add sugar gradually and continue beating until thick. Stir in coconut, salt and vanilla. Put teaspoonfuls onto greased oven tray and bake in a slow oven (130°C) until slightly coloured and set. Lift off onto wire cooler.

Gingernuts

250 g self-raising flour
1 teaspoon ginger
125 g castor sugar
3 tablespoons butter
½ cup golden syrup
1 egg

Mix dry ingredients together. Warm butter, add golden syrup then add dry ingredients and beaten egg. Mix well and place teaspoons of mixture, rolled into balls, on greased trays. Bake in moderate oven (180°–200°C) for 15 minutes or until golden brown.

Gingerbread

2 tablespoons butter
1 small cup sugar
2 eggs
1½ cups self-raising flour
1½ cups plain flour
1 level tablespoon ginger
1 level tablespoon
    cinnamon
1 teaspoon spice
pinch of salt
1 small cup golden syrup
1½ cups sour milk (to make
    milk sour, add some
    lemon juice)
1 teaspoon bicarbonate of
    soda dissolved in 1
    tablespoon hot water

Cream butter and sugar. Add eggs and beat well. Sift flours, ginger, cinnamon, spice and salt together. Warm syrup, add to milk, then add to butter and sugar mixture. Fold in flours and spices and lastly bicarbonate of soda. Put mixture in a large, flat greased cake tin and bake in a moderate oven (180°–200°C) for about 40 to 50 minutes.

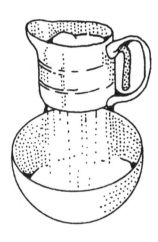

Apricot Date Bars

125 g dried apricots
hot water to cover apricots
1 cup raw sugar
2 cups self-raising flour
¾ cup coconut
½ cup chopped dates
¼ teaspoon salt
175 g butter

Soak chopped apricots in hot water for 30 minutes. Drain. Put in bowl with sugar, sifted flour, coconut, dates, salt, and melted butter. Mix well. Spread mixture into greased lamington tin. Bake in a moderate oven (180°–200°C) for approximately 25 minutes or until cooked. Remove from oven, allow to cool, and cut into squares. Top with icing of your choice (see Fillings, Icings and Sauces for suggestions).

Brandy Snaps

Makes 6 to 8 snaps

2 tablespoons golden syrup
60 g butter
⅓ cup brown sugar
½ cup plain flour
2 teaspoons ground ginger
pinch of salt

Place syrup, butter and sugar into saucepan, heat slowly until butter has melted, stirring occasionally. Sift flour, ginger, and salt into a bowl, stir in syrup and butter mixture; mix well. Drop dessert-spoonfuls of mixture onto greased trays, allowing room for spreading. Bake in a moderate oven (180°–200°C) for 5 to 7 minutes, or until golden brown. Remove from oven, cool 1 minute. With knife, lift the brandy snaps from tray. Roll each immediately around the greased handle of a wooden spoon. Allow to firm and cool on spoon handle. Just before serving, fill with whipped cream.

It's a good idea to bake only two brandy snaps at a time as two will fit comfortably onto a baking tray. If they firm up before you have time to mould them into shape, return them to the oven for a few minutes to soften.

Golden Crunch Biscuits

125 g butter or margarine
1 tablespoon golden syrup
2 tablespoons boiling water
1 level teaspoon
   bicarbonate of soda
1 cup plain flour
1 cup sugar
1 cup rolled oats
1 cup coconut

Melt butter, add syrup, water and soda. Pour onto combined dry ingredients. Drop teaspoonfuls onto a greased tray, leaving room for spreading. Bake in a very moderate oven (180°–200°C) until golden. Cool on a wire rack.

Cherry Biscuits

60 g butter
60 g sugar
1 egg
1 cup plain flour
Lemon Icing (see p. 249)
sliced glacé cherries

Cream butter and sugar, add egg and beat well. Sift in flour to make a stiff dough. Roll very thinly and cut in shapes with a fluted cutter. Place on greased trays. Bake in a moderate oven (180°–200°C) for 15 to 20 minutes. When cold, sandwich together with Lemon Icing and place a dab of icing on each pair to hold a slice of cherry.

Oatmeal Biscuits

1 cup sugar
3 cups rolled oats
2 teaspoons baking powder
2 tablespoons butter
plain flour as required
2 eggs

Mix all dry ingredients (except flour) and rub in the butter. Add well beaten eggs and enough flour to make a mixture which can be moulded into soft balls. Put on greased trays. Bake in a hot oven (230°C) for 15 to 20 minutes.

Peanut Drops

I make these biscuits a lot with Kingaroy peanuts.

3 tablespoons butter
½ cup sugar
½ teaspoon vanilla
1 egg
2 tablespoons milk
1½ teaspoons baking powder
1 cup plain flour
1 cup roasted peanuts
½ teaspoon vanilla essence

Cream butter and sugar and beat in the vanilla. Add the beaten egg and milk. Add the sifted dry ingredients and ¾ cup chopped peanuts. Drop in spoonfuls onto a greased slide and top with the remaining nuts. Bake in a moderate oven (180°–200°C) until brown.

Butterscotchies

½ cup butter
2 cups brown sugar
2 eggs
2 cups plain flour
½ teaspoon baking powder
1 teaspoon vanilla essence
1 cup coconut or walnut
　pieces

Heat butter and sugar over low heat until they begin to bubble. Remove from heat and cool. Beat the eggs in thoroughly. Add the rest of the ingredients. Place in spoonfuls onto a greased tray and bake in a moderate oven (180°–200°C) for 10 to 15 minutes.

Almond and Cherry Fingers

My grandchildren love slices with almonds and cherries.

60 g butter
½ cup sugar
½ teaspoon vanilla
1 egg
1 teaspoon water
1 cup plain flour
¼ teaspoon baking powder
few almonds and
　crystallised cherries

Cream butter, sugar and vanilla. Add egg yolk to the water, stir in the sifted flour and baking powder. Roll out thinly on a floured board and brush with egg white. Sprinkle with almond and cherry pieces and a little extra sugar. Cut into fingers, bake on a greased oven tray in a hot oven (230°C) for 10 to 15 minutes. Leave on the tray until cold.

Cinnamon Hearts

90 g butter
1/3 cup sugar
1 egg
1 1/2 cups plain flour
1 teaspoon cinnamon

Cream butter and sugar, add the beaten egg and mix thoroughly. Add the sifted flour and cinnamon and mix to a stiff dough. Roll out thinly on a floured board and cut with a heart-shaped cutter. Place on a greased tray and bake in a moderate oven (180°–200°C) for about 10 minutes. When cold, sandwich together with a little stiff Mock Cream (see p. 118) or Chocolate Icing (see p. 247). Put a dab of cream or icing on each pair and sprinkle with hundreds and thousands.

Honey Hermits

1/2 cup margarine
1 cup honey
1/2 cup brown sugar
2 eggs
3 tablespoons milk
2 1/4 cups plain flour
1 small teaspoon
  bicarbonate of soda
1/2 teaspoon each allspice
  and cinnamon
1 heaped cup raisins or
  chopped dates
1 tablespoon finely
  chopped mixed peel

Cream margarine, honey and sugar. Add beaten eggs and beat well. Stir in milk. Add sifted dry ingredients, fruit and peel. Drop teaspoonfuls onto a greased tray, allowing space for spreading. Bake in a hot oven (200°–230°C) for 10 to 12 minutes.

Honey Joys

2 tablespoons butter
2 tablespoons honey
2 tablespoons sugar
5 cups cornflakes

Place butter, honey and sugar in saucepan, bring slowly to the boil. Pour over cornflakes and mix well. Put into paper patty cases and bake in a slow oven (150°C) for 15 minutes, until lightly browned.

Melting Moments

185 g butter
1/3 cup icing sugar
1 egg yolk
1/2 teaspoon vanilla essence
1 cup self-raising flour
1 cup cornflour

Cream butter and sugar. Add egg yolk and vanilla. Beat in well. Sift flours together and fold into mixture. Place small quantities on greased biscuit trays. Bake in a moderate oven (180°–200°C) for 25 to 30 minutes. Loosen on tray with knife and leave to cool.

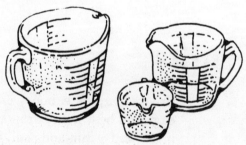

Pinwheels

125 g butter
1/2 cup sugar
1/2 teaspoon vanilla
1 egg yolk
3 tablespoons milk
1 cup plain flour
1 cup self-raising flour
1 tablespoon cocoa

Cream butter, sugar and vanilla. Add egg yolk and beat well. Add milk and flour and mix to a smooth dough. Divide into two portions, adding the cocoa (and a little extra milk if necessary) to one. Roll both pieces out thinly to the same size. Place the white over the chocolate and roll up like a Swiss roll. Chill overnight, then cut in thin slices and bake in a moderate oven (180°–200°C) for about 10 minutes.

Malties

125 g butter
1 tablespoon malt
½ cup oatmeal
½ cup sugar
*1½ cups wholemeal self-
     raising flour*

Melt the butter and combine with malt. Add to the combined dry ingredients, mixing well. Roll out quite thinly on a lightly floured board and cut into shapes. Place on a greased tray. Bake in a very moderate oven (190°C) for 10 to 12 minutes.

Apricot Almond Cookies

90 g butter
½ cup sugar
few drops almond essence
1 egg
*1 dessertspoon apricot jam
     (or flavour of your choice)*
1¼ cups self-raising flour
chopped almonds

Cream butter and sugar with almond essence. Add slightly beaten egg with jam, then stir in flour. Drop in teaspoonfuls onto a greased oven tray and top with pieces of almond. Bake in a moderate oven (180°–200°C) for 10 to 12 minutes.

Nutty Macaroons

3 egg whites
1 cup sugar
1 cup chopped peanuts
1 teaspoon cornflour
few drops almond essence

Beat the egg whites until very stiff. Gradually add the sugar. Combine peanuts with cornflour, fold into the mixture with a few drops of almond essence. Drop in teaspoonfuls onto a greased oven slide. Bake in a moderate oven (180°–200°C) for 20 to 30 minutes.

Refrigerator Cookies

¾ cup sugar
1 egg
½ teaspoon vanilla
2 cups self-raising flour
½ level teaspoon salt
125 g butter
2 tablespoons milk

Place sugar, egg, vanilla and half of sifted flour and salt in basin. Melt butter gently and add milk. Pour liquids into basin and beat 2 minutes. Add remaining flour and mix in thoroughly. Divide mixture into two portions and shape each into a roll about 2.5 cm in diameter. Roll in greaseproof paper and chill in refrigerator until firm. Cut with a sharp knife into 1 cm slices and place on greased slide. Bake in a moderate oven (180°–200°C) for 12 to 15 minutes. Store when cool in airtight containers.

AFTER FIVE BISCUITS

Lace Biscuits

Ideal accompaniment for after-dinner tea or coffee.

60 g blanched almonds
2 tablespoons liquid glucose
60 g butter
¼ cup brown sugar, firmly
   packed
⅓ cup plain flour

Finely chop almonds. Combine glucose, butter and sugar in saucepan, stir over low heat until sugar is dissolved and butter is melted. Increase heat, bring to boil, quickly remove from heat, immediately stir in sifted flour and almonds. Mix well. Lightly grease oven trays (too much greasing will cause biscuits to burn). Drop level teaspoonfuls of mixture onto trays about 8 cm apart; biscuits will spread up to 10 cm in diameter. Bake up to 5 biscuits at a time for easier handling. Bake in a moderate oven (180°–200°C) for 5 to 7 minutes, or until golden brown. Stand about 1 minute, or until edges of biscuits are firm enough to be loosened with spatula (they're difficult to remove when cold). Lift soft biscuits onto wire rack. They will become crisp on cooling. Store in airtight container.

Florentines

Makes 24

1 cup cornflakes
30 g red glacé cherries
½ cup sultanas
½ cup raw peanuts, or nuts
  of your choice
⅓ cup condensed milk
60 g dark chocolate

Combine slightly crushed cornflakes, finely chopped cherries, sultanas, roughly chopped nuts and condensed milk. Mix well. Line oven trays with greased greaseproof paper, dust lightly with flour. Drop teaspoonfuls onto oven trays. Bake in a moderate oven (180°–200°C) for 8 minutes or until edges begin to turn brown. Leave on trays to cool. Use a spatula to remove when cold. Melt chopped chocolate in top of double saucepan over simmering water. Using a spatula, spread chocolate on base of cooled biscuit. Mark wavy lines on chocolate with a fork. Let chocolate set.

Almond Bread

3 egg whites
125 g castor sugar
1 cup plain flour
100 g chopped almonds

Whip egg whites until stiff, then gradually add sugar, beating until dissolved. Stir in sifted flour, then almonds. Bake in greased loaf tin in a moderate oven (180°–200°C) for 25 minutes. When cool, remove from tin, wrap in foil and place in refrigerator for at least 2 days. Slice loaf very thinly, place on oven trays and bake in a slow oven (100°C) for 1 hour or until slices are crisp. Store in airtight container. Serve with coffee after dinner.

FILLINGS, ICINGS AND SAUCES

Stirred Custard

1 cup milk
1 egg
1 tablespoon sugar
4 drops vanilla essence
dash of nutmeg

Warm milk in a double saucepan or in a jug standing in a saucepan of water. Beat egg and sugar until thick, add warm milk. Return to double saucepan or jug. Stir with a wooden spoon until the custard coats the spoon. Do not allow it to overheat or it will curdle. Add vanilla. Cool. Place in a serving dish, in custard glasses, or use as an accompaniment to other desserts. Sprinkle nutmeg on top.

Coffee Cream

½ cup strong coffee
1 cup sugar
250 g butter

Boil coffee and sugar to a thick syrup. Set aside to cool. Cream butter, add syrup gradually, and mix well. Vanilla flavouring may be added if desired.

Apple Filling

2 large apples
rind of 1 lemon
½ cup sugar

Grate the apples into a saucepan, add grated lemon rind and sugar. Cook for 5 minutes, stirring constantly. When cold, spread on a cake such as Spiced Apple Cake (see p. 178) or Foundation Cake (see p. 189).

Lemon Jelly Filling

1 tablespoon arrowroot
¾ cup boiling water
1 cup sugar
grated juice and rind of
  lemon or orange

Blend arrowroot with a dessertspoon of water and fruit juice in a small saucepan. Pour boiling water and sugar over this paste and stir vigorously. Return to heat and boil until it thickens. When almost cold, use as a Sponge Cake (see p. 194) filling, or fill scooped-out Cup Cakes (see p. 192) and top with cream.

Nutty Filling

1 cup milk
1 rounded teaspoon butter
1 egg yolk, beaten
½ cup chopped nuts
1 tablespoon cornflour
  blended with a little cold
  milk
½ cup sugar

Heat milk and butter, add other ingredients. Gently boil until thick. Fill your favourite cake or sponge with this mixture.

Substitute Cream Filling

This filling will hold well if used in cakes and then deep frozen.

125 g softened butter
1 cup sifted icing sugar
2 tablespoons evaporated
  milk
1 egg white, beaten but not
  dry
¼ teaspoon vanilla essence

Cream butter and sugar. Add milk and egg white. Beat well for 5 minutes with electric beater. Flavour with vanilla and use as desired.

Chocolate and Honey Filling

2 tablespoons honey
2 tablespoons butter
1 cup icing sugar
2 tablespoons cocoa
3 teaspoons boiling water

Melt honey and butter in a double-boiler over hot water, stir in sifted icing sugar and cocoa. Add boiling water and mix until smooth. Use in sponges (see p. 194) for a delicious filling.

Lemon Filling

Lemon Filling can be used for Lemon Meringue Pie (see p. 144) if 2 egg yolks are added with blended cornflour. The egg whites are used for the meringue.

1 cup sugar
1 cup water
juice and rind of 2 lemons
2 rounded tablespoons
  cornflour
1 tablespoon butter

Dissolve sugar in water, add juice and rind. When nearly boiling, add cornflour blended in a little cold water. Cook for 1 minute then add butter.

Cream Cheese Frosting

A good frosting for the Carrot Cake recipe (see p. 92).

30 g butter
60 g cream cheese
1½ cups icing sugar
1 teaspoon lemon rind
1 tablespoon lemon juice
½ cup coconut

Beat butter and cream cheese until creamy. Add remaining ingredients, beating well. Spread on cake and sprinkle with coconut.

Vienna Icing

60 g butter
4 tablespoons icing sugar
2 teaspoons sherry
glacé ginger to decorate

Soften butter and beat until white. Add icing sugar, beat until creamy. Gradually add sherry, beating in well. Spread on cake and top with diced glacé ginger.

Creamy Syrup Icing

60 g butter
4 tablespoons icing sugar
2 teaspoons golden syrup
walnut pieces to decorate

Cream butter and icing sugar. Beat until smooth, then add golden syrup. Spread on cake and decorate with walnut pieces.

Glacé Icing

½ cup icing sugar
2 teaspoons lemon juice
1 teaspoon butter

Sift icing sugar into basin. Add lemon juice and butter and stir until smooth. Place basin over pan of hot water and stir until glossy. Spread over cake as required.

Chocolate Icing

30 g butter
1 tablespoon cocoa
1 cup soft icing sugar
15 mL boiling water
6 drops vanilla essence

Gently melt butter, add cocoa and blend well. Stir in icing sugar. Blend to a spreading consistency with the boiling water. Add vanilla. Spread evenly on a cake such as the Quick Chocolate Cake (see p. 60).

Coffee Icing

This is a good recipe and one of my favourite icings.

¾ cup icing sugar
1 teaspoon instant coffee
    essence
6 drops vanilla essence
2 teaspoons melted butter
1½ tablespoons boiling
    water

Sift icing sugar into a small bowl. Add essences, melted butter and very little boiling water. Beat together, add extra water (few drops at a time) until a decent spreading consistency is reached and icing is glossy. Use as required.

Fondant Icing

500 g icing sugar
3 tablespoons liquid glucose
1 egg white
flavouring and colouring of
    your choice

Sift icing sugar into large basin. Make a well in centre and add softened glucose, lightly beaten egg white and flavouring. Beat with wooden spoon, drawing the icing sugar into centre until mixture is stiff. Turn onto board dusted with icing sugar. Knead well until smooth and glossy. Colour as desired and use as required.

Rum Butter Icing

1¼ cups icing sugar
100 g butter
1 teaspoon vanilla essence
2 teaspoons rum
2 teaspoons lemon juice
colouring

Sift icing sugar. Soften and cream butter, then work in the icing sugar. Beat well. Add vanilla, rum, lemon juice, and colouring as desired. Use as required.

Orange Icing

30 g butter
1 cup soft icing sugar
2 teaspoons orange juice
1 teaspoon grated orange
  rind (optional)

Gently melt butter. Add icing sugar and beat well. Mix in enough orange juice to give a spreading consistency. Mix in rind.

Lemon Icing

1 cup icing sugar
2 tablespoons lemon juice
  or lemon essence
2 tablespoons boiling water

Sift icing sugar into saucepan. Add juice and boiling water. Stir over low heat until just warm. Use as required.

Marshmallow Topping

1 packet jelly crystals
1½ cups cold water
¾ cup icing sugar

Boil jelly crystals for 8 minutes without stirring. Cool slightly. Pour into a bowl, add sugar and beat until stiff. Use as required for biscuits and slices (see Biscuits section for suggestions).

Brandy Sauce

This goes a treat with Baked Sultana Pudding (see p. 161).

30 g butter
30 g plain flour
1¼ cups milk
1 tablespoon sugar
⅓ cup brandy

Melt the butter, add flour. Stir until smooth, cook for 1 minute. Add milk gradually, stirring until mixture boils and thickens. Add sugar and brandy just before serving.

Orange Sauce

4 oranges
1 teaspoon arrowroot
a little water
¾ cup golden syrup
8–10 sugar cubes

Rub the rind of 2 oranges onto sugar cubes and place in a pan with the juice and pulp of 4 oranges. Add arrowroot stirred smooth with a little water and the syrup. Stir over medium heat until it thickens. Serve at once.

Wine Sauce

5 egg yolks
1 cup sherry
½ cup water
1 teaspoon grated lemon
   rind
2 tablespoons sugar

Beat yolks, add remaining ingredients. Stir over medium heat until it thickens, without boiling. Wine Sauce goes very well with Basic Family Pudding (see p. 158) if you're having guests, or with Coconut Pudding (see p. 164).

Butterscotch Sauce

4 tablespoons brown sugar
1 tablespoon golden syrup
1 tablespoon water
1 tablespoon butter
1 tablespoon cornflour
blended with 2
tablespoons water
lemon or vanilla essence

Heat sugar, golden syrup, water and butter until nearly boiling, then stir in cornflour liquid. Stir until boiling, then simmer 2 to 3 minutes. Add essence and serve hot or cold.

Sweet Lemon Sauce

½ cup butter
½ cup sugar
1¼ cups boiling water
1 tablespoon cornflour
¼ cup cold water
juice and grated rind of
1 lemon

Cream butter and sugar. Pour boiling water on the cornflour, blended with ¼ cup cold water. Add to the butter and sugar. Stir over heat until well thickened. Add lemon juice and rind. Stir gently and serve.

Chocolate Sauce

1½ tablespoons cornflour
2 tablespoons cocoa
a little cold water
1 cup hot water
¼ cup sugar
2 teaspoons butter or
margarine
1 teaspoon vanilla essence

Blend cornflour and cocoa with a little cold water. Stir into hot water, add sugar and butter. Stir over gentle heat until boiling and thickened. Add vanilla. Stir gently and serve.

BREADS

Joh's mother made her own bread for most
of her married life. When I was a newly wed and
came to live at 'Bethany', Grandma Bjelke
unfailingly kept Joh and me supplied with
home-made bread.

White Bread

Joh often liked to sprinkle sugar over his buttered slice of home-made bread.

30 g compressed yeast
¼ cup sugar
2½ cups lukewarm water
1.125 kg plain flour
3 teaspoons salt
¼ cup oil
1 egg yolk
1 extra tablespoon water

Cream yeast with 1 teaspoon sugar, add 1 cup water, stir until combined. Sprinkle 1 tablespoon flour over yeast mixture. Cover bowl, stand in warm place for 10 to 15 minutes or until frothy. Sift flour, salt and remaining sugar into large bowl. Make a well in centre of dry ingredients, add oil, remaining water and yeast mixture. Mix dough well with wooden spoon. Place one hand into mixture, mix well with hands, then gather dough up into a ball. Turn out onto floured surface, knead for 3 minutes. Place dough into a large bowl brushed lightly with oil. Brush top of dough with a little oil. Cover bowl, stand in warm place for 45 minutes or until mixture has doubled in bulk. Punch down dough again, turn out onto lightly floured surface, knead for 5 minutes. Return dough to bowl, brush top of dough with oil. Cover and stand bowl in warm place for 35 to 40 minutes or until doubled in bulk. Turn out onto lightly floured surface, knead for 3 minutes. Divide dough into 4 equal pieces, knead each piece into a ball. Place 2 balls side by side into two greased 23 x 12 cm loaf tins. Stand in warm place until dough reaches top of tins, approximately 25 to 30 minutes. Brush top of bread with combined egg yolk and extra water. Bake in a moderate oven (180°–200°C) for 40 minutes or until cooked. Cool on a wire rack.

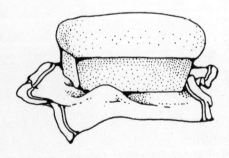

Milk Loaf

15 g compressed yeast
1 teaspoon sugar
475 mL warm milk
60 g butter
6 cups plain flour
½ teaspoon salt
extra flour for dusting

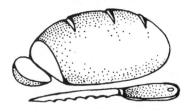

Cream yeast and sugar in a basin, cover with some of the warm milk and set in a warm place for 15 minutes. Rub butter into flour and add salt. Make a well in the centre, pour in yeast mixture and add enough of the remaining warm milk to make a dough. Knead lightly with hands until dough leaves them freely. Put dough into a clean, greased bowl. Cover with a clean cloth and place in a warm place to rise for 2 hours. Knead lightly. Break off a small piece for top and roll into a strip 10 cm long. Knead remaining dough into a round loaf. Place on a greased oven slide and glaze top with milk. Coil strip around top of dough. Brush loaf all over with milk and dust liberally with flour. Put in a warm place for 25 to 30 minutes. Bake in a hot oven (200°–230°C) for 10 minutes. Reduce heat to moderately hot (190°–220°C) and cook for a further 15 minutes.

Mixed Flour Bread

30 g compressed yeast
1 tablespoon brown sugar
3 cups warm water
2 cups plain wholemeal
flour
1 cup self-raising flour
4 cups plain flour
3 teaspoons salt

Place combined yeast, brown sugar and 1 cup of water in a warm place until bubbles form. Mix flours and salt, make a well in centre, pour in yeast mixture. Work flour in and gradually add remaining water until all flour is taken up. Turn onto board and knead for 10 minutes. Place in oiled bowl and stand in a warm place until the mixture has doubled. Turn onto board and knead again for 10 minutes. Form into 2 loaves and place in well-greased lined tins. Leave in a warm place until doubled. Bake in hot oven (220°C) for 15 minutes, reduce heat to moderate, (180°–200°C). Cook for a further 25 minutes.

Easy Bread

More families are preferring to make their own bread.

2 cups plain flour
2 cups wheaten flour
1 teaspoon salt
4 teaspoons baking powder
1 tablespoon golden syrup
2½ cups milk

Mix all ingredients together. Bake in well-greased loaf tin in a moderately hot oven (190°–220°C) for 40 minutes.

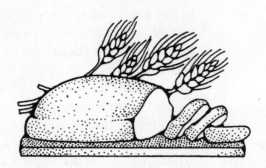

Wholemeal Bread

4 cups plain flour
4 cups wholemeal flour
4 cups stoneground flour
2 teaspoons salt
4 cups warm water
2 teaspoons honey, golden syrup or brown sugar
1 tablespoon dried yeast
milk for glazing
1 tablespoon sesame seeds

Sieve flours and salt, and place in a warm bowl in a warm place. Mix 1 cup of water with honey and add yeast. Leave for 10 to 15 minutes until mixture froths. Mix flours with yeast mixture and add remainder of water. Turn onto a floured board and knead well for about 10 minutes. Return to warm bowl. Cut crossways through dough with a knife, cover and leave in a warm place until dough doubles its bulk (30 to 40 minutes). Knead again, halve and shape into two loaves. Place in well-greased and lined tins. Cover and leave in a warm place until mixture reaches top of tins. Glaze with milk and sprinkle with sesame seeds. Bake in a hot oven (220°C) for 10 minutes then reduce to moderate (180°–200°C) and bake for a further 30 to 40 minutes.

Wheatmeal Bread

6 cups wheatmeal
2 cups plain white flour
1 dessertspoon butter
  (optional)
1 rounded tablespoon salt
1 tablespoon yeast
1 large tablespoon treacle
warm water to mix

Mix flours, rub in butter, add salt, then yeast and treacle. Add water and mix to a stiff dough. Cover basin with a cloth and place in a warm position and allow to rise. When risen, (about 1¼ hours) turn onto floured board and knead thoroughly. Return to basin, sprinkle flour on top, and allow to rise again. When well risen, turn onto board once more, cut mixture in half, knead and form into two loaves. Grease tins thoroughly, set loaves to rise before baking in a hot oven (200°–230°C) for approximately 1 hour.

Sourdough Rye Bread

Rye Bread
30 g compressed yeast
1 tablespoon brown sugar
4¾ cups plain flour
3 cups lukewarm water
4 cups rye flour
2 teaspoons salt
30 g caraway seeds
¼ cup sourdough (see
  below)
2 tablespoons oil

Sourdough
15 g compressed yeast
1 teaspoon sugar
1¼ cups lukewarm water
1½ cups plain flour

Sourdough   Cream yeast and sugar, add water. Sift flour, add yeast mixture, mix until smooth; mixture will soon start to bubble. Cover, stand unrefrigerated for two days before using.

Rye Bread   Cream yeast with 1 teaspoon sugar and 1 teaspoon plain flour. Add ½ cup water, stand in warm place until mixture starts to bubble (10 to 15 minutes). Sift flours, salt and remaining sugar; return husks in sifter to flour. Stir in caraway seeds. Make a well in ingredients. Combine yeast mixture, remaining water, sourdough and oil. Add to dry ingredients, mix well. You may need an extra ¼ to ½ cup water. Divide dough in two, then in two again. Knead each piece until smooth and round. Put two rounds side-by-side in two greased 23 x 12 cm loaf tins. Cover tins, let stand for 30 minutes in warm place until dough reaches edge of tins. Brush top of dough with water. Bake in a hot oven (200°–230°C) for 45 minutes.

Walnut Bread

4 cups plain flour
1 cup sugar
1 teaspoon soda
1 cup chopped walnuts
2 teaspoons cream of tartar
pinch of salt
1¼ to 1½ cups milk

Mix all ingredients to a fairly stiff dough. Bake in a greased standard loaf tin for 1 hour in a moderate oven (180°–200°C).

Banana Nut Bread

This bread freezes very well.

½ teaspoon salt
1½ cups self-raising flour
½ teaspoon nutmeg
½ teaspoon cinnamon
90 g butter
1 cup sugar
2 eggs
1 cup mashed ripe bananas
125 g chopped nuts

Sift together salt, flour and spices. Cream butter and sugar, then add the eggs, one at a time, beating well. Beat mixture until light and fluffy. Add sifted flour and spices and bananas to creamed mixture, combining lightly. Fold in chopped nuts. Turn the mixture into a well-greased loaf tin and bake in a moderate oven (180°–200°C) for 50 to 60 minutes. Cool in the tin and when cold wrap in foil for 24 hours before cutting.

Savoury Tea Bread

There are now many tasty variations to a bread recipe.

125 g bacon
1 small onion
2 apples
2 cups self-raising flour
pinch of salt and pepper
30 g margarine
1 egg
5 tablespoons milk

Gently fry together finely chopped bacon, grated onion and peeled apples. Allow to cool. Sift together flour, salt and pepper. Rub in margarine. Add cool bacon mixture. Beat egg and milk, stir into flour mixture. Mix well. Spoon into greased loaf tin. Bake in a moderate oven (180°–200°C) for 40 minutes. Allow to cool and serve buttered.

Mini Rolls

1 large tablespoon butter
1 tablespoon sugar
1 egg
1 cup milk
2 cups self-raising flour

Cream butter and sugar, add egg and milk. Sift in flour and mix well. Roll out and cut into small squares. Roll each piece over three times, brush with egg white or a little milk. Bake in a hot oven (220°C) for 10 minutes.

Bagels

23 g compressed yeast
3 tablespoons sugar
½ cup water
4 cups plain flour
2 teaspoons salt
½ cup lukewarm milk
1 egg yolk
3 tablespoons oil
1 extra egg yolk
extra lukewarm water
poppy seeds or sesame seeds

Cream yeast with 1 tablespoon sugar. Add ¼ cup water, stand covered in warm place until mixture bubbles, approximately 10 to 15 minutes. Sift flour, salt and remaining sugar in bowl. Combine milk, remaining water, egg yolk and oil. Add to dry ingredients with yeast mixture, mix to stiff dough. Add up to an extra ¼ cup lukewarm water if necessary. Turn dough out onto floured board, knead well. Put into lightly oiled bowl, cover, stand in warm place until doubled in bulk, approximately 1 hour. Punch dough down, knead again, divide into 15 portions. Roll each portion into rope shape approximately 20 cm long. Coil rope to make a ring, moistening ends and overlapping them. Squeeze lightly to seal. Put on greased tray, allow to stand in warm place for 10 minutes. Slide a few bagels at a time into a large saucepan of boiling water (do not let them overlap). Turn after one minute and remove with slotted spoon after boiling for one more minute. Place bagels onto greased oven tray, brush well with combined, beaten extra egg yolk and water, sprinkle with poppy seeds or sesame seeds. Bake in a hot oven (200°–230°C) for 15 to 20 minutes or until golden brown. Serve warm or cold.

Boston Bun

1 cup mashed potato
¾ cup sugar
1 cup mixed fruit
2 level cups self-raising
  flour
1 cup milk

Mash potatoes without milk, place in bowl with sugar and beat until creamy. Add mixed fruit. Sift flour and add to mixture alternately with milk. Mixture will be soft. Bake in a deep greased 18–20 cm round tin for 30 to 40 minutes in moderate oven (180°–200°C).

Glazed Buns

750 g plain flour
½ teaspoon salt
3 tablespoons butter
1 teaspoon mixed spice
1½ cups mixed fruit
½ cup sugar
2 teaspoons powdered milk
1½ cups tepid water
60 g compressed yeast

Glaze
½ cup sugar
¼ cup water
1 teaspoon gelatine

Sift flour and salt into warm basin. Rub in butter, add spice and fruit. Mix sugar and powdered milk into half of water. Crumble yeast into remaining water. Stir milk liquid into flour, add yeast mixture to make a soft dough. Knead until elastic (about 10 minutes), put in bowl and cover with cloth. Leave in warm place to rise. Turn onto a floured board, knead again. Divide into 16 parts for small buns. Leave in warm place until doubled in size. Place on well-greased trays. Bake in hot oven (200°–230°C) for 25 minutes. This mixture can also be used for loaves.

Glaze   Place ingredients in small saucepan, stir over low heat until sugar and gelatine have dissolved. Glaze after buns are cooked.

Piping batter for making crosses
¼ cup self-raising flour
2 tablespoons water
1 tablespoon castor sugar

Variation   Hot Cross Buns
Use Glazed Buns recipe.
Mix piping ingredients to make a smooth batter. Pipe on to buns after they have doubled in size, before baking.

Cinnamon Bun

1 tablespoon butter
1 cup self-raising flour
¼ teaspoon spice
pinch of nutmeg
½ teaspoon cinnamon
1 egg
3 tablespoons sugar
2 tablespoons milk
½ cup raisins

Rub butter into flour and spices. Beat egg, sugar and milk, and add to flour mixture. Add raisins. Pour into well-greased sandwich tin, sprinkle with cinnamon and sugar and small dob of butter on top. Bake in a moderate oven (180°–200°C) for 15 to 20 minutes.

Chelsea Bun

Bun
3 cups self-raising flour
½ teaspoon salt
45 g butter
1 cup milk
60 g extra butter
⅓ cup brown sugar, lightly packed
½ cup sultanas
½ cup currants
60 g chopped glacé cherries
60 g mixed peel
1 teaspoon cinnamon

Glaze
1 tablespoon water
1 tablespoon sugar
1 teaspoon gelatine

Bun Sift flour and salt in bowl, rub in butter lightly. Mix to firm dough with milk. Roll out to 30 x 23 cm oblong shape. Cream extra butter and sugar, spread over dough. Sprinkle with fruit and cinnamon, roll up lengthwise. Cut into 10 thick slices. Pack into greased 20 cm sandwich tin, cut side down. Bake in a moderate oven (180°–200°C) for 25 to 30 minutes. Brush bun with glaze while still hot.

Glaze Put ingredients in small saucepan, stir over low heat until sugar and gelatine have dissolved.

Raspberry Buns

2 cups self-raising flour
pinch of salt
2 tablespoons butter
¼ cup sugar
1 egg
4 tablespoons milk
raspberry jam

Sift flour and salt, lightly rub in the butter. Add sugar. Beat lightly beaten egg and milk then add to the dry ingredients. Mix into a light dough. Turn onto lightly floured board. Divide into 12 parts, kneading each one into a ball. Make a hollow in the centre of each. Put in a little jam. Pinch dough together to enclose jam. Glaze with a little milk. Bake on a greased oven slide in a hot oven (220°C) for 15 minutes.

Yeast Buns

Joh's mother used to make large buns with plenty of sultanas in them.

Buns
⅓ cup skim milk powder
⅓ cup sugar
1 cup water
3 tablespoons butter
40 g (2 tablespoons)
   compressed yeast
500 g plain flour
2 teaspoons salt
½ cup sultanas

Glaze
1 teaspoon gelatine
1 tablespoon sugar
1 tablespoon hot water

Buns Mix skim milk powder and sugar in a saucepan with ⅔ cup of water. Heat, stirring constantly, until boiling. Add butter and remaining water. Cool to lukewarm, then add crumbled yeast. Sift flour and salt together, add sultanas. Add skim milk mixture and mix to a soft dough (add more warm water if necessary). Knead well for 10 minutes. Place into greased bowl, cover with plastic, let stand in warm place for 10 minutes. Divide dough into 16 even-sized pieces, and shape into buns. Place on greased slides and stand in a warm place until doubled in size (20 to 30 minutes). Bake in a moderately hot oven (200°–230°C) for 15 to 20 minutes.

Glaze Glaze immediately with gelatine and sugar dissolved in hot water.

Cream Buns

30 g compressed yeast
¼ cup sugar
½ cup lukewarm milk
4 cups plain flour
60 g butter
1 cup lukewarm water
1 egg yolk
1 extra teaspoon water

Cream yeast with 1 teaspoon sugar. Add lukewarm milk. Let stand for 10 to 15 minutes until frothy. Sift flour and remaining sugar into bowl. Rub in butter until mixture resembles fine breadcrumbs. Make well in centre of dry ingredients, add yeast mixture and water, mix to soft dough. Turn out onto floured surface. Knead for 5 minutes. Place dough in lightly oiled bowl. Cover and stand in warm place for 1 hour or until dough doubles in bulk. Punch dough down in bowl. Turn out onto floured surface. Knead for 5 minutes. Divide into 12 even portions. Knead each portion of dough into a round. Put rounds on well-greased oven trays, allowing room for spreading. Stand in a warm place for 10 minutes or until half-doubled in size. Brush with combined beaten egg yolk and extra water. Bake in a hot oven (230°C) for 10 minutes. Reduce heat to moderate (180°–200°C), bake for a further 15 minutes or until golden brown. Put buns on wire rack. When cold, slit open, fill with raspberry jam and Mock Cream (see p. 118) or fresh whipped cream. Dust each bun with a little sifted icing sugar.

SCONES, MUFFINS AND DAMPER

The one important piece of advice I always give to people attempting to make scones is that you must treat them with tender loving care. Don't knead them, instead press them very lightly with your fingertips. This helps your scones to turn out nice and light.

Basic Scone

Scones are lighter if milk is at least room temperature. Warm milk slightly if taken directly from the refrigerator.

2 cups self-raising flour
½ teaspoon salt
2 level tablespoons butter
1 cup milk
extra flour for rolling

Sift flour and salt into a bowl. Melt butter and pour into flour. Add milk, gradually stirring with a knife until you have a moist dough. Turn onto a floured board. Knead lightly and then press out. Cut to size and place on floured tray. Bake in a hot oven (220°C) for 10 to 15 minutes.

Basic Scone with Cream

These are richer-tasting scones due to the cream.

4 cups self-raising flour
1 teaspoon salt
½ cup cream
600 mL milk

Sift flour and salt twice. Add cream and milk and stir with knife. Knead well, then roll out to 1 cm. Cut with scone cutter. Bake in a hot oven (220°C) for about 10 minutes. Wrap in tea towel to steam.

Variations *Cheese Swirls* Roll or press out the dough. Sprinkle with grated cheese, salt and pepper. Roll up like a Swiss roll, cut into 1–2 cm pieces. Place onto well-greased slide with cut edge up. Bake in a hot oven (200°–230°C) for 10 to 15 minutes.
Anchovy/Ham Swirls Anchovy or ham paste may be used instead of grated cheese.

Cheese Scones

2 cups self-raising flour
1 tablespoon butter
½ cup grated cheese
pinch of salt
2 tablespoons sugar
(optional)
1 egg
½ cup milk

Sift flour and rub in butter and cheese. Add salt and sugar. Moisten with beaten egg and milk. Turn out onto lightly floured board and knead quickly and lightly. Cut to size and place on greased tray. Bake in a hot oven (220°C) for 10 to 15 minutes.

Sultana Scones

3 cups self-raising flour
½ teaspoon salt
60 g butter
¼ cup sugar
1 cup sultanas
1 egg
1 cup milk

Sift flour and salt, rub in butter until mixture resembles fine breadcrumbs. Add sugar, sultanas and egg, and enough milk to give a soft dough. Place on floured surface and knead lightly. Pat out to about 2 cm thickness, and cut in 5 cm rounds. Place on greased tray, glaze with milk. Bake in a very hot oven (230°–250°C) for 12 to 15 minutes.

Date Scones

2 cups self-raising flour
½ teaspoon salt
60 g butter
¼ cup sugar
¾ cup finely chopped dates
1 egg
½ cup milk

Sift flour and salt, rub in butter until mixture resembles fine breadcrumbs. Stir in sugar and dates. Beat egg and add to dry ingredients with sufficient milk to give a soft dough. Place on floured surface and knead lightly. Pat out to approximately 1 cm thick, and, using a floured cutter, cut into 3 cm rounds. Place onto greased oven tray. Glaze tops with milk. Bake in a very hot oven (230°–250°C) for 12 to 15 minutes.

Honeyed Banana Scones

These were tested in Sheffield, England, at an afternoon tea. Everyone loved them.

1 cup self-raising flour
1 cup wholemeal self-
   raising flour
½ teaspoon salt
30 g butter
2 bananas
2 tablespoons honey
½ cup milk

Sift flours and salt into basin, rub in butter until mixture resembles fine breadcrumbs. Combine mashed bananas, honey and milk. Add to dry ingredients and work into soft dough. Turn onto floured board and knead lightly. Pat out to 2 cm thickness, cut with 5 cm cutter. Place onto greased oven tray, glaze tops with a little milk. Bake in a very hot oven (230°–250°C) for 12 to 15 minutes.

Gem Scones

60 g butter
60 g castor sugar
1 egg
2 tablespoons milk
120 g self-raising flour
pinch of salt

Cream butter and sugar, add beaten egg, then milk. Fold in sifted flour and salt. Grease hot gem iron and drop in teaspoonfuls of mixture. Cook in a moderate oven (180°–200°C) for 10 to 15 minutes.

Treacle Scones

These are delicious eaten with butter and your favourite jam.

90 g butter
1 cup self-raising flour
60 g sugar
30 g sultanas
1 tablespoon treacle
⅓ cup milk

Rub butter into flour, add sugar and sultanas. Mix with blended treacle and milk until fairly moist. Roll out lightly, cut with scone cutter. Place on greased tray. Bake in a very hot oven (230°–250°C) for 10 minutes, then reduce heat. Bake in a slow oven (150°–160°C) for a further 8 to 10 minutes.

Wholemeal Scones

125 g plain flour
2 teaspoons cream of tartar
1 teaspoon bicarbonate of
*   soda*
½ teaspoon salt
500 g wholemeal flour
2 tablespoons butter
2 tablespoons brown sugar
warm milk to mix into a
*   very light dough*

Sift plain flour, cream of tartar, soda, and salt. Add wholemeal flour. Rub butter into mixture. Add sugar and warm milk. Mix with a knife. Turn out onto a board, knead very lightly for 1 minute. Roll quickly, cut out and brush with milk. Bake on a greased tray in a hot oven (230°C) for 12 to 15 minutes.

Cinnamon Scone Whirls

2 cups self-raising flour
1 level teaspoon salt
1 level dessertspoon sugar
30 g copha shortening
milk to make 1 cup liquid
fruit and nuts for
    sprinkling on top

Place sifted flour, salt and sugar in basin. Melt copha over gentle heat and pour into measuring cup. Add milk to make 1 cup and pour onto dry ingredients. Mix to a medium dough. Roll scone dough into a rectangle 1 cm thick. Melt copha and mix in brown sugar and cinnamon. Spread on dough. Sprinkle with nuts and fruit, leaving a margin of 1 cm around the edge. Brush edge with milk and roll as for Swiss roll. Cut into slices about 2½ cm thick. Place on greased slide. Bake in a hot oven (230°C) for 15 to 20 minutes.

Variation   The slices can also be arranged in a greased sandwich tin (20 to 23 cm thick) and baked for 20 to 25 minutes to form a teacake.

Sweet Scone Turnovers

3 cups self-raising flour
1 level teaspoon salt
½ cup sugar
1 egg
¾ cup milk
90 g copha shortening

Sift flour and salt, add sugar and egg. Add milk to gently melted copha. Pour onto mixture and mix lightly to a medium soft dough. Knead lightly on a floured board and roll out to 1 cm thick. Cut into rounds with a 5–6 cm cutter. Brush top lightly with milk. Place on greased slides. Bake in a hot oven (200°–230°C) for 12 to 15 minutes. Serve with butter.

Muffins

1½ cups self-raising flour
¾ cup sugar
½ cup plain flour
½ teaspoon salt
⅓ cup vegetable oil
1 cup milk

Sift flour then sift dry ingredients together. Mix in the oil. Combine beaten egg (if using plain flour) and milk. Add to flour mixture. Stir until flour is moist. Fill greased patty cake pans two-thirds full. Bake in a moderately hot oven (190°–220°C) for 25 minutes.

For those cooks who forgot to stock up on self-raising flour!
1¾ cups plain flour
2 tablespoons sugar
2½ teaspoons baking powder
¾ teaspoons salt
⅓ cup vegetable oil
1 egg
¾ cup milk

Variations   Blueberry   Prepare muffins using ¼ cup sugar. Gently stir in 1 cup well-drained blueberries.
Apple and Sultana   Add ¼ cup chopped, dried apples and ¼ cup sultanas to flour mixture before adding liquid.
Raisin, Nut or Date   Add ½ to ¾ cup raisins, nuts or coarsely chopped dates. Stir quickly into batter.
Jam   Place 1 teaspoon jam on top of each muffin before baking.
Cheese and Caraway   Add 1 cup shredded tasty cheese and ½ teaspoon caraway seed to flour–oil mixture.

Rhubarb Muffins

1 egg
¼ cup orange juice
¾ cup low fat milk
1 stick rhubarb
2 tablespoons vegetable oil
¼ cup raw sugar
1 cup self-raising flour
1 cup wholemeal self-raising flour
½ teaspoon cinnamon

Mix lightly beaten egg, orange juice, milk, thinly sliced rhubarb, oil and sugar. Combine flours and cinnamon, gently fold into wet ingredients and spoon into greased muffin pans. Bake in hot oven (200°C) for 25 minutes.

Variation   Add ½ cup sultanas or chopped dates. Sift dry ingredients into bowl. Pour in liquids and mix with fork. Spoon into greased patty tins. Bake in moderate oven (180°–200°C) for 25 minutes.

Bran Muffins

1 ¼ cups plain flour
1 teaspoon cinnamon
1 teaspoon bicarbonate of
soda
1 ¾ cup unprocessed bran
½ cup vegetable oil
1 ½ cups buttermilk or
plain milk
1 egg

Blend dry ingredients together, make well in centre. Add oil, buttermilk and egg. Mix until well combined. Cover, refrigerate for 24 hours. Bake in greased muffin trays in moderate oven (180°–200°C) for 25 minutes.

Fruit Bran Muffins

1 cup boiling water
1 cup unprocessed bran
½ cup margarine or butter
1 ½ cups sugar
2 eggs
2 ¼ cups buttermilk or milk
1 tablespoon bicarbonate of
soda
½ tablespoon salt
1 ½ cups plain flour
2 cups bran flakes
1 cup sultanas

Pour water over bran and let stand for 15 minutes. Cream margarine and sugar, add eggs and beat well. Add buttermilk to bran mixture. Sift soda, salt and flour together, add to other ingredients. Gently fold in the bran flakes and sultanas. Cover and refrigerate for 24 hours. Bake in greased muffin trays in moderate oven (180°–200°C) for 15 to 20 minutes. Mixture will keep for up to 8 weeks.

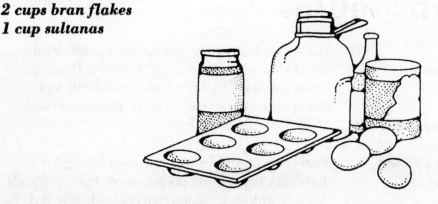

Walnut, Banana and Bran Muffins

90 g butter
⅓ cup raw sugar
1¾ cups self-raising flour
½ teaspoon bicarbonate of soda
¼ cup unprocessed bran
½ cup walnuts or dates (or both)
⅔ cup skim milk
2 mashed bananas

Cream butter and sugar. Add other ingredients, blending well. Bake in greased muffin trays in a moderate oven (180°–200°C) for approximately 15 to 20 minutes or until golden brown.

Damper

Damper's delicious served with jam or honey and whipped cream, and just as nice served hot with garlic butter.

3 cups self-raising flour
1½ teaspoons salt
90 g butter
½ cup milk
½ cup water
extra flour

Sift flour and salt into bowl, rub in butter until mixture resembles fine breadcrumbs. Make a well in centre of dry ingredients, add combined water and milk; mix lightly with sharp knife in cutting motion. Turn out onto lightly floured surface; knead lightly into round shape. Place on greased oven tray. Pat dough out to a 15 cm circle. With sharp knife, cut two slits across dough to form a cross 1 cm deep. Brush top of dough with milk, sift a little extra flour over dough. Bake in hot oven (230°C) for 10 minutes or until golden brown, reduce heat to moderate (180°–200°C) and cook for a further 15 minutes.

Wholemeal Damper

*4 cups wholemeal self-
  raising flour*
4 teaspoons baking powder
2½ cups milk
1 teaspoon salt
1 tablespoon golden syrup

Mix all ingredients together. Knead lightly and shape into a round bun shape. Bake in moderate oven (180°–200°C) for 30 minutes. Cooked damper should sound hollow when tapped on top. Serve spread with butter and golden syrup or honey.

NO-BAKE

No-bake recipes are some of the easiest recipes to make. I like making Coconut Ice (see p. 276) almost as much as Joh likes eating it. My grandchildren love to stay with Joh and me, and they all enjoy cooking, so I have also included some of their favourite recipes.

Cigars

Makes about 40

60 g copha
300 mL tin condensed milk
**250 g crushed coffee
    biscuits**
2 tablespoons cocoa
½ teaspoon vanilla
**½ cup extra coconut for
    rolling**

Gently melt the copha. Crush biscuits and mix all ingredients. Break off in small pieces and mould into cigar shape. Roll in extra coconut. Allow to set in refrigerator.

Coconut Ice

A very good recipe for Coconut Ice.

3 cups icing sugar
3 cups coconut
1 teaspoon vanilla
2 egg whites
125 g copha
cochineal

Sift icing sugar. Add coconut, vanilla and beaten egg white. Melt copha gently and allow to cool slightly. Add to mixture. Divide mixture and colour half with drops of cochineal until pink. Spread white mixture onto a well-greased flat tray. Cover with pink half. Chill and cut into pieces.

Coconut Lemon Fingers

Makes 24 to 28

125 g copha or butter
400 mL condensed milk
**250 g plain sweet biscuits
    (crushed)**
¾ cup coconut
grated rind of 1 lemon

Gently melt the copha or butter and add condensed milk. Combine all ingredients and stir well. Press firmly and evenly into a greased Swiss roll tin and allow to set. Cover with Lemon icing (see p. 249) and sprinkle with 1 tablespoon of coconut. When set cut into fingers.

Date Balls

125 g butter
1 cup brown sugar
500 g dates
1 cup coconut
4 cups rice bubbles
extra coconut for coating

Boil butter, sugar and chopped dates for 3 minutes. Remove from heat and stir in coconut and rice bubbles. When cool, roll into balls and coat in extra coconut. Store in refrigerator.

Date Fingers

12 weetbix
1 tin condensed milk
1 cup coconut
½ cup chopped dates or
*   mixed fruit*
½ cup chopped walnuts
2 tablespoons cocoa

Crush weetbix, mix all ingredients together and press into a greased Swiss roll tin. Cut into fingers and allow to set firm. Dust with sifted icing sugar if desired.

Dreams

Makes about 40

400 mL condensed milk
250 g plain biscuits
1 cup coconut
1 tablespoon cocoa
1 tablespoon orange juice
¼ cup extra coconut

Crush biscuits and mix all ingredients together. Roll teaspoonful of mixture in the extra coconut, shaping into small balls. Allow to set in refrigerator until firm.

Alsatian Cake

A no-bake dessert.

1 double layer unfilled
    Sponge (see p. 194)
125 g butter
150 g icing sugar
4 egg yolks
4 egg whites, well beaten
small glass of rum or sherry
whipped cream
cherries, nuts and grated
    chocolate gratings to
    decorate

Cut each half of the unfilled sponge through the centre, making four layers. Place bottom layer on plate, cut a ring out of the second layer, and place the outside ring on top of the first layer to form a well. Crumb the cut-out portion and the whole of the third layer. Cream the butter and icing sugar, add beaten egg yolks, 2 cups of cake crumbs and the rum or sherry. Lastly add the well beaten egg whites. Pour as much mixture into cake well as possible, then cover with top layer of sponge. Cover and place in refrigerator for 24 hours. Coat with whipped cream and decorate with cherries, nuts and grated chocolate.

Honey Bubble Crunch

125 g butter
½ cup sugar
2 tablespoons honey
4 cups rice bubbles
1 cup coconut

Boil butter, sugar and honey for 5 minutes. Stir into rice bubbles and coconut. Spread into greased slab tin and press flat. Set in fridge. When set cut into slices or squares.

Classic Country Wisdom

CONTENTS

THE HOME

Joh always had the job of collecting the eggs when he came home from school.
He told me how he would run barefoot through the grass looking for new nests
under bushes and logs. Sometimes he missed a nest for a couple of weeks and
so it was very exciting when he found 12 to 14 eggs.
A bigger surprise was when he missed a nest altogether and one day a mother
hen would appear with a family of little chickens.
I've always been glad that my kitchen catches the morning sun —
especially in our Kingaroy winters — and it also has a lovely view towards
Kingaroy, it makes it such a delight to work in. I can also watch the small
finches eating their seed as Joh has put a feeder just outside the window.

Cooking

I really enjoy cooking, and, of course, eating the results. Over the years I have met so many people interested in exchanging a recipe with me or passing on a hint about cooking.

I have included a lot of cooking hints which I have collected over the years, and which may help you. My favourite is that you should never be scared to improvise with a recipe, such as adding extra flavouring or a different herb. This often makes a dish more exciting.

Almonds and pistachios

To peel almonds and pistachios, cover the nuts with boiling water, leave for 6 or 7 minutes, then strain. Place them in a bowl and cover with cold water. When cool, drain well, and remove the skins by pressing each nut between the thumb and forefinger. Dry well on a sieve and use as required.

Aniseed

Use whole or crushed aniseeds in breads, cakes, apple pies and apple sauces. Add to cream cheese, pickles, curries and water for boiling shellfish. Mix aniseed flowers into fruit salads, and add the leaves with figs, dates and chestnuts.

Asparagus

Cook asparagus tied in bundles standing up in a saucepan; this way the tips won't go limp. After cooking, drain on a slice of dry toast.

Avocado

To ripen, place avocado in a brown paper bag for a few days.

To prevent a fresh avocado from going black when cut, rub flesh with lemon juice.

Bacon

If bacon is slimy, or too salty, rinse in hot water.

Bacon rinds added to pea soup will give that extra flavour, and they also make excellent party nibbles.

Baking powder

60 g ground rice
60 g bicarbonate of soda
140 g cream of tartar or 60 g tartaric acid

Mix together well, then pass mixture through a fine sieve.

Bananas

To ripen, place bananas in a brown paper bag for a few days. Sliced bananas won't darken if they are sprinkled with lemon juice.

Barley

Barley is valuable for thickening soups. It contains no gluten (which also makes it suitable for people with wheat allergies) and therefore isn't suitable for breadmaking, except with a mixture of wheaten flour.

Basil

Tear rather than chop basil leaves, and add at the last minute to cooked dishes, or sprinkle over salads and sliced tomatoes. Basil's rich flavour complements garlic. The leaves can be dried slowly and used for cooking in soups or as seasoning.

Batter

Let the batter for fritters, pancakes and crepes stand for 30 minutes before using to soften the starch grains in the flour. You can use 1 teaspoon of custard powder and a dash of vinegar instead of eggs in fritter batter.

Bay leaf

Include a bay leaf in a bouquet garni for flavouring stews, soups and sauces.

Add to marinades, stock, potato soup, stuffing, curry, game and poached fish liquid, and remove before serving. You can also use it as a garnish. Boil in milk to flavour custards and rice pudding.

Place a bay leaf in the *rice jar* to flavour rice.

Tape a bay leaf to the inside lid of a *flour or cereal jar* to keep the weevils away.

Berries

When there is a plentiful supply of berries, spread on trays and freeze. Once frozen, store them in freezer bags in the freezer.

Biscuits

Biscuits are fresher and more crisp if a sugar lump is placed in the biscuit tin. If biscuits have become soft, put them in the oven for a few minutes to freshen.

Bouquet garni

Bouquet garni is a sachet of herbs used for flavouring dishes such as stocks and soups. Use crumbled, dried bay leaves, dried thyme, dried marjoram and dried parsley. Place a small pile of the herbs in the middle of a muslin square and tie with a long piece of string for easy removal at the end of the cooking time.

A use for stale bread

We often went to our Bunya Mountains 'Possum Lodge' home for a short holiday at Christmas. One year Joh went home a few days before I did and when I returned my cat seemed to be missing.

After a couple of days I asked Joh whether he had seen my cat. He replied very sheepishly that the cat had been eating his little birds and so its life had come to an unhappy end.

I wasn't very happy about this as I maintained that there were hundreds of birds and only my one pussy.

Nowadays when Joh is away in Tasmania it's my job to feed the birds at home. It takes a good deal of time every morning. We have galahs, lorikeets, double-bars, finches, and occasionally a few King parrots. They are lovely birds.

I'm sure they must tell each other in bird language 'Go to Joh's — there's plenty of food there'. I often think it's their social security!

Stale bread or crusts soaked with honey are ideal for birds, and the possums love it too. I have included several hints to keep bread fresh. Alternatively it can be used up in bread puddings, which is one of Joh's favourite desserts.

You should never have to throw any bread out.

Bread

Bread is cooked when the loaves sound hollow when tapped.

When cooked, bread should be cooled on wire trays and turned upside-down.

Make *two loaves* instead of one and freeze the second loaf in a freezer bag.

To *cut* really fresh bread, heat the breadknife in boiling water.

To *freshen* stale bread, dip the loaf quickly in and out of a bowl of water. Place in a moderate oven for 5 to 6 minutes, or put bread (without wetting) into a casserole dish with the lid on and bake in a fairly hot oven for 30 minutes.

Put a potato in the breadbin to keep bread fresh.

Yeast bread must be baked in a very hot oven at first to kill the yeast. When brown, the oven heat can be gradually reduced.

Breadcrumbs

They will be finer if rubbed through a wire sieve than if grated.

Stale bread may be dried in oven and rolled or grated for crumbs for frying, or used in baked bread puddings. Breadcrumbs can also be used in puddings in place of flour, $^2/_3$ breadcrumbs to $^1/_3$ flour.

Fresh breadcrumbs can be used for thickening gravy and soup.

To *coat easily*, beat 1 dessertspoon of salad oil with each egg when preparing breadcrumbs for fish or cutlets, as it binds the crumbs.

To *evenly coat* fish or meat pieces, place breadcrumb mixture into a plastic bag, add your fish or meat and shake well.

Broccoli

Soak broccoli in cold salted water with heads down to draw out any insects. Cook with heads down and pan uncovered to preserve colour.

Butter

It's easier to cream butter in a basin which has been rinsed out in very hot water.

To *soften quickly*, grate butter into mixture.

To *remove salt*, place butter in a bowl and pour over boiling water. Leave until cold. Butter will have risen to the top and can be lifted off.

If *rancid*, butter should be washed well in fresh milk, then melted slowly over the stove. Skim the top from time to time, then strain it and leave to cool.

To *double the quantity* and make butter easy to spread, soften butter, beat with 1¼ cups of warm milk, in which 15 g of gelatine has been dissolved.

To *test for adulteration:* when heated, butter bubbles up and burns; margarine boils.

To *preserve butter when camping,* stand butter in a container of salted water and cover. Keep changing the salted water.

Beat 250 g of butter with 4 crushed cloves of garlic in a bowl until smooth to make *garlic butter.*

Sprinkle dry basil, oregano, tarragon, rosemary or any other herb you like over the softened butter (1–2 teaspoons to 125 g of butter) to make *herb butter.* Pop some grated cheese on top (¹/₃ cheese to 1 butter). Mix, wrap in foil and store in the refrigerator. Use on sliced bread sticks or over cooked meat, fish or vegetables.

Cabbage

To flavour cooked cabbage, add 1 teaspoon of plain yoghurt and a sprinkle of pepper.

To prevent cabbage *smells,* put a couple of slices of lemon in with the cabbage when cooking or put a slice of bread over the cabbage and seal with lid.

Cakes

All tins and biscuit trays should be greased with butter or fat. Scone trays should be warmed and floured, and large sponge tins should be buttered and sprinkled with equal quantities of flour and icing sugar. Fruit cake tins are buttered and lined with greased paper.

To *prevent fruit from sinking* in a fruit cake, sprinkle a little flour on the fruit.

For a *level and shiny top* on a fruit cake, brush top of cake with milk before baking.

When cooked, a cake should be elastic when pressed, and an even colour. A *small cake* which sinks or sticks means the oven is too cool, there is too much liquid, or too much sugar.

When a skewer is inserted into a *large cake*, it should come out clean and dry.

A *sponge cake* when cooked begins to shrink from the tin and is elastic to the touch. Adding 1 tablespoon of lukewarm water into the sponge mixture after adding the eggs helps make the sponge light and fluffy.

Uneven rising for sandwich cakes means the tins could be too close together which gives a poor circulation of heat.

Holes in the cake can be caused by insufficient sifting of the flour and rising agent, or it could be due to too much baking powder or an overheated oven.

Sticky top on a cake means the oven is too cool.

Swiss rolls will crack instead of rolling easily if cooked in too slow an oven.

To *keep cakes moist*, keep a loaf of bread with your cake in a tin with a tight fitting lid.

When removing cakes from the tin when cooked, wipe over cake tin with a damp cloth, or hold the tin in a sink of hot water for a few seconds, as this helps loosen the cake.

Cover wire cake coolers with paper before turning out a hot cake, to prevent the cake sticking and wire marks on the cake.

Stale cake crumbs can be used in plum puddings instead of breadcrumbs.

Cake tins

Unless badly stained, these should never be washed. This will destroy the seasoning of the tin and cause the next cake to be cooked in it to stick. They should be rubbed clean with kitchen paper as soon as the cake has been removed. The tins should still be hot and they should be wiped until every crumb has been rubbed away.

Can opener

When your can opener gets dull, try grinding a small piece of steel wool

through it. Then wash in suds and
rinse. It cleans as well as sharpens.

Capsicum

Revive a shrivelled capsicum by
cutting in half and removing the seeds.
Place in a jar of water in the fridge. It
will become smooth and crisp again
and remain fresh for several days.

Caraway seeds

Sprinkle over rich meats such as pork
and goose, and Hungarian beef stew.
It can also be added to cabbage water
to reduce cooking smells. Use to flavour soups, breads, cakes, biscuits,
apple pie, baked apples and cheese.

Carrots

When pulling up carrots, keep the earth on the carrot until needed as it
will keep them fresh.

Carrots and parsnips

Use carrots and parsnips in puddings and cake making. The natural
sweetness, colour, texture and flavour of these vegetables serve as a
substitute for sugar.

Cauliflower

A pinch of grated orange peel gives an interesting flavour to white sauce
for cauliflower.

Add 2 tablespoons of milk to the water while cooking to *whiten*
cauliflower.

Celery

The celery tops will flavour soups, while the outside stalks may be used
as a vegetable.

Cheese

To prevent mould, cheese may be wrapped in a cloth dipped in vinegar and wrung nearly dry. Cover the cloth with a wrapper of paper, and keep in a cool place. You can also place a sugar lump in the cheese dish, as the sugar absorbs moisture.

When cheese becomes *dry*, place in hot water for a few minutes.

Stale cheese can be used in savouries.

To *prevent mould in grated cheese in packets*, store in the freezer, and break off amount required. There's no need to defrost.

Chervil

Use the leaf in salads, soups, sauces, vegetables, chicken, white fish and egg dishes. Use the chopped stems in soups and casseroles.

Comfrey

Chop young leaves into salads. Cook as with spinach or in fritters. Blanch the stems and cook like asparagus.

Coriander

Use the seeds in tomato chutney, ratatouille and curries, as well as in apple pies, cakes, biscuits, and marmalade. Add whole seeds to soups, sauces and vegetable dishes. Add the fresh lower leaves to curries, stews, salads, sauces and as a garnish.

Corks

To make corked jars airtight on fruit and sauces, dip the cork in equal quantities of hot mutton fat and wax.

Corned beef

When boiling corned beef or mutton, cut up oranges (including skin) or pineapple skins to add a nice flavour.

Cream

To thin the cream so it goes further, add 1 beaten egg white to every 125 mL of cream.

Adding 3 to 4 drops of lemon juice to each cup of whipped cream will make it stiff and firm. When whipping cream for cakes, add a small pinch of bicarbonate of soda to keep cream fresh for days. Whipped cream will go further if 1 tablespoon of sifted icing sugar and 1 stiffly whisked egg white are folded in.

Crystallised flowers

A simple and quick method for crystallising whole small blooms or single petals of violets, rosemary flowers, rose petals and small, whole rosebuds. Put 1 egg white into a saucer, break it up with a fork, but do not whip. Take a dry flower, or a single petal, and with a small paintbrush dipped into the egg white, cover it completely. Shake castor sugar through a fine sieve over the flower, first on one side, then the other. As each flower is finished, spread them out on greaseproof paper laid over an oven tray. Put the flowers in a very slow oven with the door open for approximately 10 to 15 minutes, and turn as the sugar hardens. Do not leave too long or they will go brown. Store between layers of greaseproof paper in an airtight container.

Curry

Add $^1/_4$ teaspoon of cinnamon and 1 dessertspoon of brown sugar for a lovely flavour.

Custard

To make a delicious meringue on a baked custard, pop a few marshmallows into the pie dish. They will rise and melt and make a lovely topping.

To *prevent a skin* forming on custard, place a damp cloth or damp waxed paper over saucepan or dish as soon as it is cooked.

If *custard curdles*, cool slightly and whisk well.

Sweeten custard with honey or treacle; 1 tablespoon will give a delicious flavour.

Instead of 2 eggs to $2^1/_2$ cups of milk in the standard custard recipe, 1 egg and 1 tablespoon of cornflour can be *substituted*.

Custard powder
14 drops of nutmeg oil
28 drops of bitter almonds oil
1$^1/_4$ cups of cornflour
1$^1/_2$ cups of dried arrowroot

Mix well together.

Dill

Use the seeds whole or ground in soups, fish dishes, pickles, cabbage, apple pies, dill butter, cakes and breads. Add a flower head per jar to pickled gherkins and cucumbers for a flavour stronger than dill leaves, but fresher than seeds. Add finely chopped leaf to soups, potato salads, cream cheese, eggs, salmon and grilled meats, and use as a garnish. Boil with new potatoes.

Dog biscuits

We've had Sparky, our Labrador, for many years. He actually has a pedigree name, but he arrived at the time of the electricity strike — when Joh as Premier took action to stop it, hence his name.

Now John has come home with three of his dogs, including Rebel, the German Shepherd, and he and Sparky have to stake out the area that belongs to each of them. I've heard plenty of growls and fights.

I have included a recipe for cooking dog biscuits, using the liver which I used to give to the cat.
250 g liver
2$^1/_2$ cups of plain flour
2$^1/_2$ cups of wheat meal
1 cup of bran
A little water

Boil the liver and mince it. Mix with the flour, wheat meal, bran and water. Roll out and cut into squares. Bake in a hot (200°C) oven for 8 to 10 minutes.

Dripping

To *clarify*, chop dripping into a saucepan, cover with water and bring to the boil. Boil until the liquid becomes oily. Cool then strain. Put dripping into a bowl and cover with boiling water. Stir well, then leave to cool. The white dripping will form a lump on the top.

Duck

When cooking wild duck, stuff the inside with fresh eucalyptus leaves.

Eggs

To separate egg white from yolk, use a small funnel, as the white will run through the funnel and the yolk will remain inside.

To *freeze*, break a couple of eggs onto a dish, and freeze. Wrap eggs in plastic and return to the freezer.

Duck eggs may be used for cooking. One duck egg is equal to 2 small hen's eggs.

To *test for freshness*, place egg in a bowl of water; a fresh egg will sink to the bottom, and a bad egg will rise to the top.

If *short of eggs*, *substitute* eggs in a cake by adding 1 level teaspoon of baking powder to each cup of flour.

Reduce the number of eggs required in a recipe by using 2 tablespoons of cornflour for each egg omitted.

If an *egg cracks* in the boiling water, a teaspoon of salt quickly added will stop it from boiling out into the water.

When *hard-boiling eggs*, keep turning them around in the saucepan until water comes to the boil to keep the yolks in the centre of the egg. After cooking, immerse in cold water immediately to prevent a dark ring forming around the yolk. A pinch of salt in the water helps eggs set more quickly. This hint also applies to poaching eggs.

Never use eggs under a week old when making a sponge or a cake.

Eggs should be at *room temperature* when using for cooking.

Never use a plastic bowl to beat *egg whites* as traces of grease are often retained by the plastic.

A few drops of water make it easier to beat *egg yolks*.

To *preserve egg yolks* beat them up with a little cold water. They will keep fresh for several days.

In *cakes or puddings*, one egg can serve for two if yolks and whites are beaten separately.

Evening primrose

Boil the root, which tastes like sweet parsnip, then pickle and toss in salads.

Fat

A few grains of salt in hot fat stops it from spluttering.

When a fire is started by burning fat, throw a handful of salt or flour on the fire. If the fire spreads, throw a blanket over it, **but never use water**.

Fennel

Use the seeds in sauces, fish dishes and bread, and as sprouts for winter salads. Finely chop the leaves over salads and cooked vegetables. Add to soups and to stuffing for oily fish. Add young stems to salads. Slice or grate the bulb into sandwiches or salads.

Fish

When frying, put a little salt in the pan to stop it sticking.

As fish can make a saucepan *smell*, tip tea leaves into the saucepan and add water. Leave it to stand then rinse out.

Fresh water fish often have a muddy taste. Soak in strong salt and water after it has been well cleaned.

Lemon and/or vinegar added to water helps remove the smell of fish after cooking.

Flour

To test for freshness, warm flour in oven for an hour, then sift onto a plate. If it has no lumps and the flour has a pleasant smell, then the flour is good.

Fowl

An excellent way to cook an old fowl is to place a piece of bacon fat inside the fowl, and then roast or boil it. The flesh will then be quite tender.

Truffles

Makes about 24

60 g butter
2 tablespoons milk
4 tablespoons sugar
1 teaspoon instant coffee
   powder
1 tablespoon cocoa
6 drops vanilla
1½ cups coconut
extra coconut or cocoa for
   coating

Boil butter, milk and sugar. Allow about 10 minutes to cool. Add coffee, cocoa, vanilla and coconut. Roll into small balls and coat with extra coconut or chocolate. Allow to set firm.

White Christmas

1½ cups rice bubbles
1 cup soft icing sugar
1 cup dried milk powder
1 cup mixed fruit
   (including peel and
   chopped cherries)
½ cup coconut
½ cup chopped walnuts or
   other nuts
250 g copha

Sift icing sugar. Mix in other dry ingredients. Gently melt the copha, but do not let it boil. Stir into dry ingredients and mix well. Spread into greased slab tin and smooth out with a spatula. Allow to set firm then cut into small squares.

Fruit

To store ripe stoned fruit, place them in a plastic bag from which as much air has been excluded as possible. Store in the fridge. When fruit needs further ripening leave at room temperature for a few days.

Fruit or ginger cake

One dessertspoon of vinegar, in which $1/2$ a teaspoon of bicarbonate of soda has been dissolved, can be used in place of 2 eggs. Vinegar should be the last ingredient added.

Frypan (electric)

When cooking several different foods in an electric frypan, wrap them in foil first, so they remain separate.

Garlic

After buying a fresh bulb of garlic, peel the cloves, put them into a small jar and fill with oil. If stored in the refrigerator, the garlic will keep for months and the oil can be used later for salad dressing or for frying.

Gelatine

Add gelatine to the boiling water to dissolve quickly, rather than the other way around.

Geraniums

Chop the leaves of scented geraniums finely, or infuse in liquid then discard leaves, and use to flavour sauces, custards, jellies, buns, butters, jams, syrups and vinegars.

Crystallise to decorate cakes (*see* Crystallised flowers on p. 293).

To *add flavour*, place the leaves under baked apples or cakes.

Ginger (ground)

Added to stews, savouries and seasoning for poultry will aid digestion.

Golden syrup or honey

When added to a cake, the cake needs to be baked at a slightly lower temperature as the syrup can make the cake burn more easily.

Sunday lunch

My family has grown again now that John and Karyn have moved back to 'Bethany' with their three boys. One of our lovely customs at Bethany is to have all the family home for Sunday lunch. Since the family has expanded we don't have it every week, but I still have it at least once a month.

The girls and their husbands do the dishes for me after lunch, as I cooked, and the children play outside on the trampoline. We then all sit in the lounge and talk about the children, and things in general. Joh and I still love bringing the family together.

Gravy

To *make gravy*, put 1 tablespoon of plain flour into the pan in which the roast has been cooked. Stir until the starch grains of flour have burst and the flour is a nice golden brown, then add cold water. Water drained from vegetables can also be used. Keep stirring until the gravy thickens.

To *darken gravy*, add 1 teaspoon of vegemite or 1 teaspoon of soya sauce, or put 1 cup of sugar into a saucepan and heat until the sugar becomes quite dark. Cool, then add 1 cup of water. Let stand until mixture is quite thin. Store in the fridge and use mixture when making gravy, to give it a rich brown colour.

To *remove excess fat* from gravy, add a pinch of bicarbonate of soda to gravy.

Grease

To remove grease from soup or gravy, dip in small pieces of clean tissue paper, as they will absorb all the fat.

Green vegetables

Cook vegetables with the lid off to preserve their colour.

Ham

To *cook* a ham, cover with water and bring slowly to the boil. Remove any scum as it rises to the surface. Allow 15 minutes for every 500 g of ham.

To *store* ham on a plate, cover with muslin rinsed in a solution of 2 cups of water and 1 tablespoon of vinegar.

Herbs

To *make a herb oil*, fill a jar with freshly picked herbs and cover with safflower or sunflower oil. Cover with muslin and place in a warm spot for 2 weeks, stirring daily. Strain through the muslin and check the flavour. If it is as strong as you wish, bottle. If you want a stronger flavour, repeat the process with fresh herbs. Use in salad dressings, marinades, for browning meats and softening vegetables.

Savoury herbs are basil, garlic, fennel, marjoram, mint, rosemary, tarragon, thyme.

Sweet herbs are clove pinks, lavender, lemon verbena, rose petals.

To make a *herb vinegar*, Use cider or wine vinegar as a base. Bruise the freshly picked herbs and loosely fill a clean jar. Pour on warm vinegar to fill the jar and seal with an acid proof lid. Leave in a warm spot and shake daily for 2 weeks. Test for flavour; if a stronger taste is required, strain the vinegar and repeat with fresh herbs. Store as it is or strain and rebottle. Add a fresh sprig to the bottle for identification. Use in salad dressings, marinades, gravies and sauces.

You can use basil, bay, chervil, dill leaves, fennel, garlic, lemon balm, marjoram, mint, rosemary, tarragon, thyme for vinegars.

Honey

If used to sweeten a fruit salad, honey will not only give it more flavour, but also help prevent apples and bananas from going brown. When measuring honey or syrup, dip the spoon into boiling water first.

Ice-cream

When making ice-cream, cover trays with greaseproof paper, as this will prevent snow forming. Before returning to freezer, place a piece of foil on top before replacing lid. This prevents a crystallised layer forming.

Jams

Frothiness and scum on bottled jam indicates fermentation. After having removed scum, turn the jam into a clean jar.

To every 500 g of fruit used in making raspberry jam, 500 g of sugar should be allowed.

If homemade jams are *runny*, add some desiccated coconut.

Cover jams and marmalades as quickly as possible before the steam loses its power to exclude the air.

Jelly

To *set quickly*, place mould into a basin of cold salted (a handful of salt should do) water.

Jelly mould: smear mould with egg white and jelly will turn out whole or dip mould quickly into hot water before turning out.

Scissors dipped in cold water to cut jelly squares make even edges.

Lavender

Use the fresh flower to flavour jams and to make lavender vinegar.

Mix small amounts with savoury herbs for fragrant stews.

Do not use lavender for crystallised flowers (*see* p. 293) as they have a bitter taste.

Lemon balm

Finely chop fresh leaves into salads, white sauces for fish, mayonnaise, poultry and pork. Add to fruit salads, jellies, custards, fruit drinks and wine cups. Float in Indian tea. Add to blended vinegars, such as lemon balm with tarragon.

Lemons

To *preserve*, smear them all over with the white or yolk of an egg and place them on a shelf to dry, or, keep them in a jar of water, changing the water daily.

Warm a lemon before squeezing to give you almost twice the juice.

When only a *few drops* of lemon are required, prick end of lemon with a fork and squeeze out required amount. The holes will close up and the lemon will stay fresh.

To freeze *lemon juice* or *passionfruit*, squeeze and put in plastic iceblock containers.

Lemons and oranges

To keep fresh, store in sawdust.

Lemon and orange peel

Soak skins in brandy and leave for several months. Peel is ideal for flavouring cakes and desserts. Dry peel in the oven and pulverise. Store in a jar.

Lettuce

Lettuce can be cooked as a green vegetable.

To *crisp* a flagging lettuce, wash well, and place leaves in a bowl of cold water. Sprinkle with sugar. Leave awhile. Wash and drain.

You can also add lemon juice to the rinse water to crisp a lettuce.

Marjoram and oregano

Infuse the leaves as an aromatic tea. Chop the leaves for salads and butter sauces for fish. Add the leaves to meat dishes in last few minutes of cooking. Blend with chilli and garlic. Add to pizza, tomatoes, egg and cheese dishes. Stuff fresh haddock with marjoram and breadcrumbs. Rub into roasting meat. Give food a faint marjoram flavour by laying stems on barbecue embers.

Marmalade

500 g sugar to each orange
$2^{1}/_{2}$ cups of water to each orange
1 lemon to every 4 oranges

To prevent jam sticking to the pan, rub pan with cooking oil.

Meat

If it appears tough, rub a little vinegar over it before cooking, or wrap in pawpaw leaves for a couple of hours.

To *bake*, put a little water in the baking dish, then add the meat. As the water evaporates, it is replaced by the natural fats of the meat.

Tainted meat can be washed in vinegar and water.

To *fry meat without fat*, heat 1 teaspoon of salt in the pan then add meat.

When *stewing mutton*, add ¹/₂ teaspoon of ground cloves, and ¹/₂ cup of sherry. Cloves take away the mutton flavour and sherry makes it tender.

Meringue

If egg whites are allowed to stand overnight they will whip up more quickly. A pinch of salt in egg whites makes them stiffen quickly.

To prevent a *meringue topping from shrinking* and becoming moist after cooking, sift a dusting of icing sugar over the meringue before placing in the oven.

For *sticky meringues*, the oven should be cool (not too hot) and shouldn't be cooked too rapidly.

Flat meringue means insufficient beating before the sugar was added. Sugar should be added a little bit at a time, beating well each time.

Milking the house cow

In my early days at 'Bethany' Joh told me I had to learn to milk the house cow. I was horrified as I'd always been scared of cows from the days when, as a girl, I went to my uncle's dairy farm at The Gap in Brisbane. But Joh said if he was away and his mother and sister weren't there, the cow had to be milked.

I finally learnt how, but on one occasion I undid the rope that kept the cow in the bails and forgot to take off the leg rope. What a performance! I had to call for help, but we finally calmed her down.

As soon as I had household help, and Meg and John were old enough, I left the milking of the house cow to the help. Nowadays, I buy my milk in a bottle, it's so much easier.

Below I have included a couple of hints on how to preserve milk, which will be handy to people on the land, or those who go camping. There is also an interesting hint for making a milk substitute to put in your coffee.

Milk

If it becomes slightly soured, it can be restored by adding a pinch of bicarbonate of soda. If really sour, don't throw the milk out, use it for cakes. If camping and unable to keep the milk cold, scald to keep it sweet.

To *stop milk from running over* when it comes to a boil, stand a spoon in the saucepan.

To *check if milk has been adulterated* with water, put a bright steel knitting needle into the milk. If on withdrawal the milk drops off slowly, it is fresh. If it runs off quickly it has had water added.

When *out of milk* for your coffee, whisk an egg and put a small amount in each cup.

A pinch of salt will take away the unpleasant taste from *burnt milk*.

Sour milk may be used to make scones.

To make *sour milk or cream*, add 1 tablespoon of white vinegar to each 1¼ cups of fresh milk or cream. Allow to stand at room temperature for 30 minutes.

Mince

To make mince go further, add breadcrumbs or cooked rice.

Mint

When chopping mint, sprinkle the board with sugar. It helps to keep the leaves green and makes chopping easier.

Mint vinegar can be made by loosely filling a pickle bottle with mint leaves, and adding white vinegar to cover them. Cork firmly, leave for 3 weeks, then strain into another bottle.

Mints: infuse the leaf either individually, or blend mints (such as spearmint and peppermint) for a refreshing tea. Use for mint sauce, vinegar, syrups and with chocolate in rich desserts. Crystallise spearmint and applemint (*see* p. 293) as a sweet for decoration. Add fresh leaves to new potatoes, peas, fruit salads, drinks and punches.

Mint sauce
2 tablespoons of sugar
1 tablespoon of boiling water
2 tablespoons of chopped mint
2 tablespoons of vinegar

Boil sugar and water for 1 minute. Add mint and vinegar. Cool, then pour into bottle or jar.

Mixed fruit

If mixed fruit becomes dry, moisten it by steaming over hot water for 10 minutes.

Mushrooms

Fresh mushrooms don't need peeling, just wipe with a cloth.

To *test mushrooms*, sprinkle a little salt over the spongy part and leave for a few minutes. If flesh turns yellow the fungus is poisonous. If it turns black it is wholesome.

Another test is to use a silver spoon while cooking the mushrooms. The silver will be blackened if any injurious property is present.

Mussels

To test mussels, add and boil a small onion to the liquid or juice in which they have been cooked. If there is any poison present the onion will go black. If they are good, the onion will retain its colour.

Nasturtium

Both the leaves and flower buds have a cress-like flavour and add a bite to salads and sandwiches.

Nutmeg

Nutmeg should be firm. Prick with a pin to test. If it's good, the oil will instantly spread out and around the hole.

Odours

By placing a saucer of vinegar near your stove, you will reduce odours of certain vegetables during cooking. You can also add a wedge of lemon

with skin in the saucepan when cooking onions or
cabbage to prevent odours.

Oil

When oiling a pan, use a brush to wipe the pan.

Onions

Peeling under water will prevent the hands being
stained and the eyes from watering.

Oven

If an oven is overheated, place a pan of cold water on the shelf to cool
quickly.

Oysters

Keep oysters in a bucket covered with salt and water for 10 hours, then
drain. Allow to stand for 10 hours without water, then repeat the process
until required for use.

Parsley

Add raw parsley leaves to salads. Finely chop and sprinkle over
sandwiches, egg dishes, vegetable soups, fish, boiled potatoes and potato
salad. Add to mayonnaise and sauces. When cooked, parsley enhances
other flavours, but only add it towards the end of the cooking time. Use
in a bouquet garni and for decoration.

To *dry parsley*, wash well and strip leaves from the stalk. Dry in a
moderate oven until crisp. Rub with hands into a powder and sieve.
Store in an airtight container.

Wash parsley in hot water, as it *improves the flavour* and can be chopped
more easily.

Pastry

Handle pastry as little as possible to keep cool.

Uncooked pastry will keep fresh for several days if wrapped in
greaseproof paper and kept in a cool place.

For *successful pastry making*, everything must be as cold as possible.

Pastry shells cooked without a filling should be pricked to prevent their rising.

For a *lovely finish to pastry*, sprinkle pastry board with custard powder instead of flour.

Pastry will be much easier to handle if rolled between two pieces of clingwrap. The plastic film won't stick and the problem of lifting rolled pastry into a tart plate is solved.

A *pastry shell* which is to be filled with a wet mixture should be brushed with melted butter to prevent sogginess.

Pastry glaze for meat pies and sausage rolls: brush over with a well-beaten egg before baking. Fruit tarts, puffs, etc. should be brushed over with cold water and sprinkled liberally with castor sugar before baking.

Heat pie tins or containers before lining with uncooked pastry so that the pastry will brown on the bottom and be more firm.

When *cooking pies* put pie container in a baking dish so overflow will be caught in the baking dish.

Patty cakes

Add $1/4$ teaspoon of baking powder dissolved in 1 dessertspoon of boiling water to the cake mixture to make patty cakes rise in the middle.

Pavlova

Eggs must be at room temperature, and a few days old.

See Merinque on p. 302 for how to beat egg whites.

Pepper pot

To prevent clogging, place a dried pea in the pot.

Pies

When reheating savoury pies, glaze the top of the pie with melted butter, or for a fruit pie, sugar and water. They will taste as if they are freshly baked.

Plastic film wrap

To prevent plastic film wrap sticking together, keep stored in refrigerator as this makes it easier to handle.

Playdough

Now that Karyn and John and their three little boys are back at 'Bethany', the boys go to the local playgroup once a week. Playdough is a very important part of their morning's activities, and Karyn, who is an early childhood teacher by profession, is used to making the playdough for the playgroup. She told me that you can use food colouring to give the playdough different colours.

1 cup of salt
2 cups of plain flour
2 cups of water
2 teaspoons of oil
4 teaspoons of cream of tartar

Cook all ingredients over a low heat, stirring until the dough forms a ball in the middle of the saucepan. Store in the fridge.

Pork

Rub with vinegar before baking so that the crackling will be nice and crisp. You can also rub the pork with flour and salt to achieve the same result.

Potatoes

Store potatoes in a cool dark place so that they don't go green. If they do, don't use them.

Baked potatoes: to have in a hurry, boil in salted water for about 10 minutes, drain, then place in the oven.

Fluffy potatoes: mash with $1/2$ teaspoon of cornflour and a little milk and butter.

Mashed: when mashing add $^1/_4$ teaspoon of baking powder to the potatoes. This makes them light and fluffy.

Potato cakes: one tablespoon of vinegar in the frying oil will prevent the cakes from becoming too greasy when cooked.

Poultry

A spoonful of vinegar in the water into which meat or fowls are boiled makes them tender. You can also mix together $^1/_2$ teaspoon of bicarbonate of soda and 1 teaspoon of vinegar and rub over tough poultry.

To *keep poultry fresh* put a peeled onion inside the bird. It will help keep the bird fresh for a day or two before cooking.

Preserving fruit or vegetables

Fruit or vegetables should not be packed into bottles with syrup or water and left overnight before sterilisation, as they will ferment. They should be sterilised immediately after being packed into bottles.

Pulses

Soak *lentils* for 2 to 3 hours then cook slowly for $^3/_4$ to 1 hour.

Soak *beans* for 12 hours then cook for 1 to $1^1/_2$ hours.

Pyrethrum

Use the raw young leaves in salads or stir fries. They taste similar to cress.

Raisins

A little butter rubbed on both sides of a knife will prevent the raisins from sticking when cutting them into small pieces. If using a blender, a few drops of lemon juice should be wiped over the blade.

Rice

Cook extra rice to be used during the week for soups, stuffed vegetables, salads and casseroles.

To *whiten and separate rice grains* during cooking, a squeeze of lemon juice over the rice works wonders.

If *added to boiling water*, rice need not be stirred while cooking. If rice is stirred it will have to be stirred continuously until cooked.

See spaghetti hint on p. 311 for cooking instructions.

Rissoles

To make light rissoles, add rolled oats to mince and mix together with $1/2$ cup of self-raising flour mixed with a little water. Use an ice-cream scoop rinsed in cold water to shape the rissole.

Rosemary

Crystallise for a garnish. Mash with sugar, mix with cream, and add to a fruit puree. Add the leaves to meat dishes, especially lamb and pork. Use rosemary to flavour baked potatoes and to make a herb butter for vegetables.

To *preserve*, dry sprigs and branches and strip off leaves before storing.

To *release the aroma*, crush leaves just before use. Use the stems (with leaves removed) for barbecue skewers.

Sage

Use flowers in salads. Use leaves for a light tea. Mix the leaves with onion for poultry stuffing. Cook with rich, fatty meats; pork, duck or sausage. Blend into cheeses. Make sage vinegar and sage butter. Dry leaves slowly to preserve best flavour and avoid mustiness.

Salt

To prevent salt caking in salt shakers, add some ground rice or store in the refrigerator.

If a *soup or gravy is too salty*, add 1 teaspoon of brown sugar and the briny taste will disappear. If a soup or stew is too salty you can reduce it by dicing and adding a potato.

Sandwiches

To *keep fresh*, cover sandwiches with a damp, clean cloth.

Sauce

If a vegetable sauce is a little too sweet, add some lemon juice or pepper.

Scones

A friend of mine who is a good cook decided to make some pumpkin scones from my recipe. The next time I talked to her she said it had been a failure. I couldn't believe it, and when I chided her she said she felt it was because she had used hot pumpkin.

Now when I write out my recipe, I always stipulate mashed (cold) pumpkin.

Heavy or dense scones means that the oven is too cool, or there is too much liquid.

Seasoning

Season food with garlic or herbs to reduce your intake of salt.

Self-raising flour

2 kg of plain flour

2 tablespoons of bicarbonate of soda

1/4 cup of cream of tartar

Sift well.

Shallots

To store shallots, hang them up in strings but don't keep them in the pantry.

Sorrel

Add to salads (reducing vinegar or lemon in dressing). Cook as with spinach, changing the cooking water to reduce acidity. Sorrel can be used to season vegetable soups, omelettes, lamb and beef dishes, and also in sauces for fish, poultry and pork.

Soup

Make a double quantity of soup and freeze half.

To *remove fat* from soup, if using bones and meat as a base. Allow the soup to go cold. The fat will rise to the top and can be scooped out.

When cooking *split pea soup* add a slice of bread to stop peas from sinking to the bottom of the saucepan.

Soup cubes are ideal for flavouring gravies, soups, stews and casseroles. Crumble a couple of cubes into the ingredients for extra flavour.

Soya bean flour

Use soya bean flour for bread, puddings and cakes. It is also useful for thickening sauces and gravies.

Spaghetti

A few teaspoons of cooking oil or a teaspoon of butter added to the water in rice, noodles or spaghetti will prevent the water from boiling over and strands from sticking together.

Spices

Buy spices in small quantities as they lose their freshness and aroma if kept for too long.

Spicy food

Often recipes using chilli or curry powder can be cooled by adding a handful of sultanas and leaving it to simmer a little longer.

Sponge

To make it light, put a tablespoon of warm water in the cake mixture after adding the eggs.

Sponges and pavlovas need light and fluffy eggs. Leave the eggs in a basin of cold water for 1 hour before beating.

Stewing apples

Boiling the sugar and water first when stewing apples helps prevent the apples from going mushy.

Stoned fruits

Don't stone fruits until use as they oxidise and develop an unpleasant colour and taste.

Sugar

When storing sugar, put a slice of bread in the container to stop it becoming hard.

To *test sugar*, burn a little in an iron ladle. Pure sugar will burn away whereas impure sugar will leave a residue.

Tansy

Stew the leaves with rhubarb, or rub on meat for a flavour similar to rosemary.

Tarragon

Use to flavour vinegar and vinegar blends, and for tartare and hollandaise sauces. Add shredded leaf to avocado fillings, mayonnaise for fish dishes, salad dressings, light soups, tomatoes, omelettes and scrambled eggs. Make a herb butter for vegetables, steaks, chops and grilled fish. Rub tarragon onto roast chicken or mix with chicken stuffing.

Tarts

To prevent the jam from becoming sticky and dry, sprinkle with cold water before baking.

Tea

To test the quality of tea, throw a pinch into the fire. The bluer the flame the better the tea.

Thyme

Add to stocks, marinades, stuffing, sauces and soups. It aids digestion of fatty foods and suits food cooked in wine, particularly poultry, shellfish and game. Add to chicken, fruit salads and jams. It is also used to flavour beef.

Tinned food

To test a tin for freshness tap the bottom of the tin. If it makes a loud noise the tin is not airtight so the contents will be unsafe to eat.

Tomatoes

Freeze when in plentiful supply by washing and sealing them in plastic bags.

To make *sun dried tomatoes*, slice tomatoes thinly, place on aluminium foil and place in sun to dry. When dry, they should be rubbery. Pack them into jars and cover with olive oil to which you can add garlic or basil. Keep jars in a cool, dark place.

Miniature tomatoes can be stored whole in oil but only if they are completely perfect.

To *peel tomatoes easily*, drop into boiling water first.

To prevent *tomato sandwiches* from going soggy, dip slices of tomato in milk, then drain on kitchen paper.

Vegetables

If vegetables such as lettuce or parsley are limp, plunge in boiling water, then rinse in cold water, and serve.

Use vegetable water for making gravy or soup.

Vinegar

Add vinegar to meat dishes, such as stews, to improve the flavour.

Cleaning

How many of us like cleaning? It's so repetitive. Over the years I have been fortunate to have someone to help me in the home, and it was wonderful to come home from the Senate each weekend and know that the house was clean and my ironing done.

However, now that I have retired I will have more time to do my own home cleaning, and I am glad to use all of the following helpful hints.

My own experience as a wife and mum, and as manager of the household finances, has helped me to appreciate the difficulties faced by all families. In this section on cleaning, I have included time-tested, effective and inexpensive ways to make things look as good as new.

We all know that commercial cleaners are available in supermarkets and most stores. However, many of the suggestions in *Classic Country Wisdom* use common ingredients normally kept in your cupboards at home.

All-purpose cleaner

This cleaner is easy to make and very effective. I hope you're satisfied with the results.

3 tablespoons of cloudy ammonia
6 tablespoons of bicarbonate of soda
3 tablespoons of vinegar

Mix ingredients together. This cleaner can be used on most surfaces, then wiped off with clean water.

Bathroom

Mix equal parts of salt, borax and kerosene into a paste, cover the *bath*, then rub with a soapy cloth, followed by a dry cloth. Equal parts of brown vinegar and kerosene can also be used.

Rub *porcelain sinks* with kerosene and rinse with warm soapy water.

For a *sweet-smelling* bathroom, pour a few drops of an essential flower oil onto the hot tap spout and turn it on for a few moments to release the fragrance. The floral aroma will fill the room for some time.

Dab turpentine or kerosene onto a cloth, wipe *surfaces* thoroughly, then rinse well. Salt can also be used as a cleaning agent.

To clean out *pipes* beneath the sink, put a small handful of bicarbonate of soda in the sink, then pour over half a cup of vinegar. Leave for half an hour, then rinse with boiling water.

To clean the *toilet bowl*, add 1 cup of vinegar and leave to soak. Lemon juice can also be used as a cleaner. (Neither will damage septic systems.)

Blinds

Bead blinds may be soaked in hot water and borax, then rinsed in warm water and dried. The strings must be stretched while drying or they will dry unevenly.

Linen blinds may be cleaned by wiping them with a piece of bread, or, if dark, sponged with warm vinegar and water.

Venetian blinds may be cleaned with warm soapy water and dried. The slats should be wiped with linseed oil.

Books

Use the white of an egg to repair torn pages in a book. Egg white can also be used to glue back on small pieces of wood chipped off furniture.

Boots

To *clean* and *revive* boots, brush leather with warm soap, and allow to nearly dry. Wipe off soap with damp cloth. Allow to dry thoroughly, then polish.

A small amount of methylated spirits wiped over *brown boots* removes stains and gives them a good polish. Only use methylated spirits occasionally, otherwise it will dry out the leather.

For *grease stains*, make a paste of fuller's earth with a little water, then rub onto stains. Leave to dry, then wipe off.

Salt water stains can be removed by mixing a lump of washing soda into very hot milk, then rubbing the mixture over the stains. Dry the boots then polish with boot polish.

To remove *stains from brown boots*, cut a piece of lemon and rub it into the boots, then polish with brown polish. A banana skin also acts as a good polish for brown boots.

To prevent *scratches*, spread an egg white over the leather and allow to dry. Polish with a soft cloth.

To *waterproof* boots and shoes, melt together 2 parts of beeswax and 1 part of mutton fat, and apply to the leather at night. Wipe the boots with a flannel the next morning. The boots will not polish so well at first, but after the polish has been used several times they will shine brilliantly. A coat of varnish will render the soles waterproof and will prolong their life.

To *blacken brown boots*, mix equal parts of black ink and blacking (used to black the stove). Rub over the boots.

To *soften* boots and shoes after they have been put away, wash them well in warm water and then rub in castor oil. Almost any oil will do, but castor oil gives the most supple result.

Bottle

Drop a tablespoon of rice into the bottle, pour in cold water and shake briskly.

Brass

Use a vinegar and salt or a vinegar and bicarbonate of soda paste, to be rubbed over the brass item with half a lemon or a mixture of salt and wood ash. Rinse and dry. A coating of vaseline or olive oil will help prevent tarnishing.

To clean verdigris on *brass taps*, clean with an old toothbrush dipped in ammonia. Toothbrushes are useful for cleaning around taps and hard-to-get-at places.

Bread bin

Sprinkle a teaspoon of bicarbonate of soda into the breadbin and cover with greaseproof paper. This will remove any stale odour.

Carafe

To remove any residue in a carafe, mix in equal quantities cooking salt, washing soda and vinegar. Add some tea leaves and eggshells. Pour the mixture into the carafe and shake well, then rinse.

Carpet

Sprinkle salt or bicarbonate of soda over *mud marks* and leave to dry, then vacuum.

Stains can often be removed by dabbing with vinegar mixed into soapy water.

To *clean and brighten*, salt can be sprinkled onto a carpet, brushed, and then vacuumed. Rubbing a carpet with strong ammonia water will also give it new life and help to remove stains.

To *deodorise*, sprinkle with bicarbonate of soda then vacuum.

To *destroy moths*, place a damp cloth over the area and press a hot iron over the area until the cloth is dry. The moths and eggs should then be destroyed.

To *remove ink*, wash the stain immediately with skim milk. Plenty of milk must be used and rubbed into the carpet vigorously with a piece of clean flannel, pouring the milk directly onto the stain. You can also use a cut lemon, which will give the same effect. Allow to dry and then vacuum.

To *remove soot*, sprinkle salt over soot and leave for a short time, then vacuum.

To *repair burn holes*, squeeze household adhesive into the hole. Pluck from carpet pieces of pile in matching colour, press into the glued burn hole, let adhesive dry, then brush pile gently.

Ceilings

When blackened with smoke, ceilings can be cleaned with warm water and washing soda.

Chopping boards

Chopping boards on which *onions* have been cut can be rubbed with vinegar or lemon before scrubbing.

To remove odours from cutting boards, rub with salt and rinse in cold water.

Chrome

Rub chrome with vinegar, then wipe off with a damp cloth. Rub clean with a soft dry cloth.

Concrete

To remove oil stains, pour a little kerosene over the oil then cover with sawdust. Leave for a few minutes and sweep clean. Hose area immediately.

Copper

Rub *copper* with vinegar then polish with a dry cloth, or rub copper with Worcestershire sauce, then buff. If articles are not in regular use, a film of vaseline helps preserve copper and brass.

Fill a *copper kettle* with hot water and rub with sour milk to clean the outside.

Pan cleaner

2 tablespoons of strong (cider) vinegar
1 tablespoon of salt

Rub the pan with this mixture, then rinse and dry thoroughly.

Corks

A cork dipped in paraffin is effective in removing rust.

Cups (china, tea and coffee)

A small squeeze of toothpaste onto a piece of damp cottonwool or sponge will remove tea stains from delicate china, as well as marks from laminex. It will also help remove nicotine stains from fingers. Stains can also be removed by rubbing the inside of the cup with plain salt, or salt and lemon juice, or salt and vinegar.

Decanters

To wash out, crush eggshells and place them in the decanter with warm soapy water. Swirl around briskly, then rinse and dry. You can also add raw chopped potato and vinegar, shake well, then rinse in cold water.

Diamonds

Wash in hot soapy water with a few drops of cloudy ammonia. Scrub gently, rinse, then dip into alcohol for a good shine.

Dishwasher

I still don't have a dishwashing machine in my

kitchen. In any case I don't know where I would fit it, although Joh is always promising to enlarge the kitchen. However, I have included a hint to clean a dishwashing machine as my daughters have them and most young marrieds seem to start off with one. I don't think it hurts the young ones to do the dishes after tea, as many a lively discussion has been had while leaning over the kitchen sink.

To *rejuvenate your dishwasher*, simply pour in half a bottle of vinegar and run full cycle.

Disinfectant

Teatree oil added to cleaners or in the rinsing water is a natural disinfectant.

Disinfectants can also be made with the leaves of eucalyptus, lavender, sage and thyme.

To *clean sinks and bathrooms*, use rosemary to make a disinfectant. Boil leaves and stems for 15 minutes in 2 cups of water. Strain and then use liquid. Add washing up liquid to *get rid of grease on surfaces*. It can be stored in the fridge for a week.

Duster

To make an oiled duster, soak an old, soft clean cloth in kerosene, wring it out and allow to dry. This will gather up the dust and give a polish to mirrors and glass.

Ebony

To restore and clean ebony, rub with olive oil.

Enamel

Make a *paste of salt and vinegar* and rub over enamel. Rinse well.

An *enamel bath* can be cleaned by washing with turpentine or salt, then rinsing.

Fenders and stoves

Old *pieces of velveteen* give a brighter polish than using a brush or leather.

Brushes used to black lead stoves can be washed in warm water to which bicarbonate of soda has been added.

Fire bars

To clean and prevent fire bars from turning red, rub with a raw onion, then apply the black lead.

Floors

Timber floors which have been sealed can be cleaned with cold tea on a mop.

A little vinegar in the bucket of water with the detergent helps to remove any grease from *kitchen floors*.

Polish

1 rounded tablespoon of beeswax

1 tablespoon of pure soap

1 cup of turpentine

1 cup of boiling water

Shred beeswax and soap. Add turpentine and leave for 24 hours. Pour water over and mix well.

Economical floor polish is made by melting down any odd candle ends which are too small for burning. When the wax is quite liquid, remove any bits of wick, and add turpentine in equal proportion to the melted candle grease. Warm slightly before using.

Formica

Formica is best wiped over with a cloth wrung out in hot water with a little detergent added. Wipe again with a cloth to which a little methylated spirits has been added.

Fountain pen

To clean pull apart and soak all parts in vinegar for 30 minutes. Rinse clean.

Fridge or freezer

To keep fridges and freezers *smelling fresh*, sprinkle a few drops of lemon or vanilla essence onto a damp cloth and wipe the interior walls and shelves.

To *dispel odours*, place a small container of bicarbonate of soda inside the fridge.

Frypan (electric)

Soak electric frypans with ammonia and water.

If the *bottom has become stained*, remove the legs and place a towel soaked in ammonia over the pan. Wrap the pan in a plastic bag, with the handle protruding. Leave overnight and then scour.

To *restore its shine*, boil half a lemon or apple peel in the pan, then rub with crumpled foil.

Furniture

Bamboo furniture can be cleaned with a soft brush dipped in salted water. Dry with a soft cloth, then rub over with a little linseed oil.

To *remove stains*, rub with equal parts of methylated spirits and olive oil. The inside of banana skins will clean old *(unvarnished) wood*. Polish with a soft cloth. It will also remove scratches.

Scratches can be removed by mixing equal parts of linseed oil and turpentine. Dip a soft cloth into the mixture and rub into surface. Polish with a soft cloth.

To *disguise scratches on wood*, halve a walnut and rub over the scratch. The oil will help disguise the mark.

To *remove dents*, wet the damaged part with warm water, double a piece of brown paper several times, soak it in warm water, and lay it on the dent. Apply a warm (**not** hot) iron until the moisture has evaporated. If the dent is not raised to the surface, repeat the process.

Upholstered furniture: to remove stains, warm a bowl of bran in the oven, and rub well into the soiled parts. Vacuum off the bran then sponge area and leave to dry.

An *egg white* can be used to glue on small pieces of wood that have been chipped off furniture.

To remove *texta pen* from a *vinyl lounge*, rub with methylated spirits or bicarbonate of soda on a damp cloth. Make sure you test a small area on the back of the lounge first as it may fade the colour.

To remove *white heat marks* on furniture, rub with a mixture of 1 dessertspoon of olive oil and 1 small teaspoon cooking salt, or rub with a paste of water and cigarette ash.

To remove *white water marks from furniture*, apply mayonnaise and rub it in. Let stand for an hour, then wipe clean with a soft cloth.

To preserve *garden furniture*, rub occasionally with linseed oil to prevent timber cracking.

Basic furniture polish
1 cup of olive oil
$^1/_2$ cup of strained lemon juice

Pour into a jar and shake well. Apply to furniture with a damp cloth.

Old-fashioned furniture polish
It's safe to use on any furniture, especially antique furniture. Shred the beeswax and add as much turpentine as necessary to dissolve the wax to a moderately thick solution. You can also use paraffin and turpentine, mixed in equal quantities, or linseed oil, turpentine and methylated spirits mixed in equal quantities. To any of these can be added a few drops of essential oil for a lovely fragrance.

Marjoram furniture polish
1 cup of beeswax
$2^1/_2$ cups of turpentine
$1^1/_2$ cups strong infusion of marjoram
(or lavender)
1 tablespoon of olive oil based soap, grated
A few drops of oil of marjoram or lavender

Grate the beeswax into the turpentine and leave to dissolve for two days. Bring the mixture to boiling point and stir in the soap until melted. Allow this mixture to cool, then slowly add the beeswax mixture, stirring until it resembles thick cream. Stir in a few drops of essential oil (rosemary or lavender flowers can be used instead of marjoram) for fragrance.

You can also add *lemon balm juice* to furniture polish for a lovely lemon fragrance, or you can mix equal parts of methylated spirits, brown vinegar, linseed oil and turpentine. Add a few drops of essential oil of your choice for a nice fragrance.

Furniture reviver

1 cup of turpentine

1 cup of linseed oil

1 cup of brown vinegar

Pour into a bottle and shake well before each use.

Gas fire

To clean, sprinkle with salt when cold. When the gas is lit it will burn the salt away and leave the gas fire clean.

Glass

Use hot vinegar to remove paint spots. A few drops of lemon juice in the rinsing water will add a lustre to glassware.

Wash *cut glass* in warm soapy water, using a small brush or toothbrush to get into any difficult areas. Rinse in cold water with a little vinegar, dry with a linen cloth.

Glass-topped tables can be wiped with white vinegar or methylated spirits. Dry with a newspaper.

Tea leaves can be used as a scourer for *jars*. Pour teapot dregs in and shake well, as the warm tea will soften any remains.

Labels can be removed by rubbing with eucalyptus oil then washing it off with hot soapy water. Eucalyptus oil will also remove glue.

To clean *glass or crystal*, add a few drops of ammonia to the rinsing water to produce a shine.

Grouting

Scrub with an old toothbrush and bicarbonate of soda.

Insect repellent

To repel *moths*, put dried lavender flowers in sachets and bundles to scent drawers and to protect linen from moths.

Put cinnamon bark pieces and crumbled mint into muslin bags to help keep *moths and silverfish* away from cupboards and drawers.

To repel *cockroaches* put slices of fresh cucumber onto shelves, or mix borax and sugar and put onto shelves.

Iron

You can clean the *underneath* of an iron by wiping it with a cloth soaked in cold tea. This will remove stains immediately.

Iron kitchen utensils that have developed rust inside can be treated by putting potato peelings inside them, and adding water and a lump of bicarbonate of soda, then boil.

Ivory

Lemon dipped in salt removes watermarks from ivory. You can then rub with a good furniture polish (*see* p. 323).

Jewellery

Ammonia can be used to give jewellery a sparkle.

Gold jewellery can be soaked in a little cloudy ammonia for 10 minutes. Scrub gently with a soft toothbrush, then rinse.

For *silver jewellery* bring to the boil 1 dessertspoon of bicarbonate of soda and some aluminium foil in a saucepan of water. Dip jewellery into mixture and rinse.

Knives

To whiten *bone handles*, dip half a lemon in salt and rub on the handles, then wipe clean. You can also try toothpaste rubbed on and wiped off. Don't immerse handles in water or in the dishwasher.

To secure *knife handles*, make a mixture of equal quantities of resin and brick dust. Fill the hole in the knife handle, warm the tang of the knife and press into the hole in the handle.

Stick *rusty knives* into soil for 60 minutes, then rub well with a damp cloth dipped in ashes. Rinse well.

Lacquer

Wipe lacquered surfaces with sour milk or lemon juice and dry with a soft cloth.

Leather

To remove stains, use a *vinegar and warm water solution*, then rub with olive oil.

Rub *bags* well with the inside of a banana skin, and polish with a soft cloth.

Patent leather can be cleaned with butter on a cloth, then polish with a dry cloth.

A *leather lounge* is revived by polishing it with linseed oil and vinegar, in portions of two to one.

Upholstery may be revived if washed over with a cloth wrung out in warm water, to which a little vinegar has been added. To restore the polish, 2 egg whites can be beaten up with a few drops of turpentine. Rub into the leather with a soft cloth, then polish.

Reviver

³/₄ cup of vinegar

1¹/₂ cups of boiled linseed oil

Mix and shake both in a bottle until they are the consistency of cream. Rub a little into the leather and polish with a soft cloth.

Lino

Wash lino with *warm soapy water* to which vinegar can be added, but do not add any strong cleansing powder of an alkaline nature as it acts on the oil. The surface can be renewed by rubbing in linseed oil or wax polish.

To *remove built-up polish and/or paint spots* from lino use steel wool moistened with kerosene. This will also remove any paint spots.

When *fitting lino* on the floor before gluing or tacking in place, leave for several days. This allows the lino to stretch and prevents bulges later on.

For many years I had a plain brown lino on the kitchen floor. It looked very nice when it was cleaned but as soon as it was walked on the foot marks and dust showed up immediately. When choosing lino for the kitchen, or indeed any other busy part of the house, keep away from the dark colours. It's best to pick a lighter coloured lino, preferably one with a pattern or a speckled effect so that it doesn't show the marks and doesn't have to be washed every two days.

Mahogany

Mahogany is often subject to cloudiness known as bloom. Gently rub with hot water and vinegar and then with 2 cups of warm water, to which 1 dessertspoon of linseed oil and 1 dessertspoon of mineral turpentine has been added. Polish with a soft cloth.

Marble

You can rub *olive oil* onto the marble and rub down thoroughly with a soft rag or a solution of ¼ cup bicarbonate of soda in 500 mL of water. Scrub the marble well.

Another cleaning method is to *crush cuttlefish and add to beeswax*. Rub the mixture over marble, then polish, or you can use a little borax added to hot water.

Cleaner

1 part of pumice stone, powdered
1 part of whiting
2 parts of washing soda, powdered

Mix to a paste with hot water. Cover marble and let dry, then wash off. This is a very effective cleaner.

Marcasite

Rub firmly with soft tissue paper to clean.

Millet broom

To preserve, soak the broom in warm water in which plenty of salt has been dissolved. Wrap a stocking around the bristles to stop them spreading, then dry thoroughly.

Mirror

Rub mirrors with a pad of soft tissue paper moistened with methylated spirits.

Mop

Soak a mop for half an hour in hot water with 2 tablespoons of washing soda, to remove any grease and oil. Rinse well.

Oak

Polish

1 teaspoon of beeswax

1 teaspoon of brown sugar

$2^1/_4$ cups of warm beer

Dissolve beeswax and sugar in beer. Rub mixture on oak while still warm, then allow to dry. Polish with a soft cloth.

Onyx

To remove marks, powder a cuttlefish and mix to a paste with methylated spirits. Rub over the area, and wipe and polish with beeswax.

Oven

Heat the oven until warm, turn it off and place a small container of *cloudy ammonia* on the middle shelf, and a bowl of water on the lower shelf. Leave overnight and wipe down with warm soapy water. Do *not* inhale the cloudy ammonia.

You can also make a paste of *bicarbonate of soda and water* and apply to the inside of the warm oven. Leave to dry and clean off with hot water. The oven exterior and around the hot plates can also be wiped with bicarbonate of soda.

Paint brushes

Hot vinegar will soften *paint brushes*, as will a mixture of half methylated spirits and half turpentine. Clean brushes in turpentine after use. If storing, rub the bristles with linseed oil after cleaning thoroughly.

Paste

To keep paste moist, wet a rag and leave it in the covered paste bottle.

Paintings

Clean *oil paintings* by rubbing over the surface with half a raw potato. Slice off soiled surface of potato and repeat.

Two coatings of clear shellac will *preserve pictures* and they can be framed without glass.

To keep flies off *picture frames*, boil three or four onions and strain. With a soft brush paint the liquid onto the frames. It won't damage the frames at all.

Rub *gilt picture frames* with a cloth wet with warm turpentine (warm by placing the turps bottle in a container of warm water). Allow the frame to dry for a few days. You can also wipe frames with vinegar and water. Dry and polish well.

Pearls

Shake in a bag of uncooked rice to clean.

Pewter

When cleaning with *whiting*, the pewter should first be moistened with linseed oil and turpentine.

You can also *polish* pewter with cabbage leaves, then shine with a soft cloth.

Piano

Keep the keys clean from dirt and perspiration by rubbing them with a chamois wrung almost dry. Dry immediately with a soft cloth. Don't let any moisture get between the keys.

To *whiten keys*, brush them carefully with lemon juice or methylated spirits.

Porcelain

Cleaner

4 dessertspoons of flour

4 dessertspoons of vinegar

8 dessertspoons of peroxide

Mix. Rub this mixture into the stains, leave for a few hours, then rinse.

Paint spots on tile or porcelain can be removed by soaking a piece of cotton wool in nail polish remover and rubbing the spot.

Putty

Easily removed from windows if softened with turpentine then scraped off. Wash with warm water and borax afterward.

To soften *dry putty*, add linseed oil.

Rush chair

This hint is for renovating rush-seated chairs which have become dirty with age or use, but are otherwise in good condition. The framework and seating should be scrubbed with warm soapy water to which a little washing soda has been added. Rinse thoroughly and allow to dry slowly. The woodwork should be rubbed with an oily (Scandinavian or linseed oil) rag.

Satin shoes

To clean satin shoes, rub with petrol on a cloth.

Saucepan

Stains on aluminium and enamelled saucepans can be removed by dipping cork in damp salt and rubbing the stain to remove.

Ashes from the fire can be sieved and made into a paste with water and used for *cleaning the outside* of saucepans.

Never clean with soda water or put soda in them as it darkens aluminium.

To *prevent staining when boiling eggs*, place a piece of lemon rind or a pinch of cream of tartar or vinegar into the aluminium saucepan.

A pan used to *cook scrambled eggs* is easily cleaned with common salt on a scourer or damp cloth.

If your saucepan's *badly burned* it can be cleaned by pouring over a little olive oil and heating gently. Pour off the oil and clean in the usual way.

Make a paste of *bicarbonate of soda with water.* Coat the dish, then wash.

Fill the saucepan with *salt and water* and leave to stand for 24 hours. Bring the water slowly to the boil. The burned particles should come off without any difficulty.

Coat the inside with full strength washing detergent and leave to soak before washing.

To *seal cast iron pans*, wipe with olive oil and place into a warm oven for 30 minutes. Repeat if necessary when you need to clean the pan. Pan should only be wiped.

Silicon pans can be sealed by wiping pan with olive oil and placing in a warm oven for 30 minutes. Repeat if you need to clean the pan. Pan should only ever be wiped.

Shower

Soak the shower head in vinegar overnight to remove any corrosion.

Rub *shower recess* down with a damp cloth and bicarbonate of soda.

Silicone

Never use a silicone-based polish on antique furniture.

Silver

A paste of whiting and methylated spirits will remove the *worst tarnish.*

To remove *tarnish*, crumple some aluminium foil and place in a bucket with 1 tablespoon of washing soda and 2 litres of boiling water. Add the silver and leave until the tarnish has disappeared. Rinse and dry.

You can clean silver, copper and brass by rubbing them with a lemon cut in half and dipped into cooking salt. Wash items in warm soapy water and dry.

Use cooking salt to remove *egg stains* from silver spoons. Make sure you rinse thoroughly as salt erodes silver.

To help *prevent silverware from tarnishing*, wrap it in foil, black tissue or material, as sunlight causes tarnishing.

Silver used for a fish meal should be washed in cold water and soap before being washed in hot water.

Sink

Rub with vinegar. Vinegar will also remove lime deposits around the water taps.

Shoes (black suede only)

Mix equal quantities of black ink and olive oil, then rub into the suede with a stiff brush.

Slate

Wash with hot water and washing soda.

Smells

Put a little soda in a jar and sprinkle with ammonia and a few drops of lavender oil. Add 3 tablespoons of boiling water and leave uncovered. Dried lavender stems can be used as incense or scented firelighters.

An open dish of vinegar placed near the stove will remove *cooking odours*.

To remove *tobacco smoke*, add 2 tablespoons of cloudy ammonia to 2 cups of boiling water and leave overnight. Mint leaf oil will also help overpower tobacco smells; or burning sage on embers to deodorise a room.

Sorrel

Use juice of leaves to bleach rust, mould and ink stains from linen, wicker and silver.

Sponges (foam rubber)

To give your sponges a new life, add 1 tablespoon of ammonia to 2 cups of boiling water. Add the sponge and let it soak for about one hour. Squeeze sponge as dry as possible and change the water. Add 1 teaspoon of ammonia to the fresh hot water, squeeze the sponge in this several times, then rinse in plenty of cold water.

Stainless steel

Wipe with lemon juice or cream of tartar in very hot water and then wash.

Straw hats

If stained, rub a little fuller's earth into the hat then brush out. To stiffen the straw and give it a gloss, wipe the brim with one beaten egg white.

Taps (brass)

See Brass, p. 318.

Tar on cars

Dripping will dissolve the tar and prevent scratching.

Thermos flask

Smells can be removed by adding 1 teaspoon of bicarbonate of soda to hot water and leaving it to soak in the flask.

Tiles

Clean with equal parts of brown vinegar and kerosene.

Tin kettles or pans

Pour water and borax into rusty tin kettles and pans and boil. Scour afterwards.

Tins

Brown paper moistened in vinegar will polish your tins.

Umbrella

Clean *umbrella silk* by putting 1 tablespoon of sugar and 1 cup of boiling water into a bowl. Wash down from the ferrule. Leave it to dry open, and in a shady area.

Clean *mud stains* by rubbing stains with a cloth dipped in methylated spirits.

Urine

Cleaner

¹/₂ cup of methylated spirits

¹/₄ cup of cloudy ammonia

¹/₄ cup of glycerine

Wring out a cloth in warm water. Apply mixture to cloth and sponge over stain. You can also sponge white vinegar onto the stain, then dab with crushed Steradent tablets.

Wallpaper

To remove grease from wallpaper, apply a thick layer of fuller's earth or baby powder and leave for about four hours, before brushing off. If any marks remain, repeat the process.

Walls

To wash painted walls, add 1 tablespoon of bicarbonate of soda to 4 cups of warm water and use to rub on walls with a cloth. Rinse with a cloth rinsed in clean water.

Washing-up water

A little washing soda in the water will soften the water and save soap.

White cleaner (for canvas shoes)

1 dessertspoon of whiting

teaspoon of boiled starch

¹/₂ teaspoon of salt and a squeeze from a blue bag

Mix together. Add enough water to make a paste. Apply to the shoes with a brush and allow to dry.

Windows

Add 3 tablespoons of vinegar to 1 litre of warm water and wash windows with a sponge. The windows will need no drying or rubbing.

Cleaner 1

2¹/₂ tablespoons of cornflour

¹/₂ cup of cloudy ammonia

¹/₂ cup of brown vinegar

Shake well to combine, then apply to windows using a slightly damp cloth. Clean off with newspaper.

Cleaner 2

3 tablespoons of ammonia

1 tablespoon of white vinegar

1¹/₂ cups of water

Mix together, place into a spray bottle, and shake well. Use as required. You can also combine equal parts of water, methylated spirits and kerosene and apply with a soft cloth.

Wood

To clean *wood surfaces* in the house, use detergent in hot water.

Unvarnished wood can be cleaned by rubbing the inside of a banana skin in a circular motion. Allow to dry, then buff with a soft cloth.

To clean timber floors, *see* Floors, p. 322.

Laundry

I used to help mother with the washing when I lived at home, and she made sure I knew what to do in the laundry when I married in 1952. Her advice to me was 'Don't use a washing machine, make sure you use a copper and boil your clothes to keep them clean'. Mum never had a drier — the clothes went on the clothes line to dry in the sun and wind. I still like to do that today.

Washing day at 'New Farm' in the 1950s meant washing clothes by hand, boiling them in a copper with washing soda, draining them and then rinsing them twice — first in clear water, and then in a tub of blue water.

As far as following Mum's advice about using a copper for washing our clothes, I must admit that I didn't follow it for too long. Joh and his family had a washing machine at 'Bethany', and I gradually changed from boiling my clothes to using the washing machine — the clothes still came out nice and clean.

Ammonia

On wash days, add ammonia for a whiter and brighter wash.

Anti-moth herbs

Take a handful each of lavender, rosemary and thyme and mix with 14 g of crushed cloves and a small piece of lemon peel. Put in a small cloth or muslin bag and place in cupboards and drawers to repel moths.

Belts

To avoid tangles when washing by machine, place belts in old pantihose and tie the waist.

Blankets

Keep blankets and other woollen articles free from moths by adding a block of *camphor* to the final rinsing water.

To *clean* blankets dissolve 2 large tablespoons of borax or ammonia in $2^1/_2$ cups of water, and, when dissolved, add it to the warm soapy water in which the blankets are to be soaked. Put one blanket at a time into the liquid, and leave to soak for a short time, then wash. While blankets are drying on the line, shake occasionally until dry.

Calico

To waterproof calico, brush raw linseed oil sparingly on the garment and dry well. Allow two to three coats for a thorough waterproofing.

Cement

Remove cement from overalls or clothing by putting them in a washing machine with soapy water and one or two packets of Epsom salts. Leave for 10 minutes, then rinse well.

Chair covers

Slip covers that have been washed should be sprayed with starch. They will then be easier to clean next time.

Chamois leather

When washing chamois, only use tepid water. Stretch chamois before drying.

Chiffon

To wash chiffon, squeeze through
warm soapy water, and rub gently.
Rinse in warm water with a dash of
ammonia. Squeeze out water and
dry in sun. Iron with warm iron
while damp.

Chintz

To wash chintz, add bran water to the washing water. Bran water is
made by boiling $1^1/_4$ cups of bran in a muslin bag in 5 cups of water for
half an hour. This helps to stiffen the material and revive the colours.

Clothing (black)

To remove any *shine*, rub cloth well with a cloth dipped in turpentine, or
cold tea, then expose the clothing to the air.

To *restore a black dress*, dust and brush and remove any stains. Sponge
with hot water and iron on the wrong side.

To *clean black felt hats*, rub over with benzene and hang in the open air.

White blouses with *coloured embroidery* likely to run should be soaked
for 2 hours in salt and water or vinegar and water before being washed.
The salt must be thoroughly dissolved and absorbed by the water. The
proportion of either salt or vinegar is 1 tablespoon to each litre of water.

To *prevent clothes from fading*, add a handful of salt to the water in which
blue things are to be washed; a tablespoonful of alum for green materials;
a little strained tea for all shades of brown; a few drops of red ink for
pink and red; and a few drops of vinegar for black.

To *prevent colours running*, add vinegar to final rinsing water as it will
help set the dye.

Collars

To clean grease from *velvet collars*, rub a cloth dipped in ammonia over the
collar.

To prevent unnecessary wear and tear on *shirt collars*, moisten the
soiled area, sprinkle with 1 teaspoon of sugar and leave overnight.

Collars will rinse clean and stay looking new much longer if treated in this way.

Creases

I often have to press Joh's trousers, though not quite so often as when he was Premier. He always likes the creases to be sharp. I believe the hints in this section will be helpful as the men in the family like their trousers well pressed.

When travelling, hang *crumpled suits* in the bathroom and fill the room with steam, which will help remove creases.

Firm creases can be achieved by rubbing soap on the inside of creases and seams of woollen materials during ironing. This ensures sharp creases and flat seams.

Dresses

Turn children's dresses inside out when hanging them out to dry. The hem then fades to match the dress, so there's no darker band when it's let down. *See also* Hems on p. 342.

Eiderdown

To wash an eiderdown, add 1 tablespoon of ammonia to warm soapy water. When rinsing, add another tablespoon of ammonia. Shake eiderdown every so often as it dries.

Felt hat

To restore *stiffness* to the brim, dampen it thoroughly with methylated spirits, mould into shape, then dry in the sun.

Flannel (coloured)

Wash flannel in warm soapy water with a little salt. Rinse in salt and water, then shake out and dry in the shade.

Fur coat

Hang a fur coat in a dark place with naphthalene flakes. Comb through fur with a metal comb after use, as this also helps keep the fur free from moths.

Cleaning a fur coat can be done by a professional, or if cleaning at home, fill a bowl with bran and heat in the oven. Rub bran into the fur then brush or beat out. A damp towel can also be wiped over the fur and the fur hung near a draft to dry before storing.

Georgette

Georgette is inclined to shrink but can be pulled into its original shape while still damp.

Gloves

White washable leather gloves can be washed in warm water to which a little ammonia has been added. Then wash in warm soapy water. Do not squeeze. Fold between two towels and dry slowly.

Grease

To remove *candle grease* from clothing. As soon as the wax is dry, remove as much as possible with a knife. Place a piece of blotting paper or brown paper on each side of the greasy patch and press with a hot iron. Any remaining traces may be removed with the aid of a little paraffin or eucalyptus oil.

To remove *car grease* rub stain with butter, leave for an hour, then wash in warm soapy water.

Common grease stains may generally be removed by washing in borax and water. You can also, before washing, rub each side of the material with talcum powder, then put brown paper or blotting paper on each side of the material and iron with a warm iron.

Put $1/2$ cup of shredded washing soap and $1/2$ cup of kerosene into hot water to wash *greasy overalls*.

Handkerchiefs

When soiled, handkerchiefs can be soaked in $1/2$ a bucket of warm water and 1 tablespoon of borax.

Hems

When a crease remains after letting down a hem, dip a cloth in vinegar, place on crease and press with a hot iron. *See also* Dresses on p. 340.

Irons and ironing

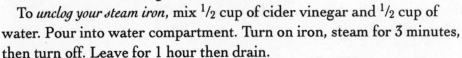

To clean an iron, rub a mixture of salt and vinegar on to the iron's surface or a cut lemon before turning it on. For *stubborn marks*, clean with steel wool and vinegar while iron is warm.

To *unclog your steam iron*, mix $\frac{1}{2}$ cup of cider vinegar and $\frac{1}{2}$ cup of water. Pour into water compartment. Turn on iron, steam for 3 minutes, then turn off. Leave for 1 hour then drain.

Trousers or slacks: when pressing pants, use a cloth which has been starched and dried before you dampen and iron over it. The creases then last much longer.

Embroidery: place face downwards on a folded up flannel while still damp to iron.

Coloured silks and *embroidered wool* should be ironed on the wrong side.

Silk should never be allowed to dry completely before ironing.

For *scorch marks* on woollens, *see* Woollens on p. 349.

Iron *pique* and *applique* on the back.

Lace

Antique lace and delicate small lace pieces can be put in a jar of warm soapy water and shaken vigorously.

To *iron*, cover lace with clean white tissue paper and press gently.

To give *doyleys* and *tablecloths* a natural buff colour, rinse in cold tea.

Linen

Wine stains can be removed by holding the stain in a little boiling milk until the spot fades to the point where it can be washed out completely with soap and water. If this is not effective, a little salt and a few drops of lemon juice may be applied.

Scorch mark remover
$1^1/_4$ cups of vinegar
$^1/_4$ cup of fuller's earth
15 g of shredded white soap
Juice of 2 onions (peel and slice onions then pound or squeeze them)

Mix ingredients, then boil them until they form a thin paste. Spread over the marks. Allow to dry, then wash it out.

Another *method*, provided the linen threads are not actually burned, is to rub the affected areas with lemon juice and allow to dry in direct sunlight.

Mildew

To remove mildew, leave the article to soak in milk overnight, and in the morning place it in the sun to dry. Wash in warm soapy water, rinse and dry.

Moths

Put dried *lavender* flowers in sachets and bundles to scent drawers and to protect linen from moths.

Put *cinnamon bark* pieces and crumbled mint into muslin bags to help keep moths and silverfish away from cupboards and drawers.

Dry some *orange peel* and leave it lying loose in drawers and wardrobes to repel moths.

Pantihose

Use *old pantihose* to hang jumpers on the clothes line. Thread them through one arm of jumper, across the shoulder and through the other arm. This avoids peg marks.

Soak *new pantihose* in gelatine and warm water before use to prolong their life.

Pillows

To wash pillows make a muslin bag a bit bigger than the pillow. Remove down or feathers, put them in the muslin bag, and sew up the end. Squeeze through warm soapy water, then rinse thoroughly in warm water. Squeeze out water and hang to dry.

Rain spots

To remove rain spots from material, hold garment over steam from a boiling kettle. Shake in the steam until moist and then shake until dry.

Ribbons or ties

To clean ribbons or ties, sponge gently with warm water and ammonia. Spread lengthwise on a table, cover with a thin cloth, and iron until dry.

Rubber

After a shower or bath, soak *mat* in cold water with a handful of salt or borax.

A little talcum powder sprinkled inside makes *gloves* much easier to put on. To prolong their life, turn them inside out after a couple of weeks and use on opposite hands.

Salt or vinegar

Added to the final rinsing water, salt or vinegar tends to revive colours where faded.

Satin (black)

To renovate satin, peel and chop two potatoes, cover with water, add a pinch of salt, then leave overnight. Sponge on right side of satin with water mixture. Iron on the wrong side.

Shower curtain

Wash with vinegar or soak in salt water to help prevent mildew. After washing, spray with a waterproof spray to revive.

Silk

Coloured silks can be rejuvenated after washing by adding 1 tablespoon of salt and 1 tablespoon of vinegar to the last rinsing water. The salt sets and the vinegar brightens the colours.

Methylated spirits in the washing and rinsing water keeps *silk blouses* white. A tablespoon of methylated spirits to 4 cups of water should be used. If a little stiffness is required put a little dissolved sugar in the rinse water.

Black silk is improved by soaking for a short time after rinsing in deep blue water.

Scorch marks, *see* Woollens on p. 349.

Soap

> *2 cups of resin*
> *12 cups of fat*
> *1 tablespoon of borax*
> *1¹/₂ buckets of water*
> *2 cups of caustic soda*

Boil resin, fat and borax in water for half an hour, then remove from heat. Add soda (wear gloves and don't let soda touch your skin). Leave to set. Cut into bars and leave for a month before use.

If your wash is too soapy, add 1 tablespoon of vinegar to the suds and they will quickly disappear.

Socks

To keep socks white, soak in warm water with 2 tablespoons of cream of tartar overnight, then wash in hot soapy water with a tablespoon of kerosene.

Stains

Wash acid off immediately with a solution of ammonia or washing soda.

How many times have you put on a clean tablecloth and served beetroot for lunch? This hint for removing beetroot stains will be very useful. To remove *beetroot* from washable clothing rub with a slice of lemon and launder as usual.

On many occasions Joh has left biro pens in his shirt when travelling by plane, and as you know they leak, sad to say, and can ruin a good shirt. It's good to know how to treat the stains so that the shirts can be recycled. *Biro and felt tip pen* stains should be treated immediately with methylated spirits, then washed in very hot water with plenty of laundry detergent. You can also spray biro stains with hairspray and then wash.

A cup of lemon juice in a bucket of water; or 1 cup of cloudy ammonia in a bucket of water; or 1 cup of salt in a bucket of water make *bleach.*

Soak *blood* stains in several changes of cold water. Wash in cold soapy water and rinse in warm water. If a stain still remains, add a few drops of ammonia to the water, or swab with hydrogen peroxide or household bleach and rinse well. Never use hot water.

Put ice on *chewing gum* until it freezes and can be loosened. Eucalyptus oil is also effective at removing gum without damaging the fabric.

Sponge spilt *cocoa* at once with cold water. Do not use hot water.

Swab *coffee* with cold water, then rub detergent gently into the fabric and rinse well, or pour boiling or very hot water through the stain, then wash in warm soapy water and rinse. If the stain has set, loosen it with glycerine, then cover it with borax. Pour boiling water through it again. On non-washable materials, rub a little glycerine into the stain and rub with cleaning fluid.

Rub *cosmetic* stains with glycerine then wash in warm water with washing soda.

Soak cloth stained with *egg* in cold water before washing.

Cover *fruit* stains with salt and soak in milk before washing, or wash the stain in kerosene.

To remove bad *grass* stains or *tree sap* from cotton fabrics, soak stains in the following: 1 tablespoon each of glycerine and kerosene with 1 dessertspoon of Epsom salts. Mix all in a bottle and shake to dissolve Epsom salts. Cover stains with mixture and roll fabric up. Leave for several hours, then wash in usual way. Grass stains can also be removed by sponging with eucalyptus oil.

To remove *grease,* cover spot with brown paper and press with a hot iron. You can also wet the fabric and rub with bicarbonate of soda. Repeat if necessary, then wash garment in warm soapy water.

Soak *ink* stains in milk.

Remove stains from *leather* using a solution of vinegar and warm water. To finish, rub with olive oil.

Soak *lipstick* stains in milk then wash in warm soapy water.

Soak *nappies* in a strong solution of bicarbonate of soda, dissolved in warm water.

Use eucalyptus oil to remove *tobacco* stains.

Dip *paint* on clothes in turps and then in ammonia.

To remove *perspiration* stains, soak clothing with lemon juice, then wash in warm soapy water. You can also soak perspiration stains in 2 tablespoons of bicarbonate of soda in $1/2$ a bucket of water for a few hours.

Soak *rust* stains in lemon juice or sour milk to which bicarbonate of soda has been added. Leave to dry, then wash in warm soapy water. You can also wash area in kerosene.

Salt heated in the oven and rubbed into serge or gaberdine will remove stains and grease spots.

Soak *sheets* for 2 hours in cold water with 3 tablespoons of borax.

To remove *tea* stains, rub borax over stain and steep in boiling water.

Freshly cut tomato is also good rubbed on common stains.

Rub salt on *wine* stains and pour boiling water over it.

Urine on mattress, see p. 335 in the Cleaning section.

Starch

2 cups of starch
2 cups of cold water
6 cups of boiling water
2 dessertspoons of borax

Mix starch and cold water. Add boiling water and borax and mix well. Allow to stand for 3 days.

Static

To avoid static, soak garment in fabric softener and then rinse well.

Stockings

Put *odd stockings* in a pot and boil for a few minutes with $1/2$ teaspoon of salt. Leave until cold. Rinse then hang them out to dry. All the stockings will be the same colour.

To wash *black stockings*, add 1 teaspoon of malt vinegar to rinsing water. This will stop the colour running.

Suede

To clean *collars and cuffs*, dip a soft brush into petrol and brush until all the dirt is removed. Finish by using a good suede cleaner.

To remove *grease from suede*, sponge stains with vinegar. Allow to dry, then brush with a suede brush.

Suits

Moisten a cloth with turpentine and rub over the suit. This will also remove shiny areas. Hang outside to remove any odour.

Taffeta

Wash taffeta in warm water in which 2 tablespoons of salt have been dissolved. Wash again in warm soapy water. To stiffen add $1/2$ teaspoon of borax to the rinsing water. Don't wring. Press before taffeta dries.

Tar stains

Soak a piece of cloth in eucalyptus oil and rub on the stain. It's also suitable for delicate materials.

Tea towels

Soak new ones in cold water and $1/2$ a packet of Epsom salts before using.

Velvet

Freshen in appearance by steaming (press the iron's steam button while it hovers over the fabric without

ironing or touching the fabric). Never iron velvet on the right side as it scorches easily.

Velveteen

To *wash*, add a small amount of ammonia to warm soapy water. Dip velveteen into the water several times. Rinse well in warm water with a little ammonia also added to the rinse water. Don't rub. Do not wring either; allow to drip dry.

To *revitalise* the pile, steam the fabric with the iron without touching it, or hold it over a saucepan of boiling water.

Washing machine

To clean, fill the machine with warm water and pour in 1 bottle of vinegar. Leave the machine to run full cycle.

Woollens

Wool mix

3 cups of Lux flakes
1 cup of methylated spirits
1 cup of eucalyptus oil

This is good for washing woollens and blankets. Place in a jar and shake well. Add 1 tablespoon of mix to warm water. Soak garments. Do not rinse.

Never rub woollens when washing them. Squeeze wool by hand through the wool mix.

To remove *ink* stains rub the woollen with green tomato.

Scorch marks in woollens and silks should be smeared with borax and glycerine, and left for an hour, after it's been carefully washed. They should disappear if the scorch marks are fresh and not too deep.

For added *softness*, add 2 tablespoons of glycerine to lukewarm water when rinsing, or 1 teaspoon of olive oil or eucalyptus oil can also be used.

To clean a *white shawl*, stretch it out on a table. Sprinkle with finely powdered starch. Fold, rub together, then shake out.

Zippers

If a zip doesn't work smoothly, rub a candle up and down the teeth of
the zip.

Miscellaneous

Adhesive paste

This paste will keep for months.

3 teaspoons alum
2¹/₂ cups boiling water
500 g flour
Few drops of oil of cloves

Dissolve alum in water, thicken with flour, add oil of cloves; boil and bottle.

Ants

Scatter fresh or dried mint leaves in cupboards to deter ants or sprinkle talcum powder on the shelves. Destroy nests with boiling water. To soothe an ant bite rub the area with camphorated oil.

Boat keys

Fasten keys to a large cork and if dropped overboard they will float.

Borers

Paint furniture with turpentine.

Broom and mop handles

Paint the socket and while the paint is still wet put the handle in firmly. Allow to dry.

Candles

Will burn better and last longer if placed in the freezer for 2 hours before use.

Car battery

Have you ever gone to start your car and had a flat battery? It has happened to me on a number of occasions and I always look for jumper leads. However the hints about batteries in this section will be of great assistance if you have trouble with starting your car.

When connecting terminals red to *plus*, black to *minus*. When charging battery take tops off the battery cells and check that the water levels are correct. Fill with distilled water.

To *clean battery terminals*, add 1 teaspoon bicarbonate of soda to $^1/_2$ cup warm water. Stir and tip over terminals.

Car freshener

Sprinkle a few drops of essential oil on a tissue and place it in an air vent inside the car. To help remain alert use basil or peppermint or one of the citrus oils to refresh the air.

Carving knife

To sharpen, hold the steel in the left hand, which should be on a level with the elbow, pointing the steel towards the right shoulder, and hold the knife upright in the right hand. Place the hilt of the knife's edge at the top of the steel, and draw the blade downwards the whole length of both steel and knife, first on one side and then on the other, that is so that the point of the knife finishes at the hilt of the steel. The blade should be almost flat on the steel, with the back slightly raised, but with only the edge touching it.

Chimney

If *chimney is on fire* throw a large amount of salt on the fire and this will extinguish the flames.

Clothing on fire

If one's clothing should become ignited, wrap a blanket, a carpet, or woollen article tightly around the person, or roll over and over on the floor.

Cockroaches

Put slices of fresh cucumber onto shelves or mix borax and sugar and put onto shelves.

Corks

Use a cork to fill a knot-hole in a floor board, then sand back.

Cricket bat

Brush linseed oil on surface of front of bat from bottom to about 30 cm upwards. Do this once a month. Store upright. Oil will soak through to back.

Damp beds

Place a mirror between the sheets, where it should remain for a few minutes. If, when removed, the glass is misty the bed is damp.

Door creaking

Rub the hinges with the lead of a pencil or a lump of dripping.

Drawers

To prevent sticking, a bar of hard soap should be rubbed over the lower edges of the drawers and on the grooves in which the drawers slide. The parts so treated must then be polished to ensure efficient working.

If *drawer knob* becomes loose, wind a few strands of steel wool round the screw before putting it back in the hole.

Enamel

For home-made, crush a piece of coloured sealing wax. Place in a jar with a small amount of methylated spirits. Shake well until wax has dissolved. Then use as required.

Enamelware

To stop leaks mix a small amount of bricklayer's cement to a thick paste. Fill the holes. Allow to dry for 3 days. Rub area with an emery cloth.

Fire

To brighten up a fire create a draft by holding an open newspaper in front of the fireplace until the fire draws.

Fish-hooks

Before storing smear the jar and lid with petroleum jelly to prevent rusting.

Fleas

Scatter fresh or dried mint leaves around or under beds to deter fleas.

Flies

Place pots of *basil* on windowsills to deter flies or hang bunches of tansy indoors. Can also use *lavender* to discourage flies. Put a sponge in boiling water then lay on a saucer. Pour some drops of oil of lavender onto the sponge. Keep sponge moist with hot water.

Beer or treacle in a saucer, or treacle smeared on sheets of paper, will attract and kill flies. Frequently wash window and door frames with disinfectant or paraffin.

At a *barbecue* take a jar of strong lavender water and leave open on the table.

Fog-free mirror

Will be yours in the bathroom despite steam if you rub the surface with equal parts of glycerine and methylated spirits.

Garbage tin

Will make a good incinerator for the back yard. Stand on some bricks.

Glue

When dried in the bottle, add a little vinegar to soften.

Hens

To cure broody hens in the early stages remove hen to a coop with slatted floor which allows free current of air beneath. In such a coop it is impossible for a hen to sit with any comfort and being obliged to roost, will quickly lose the desire. A few days confinement should cure her and she should resume laying shortly thereafter.

To help prevent hens from eating their eggs put a small amount of vinegar in the drinking water and also give them plenty of crushed shells.

Hot-water bottle

Fill with crushed ice and use to keep food cool on a picnic.

Insects

Put dried sage leaves or lavender among linen to discourage insects.

Leaking pipes

Make a paste of one part whiting, one part soap. Rub over the leak and leave to dry. Or fill the area with putty and bandage with some linen.

Macaroni

Buy for a rainy day to keep children busy. Macaroni can be threaded on string or fishing line and painted. Makes lovely necklaces and bracelets.

Mice

Use the seeds of aniseed plant as a bait in mouse traps. Can also scatter fresh or dried mint leaves around food to deter mice. Use socks dipped in turpentine to block up mouse holes.

Nail holes

To fill, mix some sawdust with some glue. Stir until it forms a stiff paste. Fill the hole with the paste. Allow to dry, sandpaper the area gently and then paint over.

Opaque glass

To make a window opaque rub toothpaste over the glass and allow to dry.

Paint

To rid a newly *painted room of smell*, leave three or four sliced onions in a basin in the closed room.

To prevent a *skin* forming on an opened can of paint, pour in enough linseed oil to cover surface. To use paint, just stir in the oil.

Avoid *paint drips* on floor and clothes when painting ceiling. Cut an old tennis ball in half and push the brush handle through the opening in it. Any trickles of paint will be caught in the cup.

For *paint stripper* blend together 8 tablespoons of starch and 3 cups of cold water. Add 5 cups of boiling water. Stir until clear. Add 8 cups of cold water and 8 tablespoons of caustic soda. When mixing and using make sure you wear gloves and don't get it on the skin. When applying to the timber, leave on as long as possible but scrape at regular intervals to make sure timber is not being damaged.

The importance of having a notebook

In 1949 I became secretary to the Main Roads Commissioner, and my sister Margaret told me she didn't think I'd ever be able to hold the job down as my memory wasn't good enough.

When I started work in the Commissioner's office, I decided to write down all my messages in a notebook and when I completed each one, crossed them out.

When I left the Main Roads and the Commissioner was speaking at a farewell function for me, what did he praise — my excellent memory!!

The discipline of using a notebook, which I recommend to anyone finding it difficult to remember things, proved a handy one at home too. Joh was a member of Parliament for 41 years and I was married to him for 36 of them, so I just had to take accurate messages.

Paste for scrapbooks

To a cup of starch, add sufficient cold water to make a smooth paste. Add boiling water until the paste is clear and jelly like.

To make *paste for paper hanging* mix flour and water to the consistency of cream. Boil, stirring all the time. Cool and use as required.

Pictures

Two coatings of clear shellac will preserve pictures and they can be framed without glass.

Pipes and taps

To stop them freezing in frosty weather, keep taps slightly dripping.

To *thaw* pipes and taps, heat house bricks in the oven. Place next to the frozen pipes. This will thaw pipes slowly. Or pour boiling salted water over the pipes and taps.

For *blocked pipes* make a mixture of soda and salt put down the pipe as far as possible then flush in an hour with boiling water.

Potato peelings

Dry in the sun then wrap in newspaper and use in the fireplace. They burn for a long time.

Putty

To soften dry putty, add linseed oil.

Rings

To remove a tight ring, wash the hand in cold water rubbing the joint of the finger with plenty of soap then carefully ease the ring over the knuckle. Never use hot water as the heat will cause the finger to swell.

Sagging cane chair seat

Can be rejuvenated if you wash seat with warm salt water and lemon juice. Rinse thoroughly in salt water then dry in the sun.

Scent balls

Cut a candle up. Place in a tin. Sprinkle some perfume or oil of lavender over the pieces. Melt while stirring. When the wax is firm but not hard, roll into balls and leave to set. Or pour into egg cartons to set.

Screws

If screws are well greased before being inserted into wood they will not rust for a considerable length of time and can be easily removed.

Sink waste container

Use a flower pot for waste; the hole at the bottom allows for drainage.

Squeaking floorboard

To stop, sprinkle talcum powder into the crack.

Steel knitting needles

To remove rust, soak the needles in vinegar overnight. Then rub needles with a flannel.

Sticky tape

To remove sticky tape from wrapping paper run warm iron over tape and it will lift off. Wrapping paper can also be smoothed over and used again by running over paper with warm iron.

Teapot

To prevent a metal teapot from becoming musty, clean and dry then put a lump of sugar inside.

Thyme

Mix essential oil with alcohol, then spray on paper and herbarium specimens for mould protection.

Trousers for children

When shortening put press studs around the inside of the hem instead of sewing the hem. Let down when washing. This will avoid a hem mark when lengthening.

Wasps (to trap)

Leave a jam jar with a little jam in the bottom near the wasp. When the wasp is trapped fill jar with boiling water.

Windows

Before painting windows, cover glass with metal polish, then after painting the spots will wipe off easily.

Windscreen

If the windscreen of a motor car is rubbed with a cut raw apple or potato, it will not become blurred.

Wood stoves

If the surface of a wood stove is cracked, make a paste of wood ash, common salt and water. Plaster over the crack.

THE FAMILY

Our son, John, has just moved back to manage 'Bethany' with his wife Karyn
and their three boys, Christian 4 years, Joshua 2 years and Samuel
who is still only a baby.

The boys love to play with their trucks and cars so Joh decided to build them a
sandpit near the kitchen, so Karyn can keep an eye on them. It is under a nice
shady tree and Joh dragged four big logs for the walls and had 12 cubic yards
of sand brought in making it about 2 metres deep.

Christian then decided he could improve the sand pit by filling his trucks with
red soil and bringing it over and tipping it into the sand. Grandpa wasn't very
happy about this when he saw what they were doing to the lovely sandpit he
had made for them.

Health

I believe that prevention is better than cure but you must remember if the family is really sick, consult your doctor. Immunisation is a contentious issue today, but local councils provide, on a regular basis, the opportunity to have children immunised against diseases such as polio, whooping cough, measles, etc.

My husband Joh is an example of where, if immunisation had been available, he would have been spared having polio. Polio struck him when he was 8 years old and he is indeed fortunate that he had parents who worked hard with him to finally ensure all he was left with was a small limp. Had immunisation been available then he would probably not have contracted polio.

A close shave!

Joh was managing 'Bethany' for his father who had been ill for a number of years, and he often told the story about the insurance agent who was always after him to take out a life insurance policy, and Joh always found it very hard to get rid of him.

One day he was ploughing the paddock when he suddenly saw the agent appear dressed in a very smart suit, but slowly being covered in dust, as he made his way across the ploughed area to see Joh. He was still very anxious to sell Joh a policy, so when he persisted Joh said 'I'll take out a policy on my father'. With a smile the agent took out his note book to take down the details.

'Your father's age', he asked. Joh answered '60 years of age'. 'State of health', he continued. 'Well', said Joh, 'he's all right at the moment but recently he had a bad heart attack'. He looked up at Joh as he put his book back in his pocket and said 'Perhaps I'll come back another day'. The interesting point was that Joh's father lived for another 25 years and it would have cost Joh a fortune.

Aloe vera

Crush sap from fresh leaves or slice them and apply as a poultice for chapped skin and dermatitis.

Aniseed

Infuse the seeds as an antiseptic tea for colds, coughs, bronchial problems and nausea.

Arthritis rub

Mix $1/2$ cup chopped parsley with $1/2$ litre methylated spirits. Leave for 14 days and then strain. Rub on affected areas.

Basil

Steep a few basil leaves in wine for several hours as a tonic. Infuse as a tea to aid digestion.

Bath water

To check water for baby or invalids, immerse your elbow. When running a bath put cold water in first, then add hot water.

Bay leaf

Infuse bay leaf as a digestive aid and to stimulate the appetite. Massage blended essential oil around sprains and into rheumatic joints.

Bleeding nose

Treat by sitting down and applying pressure to the nostril from which blood is oozing and place a cold compress (ice in cloth or cloth wet with cold water) on bridge of nose. It is better not to lie right down.

Bruises

Make a paste of dry starch of arrowroot and cold water and cover the bruise.

A burnt rubber boot

When John was very young he loved to go with Joh everywhere on the farm.

On one occasion Joh was burning old tree stumps and John was supposedly 'helping Dad'. All of a sudden Joh heard a great yell and a burning coal had fallen into John's rubber boot. Joh brought John home at a great pace, and we needed to apply one of our home remedies.

I'm sure you will find the hints for burns useful if you have the problem we had with John.

Burns

Run cold water over simple burns until the skin is as cool as the surrounding skin. Raw potato applied to simple burns will give great relief immediately.

Raw egg white will help prevent blistering if applied to a burn.

For *simple burns*, for example, from touching a hot iron in the wrong place, or grasping an overheated saucepan handle, gently pat lavender oil over the sore part. This will not only take away the pain, but will help to heal the skin tissue.

Cold tea also helps soothe simple burns.

For *serious burns*, seek medical help.

Chamomile

Infuse chamomile flowers as a tea for a general tonic and sedative. Apply a compress to treat wounds and eczema. Use in a bath to relieve sun or windburnt skin.

Caraway seeds

Chew these raw or infuse to aid digestion, promote appetite, sweeten the breath and relieve flatulence. Safe for children.

Chafing

Methylated spirits should be rubbed on the area and then powder with a non-perfumed talcum powder.

Chapped hands

To prevent hands from becoming chapped, rub with the following mixture: equal quantities of glycerine and methylated spirits, mixed well together. Add a few drops of your favourite perfume or rinse hands in a little vinegar and let it dry on the hands.

Chervil leaf

Eat chervil leaf raw for additional vitamin C, carotene, iron and magnesium.

Infuse as a tea to stimulate digestion and help circulation disorders.

Chest colds

For chest colds, finely chop 1 garlic and put into a jar of vaseline. Stand in a warm area for a few days. Massage freely into back and chest.

Chilblains

A mixture of bicarbonate of soda and vinegar applied to the affected area helps. To stop the itch, rub a raw onion over the affected spot or mix 1 tablespoon of honey with 1 tablespoon of glycerine, the white of an egg and enough flour to make a paste. A teaspoon of rosewater or lavender may be added. Wash the affected parts with warm water, dry and spread on paste. Cover with a piece of linen or cotton material.

Chives

Chives are excellent as an appetite stimulant.

Comfrey

Make a poultice with the fresh leaves for rough skin, aching joints, sores, small burns and cuts.

Common cold

To bring relief from a cold, grate horseradish and inhale the fumes that arise, or a spoonful of Vicks Vapour Rub added to boiling water and inhaled will aid congestion.

Constipation

Figs or stewed prunes are invaluable for curing constipation.

Cooking for invalids

Barley water

1 tablespoon sugar

1 heaped tablespoon of barley

grated rind of 1/2 lemon

5 cups of water

Simmer barley and water for 1/2 hour. Stir in the sugar and grated lemon. Strain mixture. Serve cool.

Eggnog

1 egg yolk

1 teaspoon of sugar

1/2 cup of warm milk (or water)

1/2 teaspoon of brandy (optional)

Beat all ingredients together and serve.

Cup custard

1 egg

1/2 tablespoon of sugar

Milk

Vanilla flavouring

Beat egg and add sugar. Put in a cup and add milk and vanilla. Put the cup in a dish of hot water and bake in a moderate oven (180°C) until just set. Sprinkle nutmeg on top of custard. Serve.

Steamed custard (for invalids and children)
1 egg beaten with 2 teaspoons sugar. Add $1^1/_2$ cups milk. Place in small basin and put into saucepan of boiling water. Boil for 10 minutes.

Coriander

Chew or infuse seeds as a tea for a digestive tonic and mild sedative. Add essential oil to ointments for painful rheumatic joints and muscles. It can also be used to flavour various medicines.

Corns

To *cure* corns, take equal parts of a roasted onion and a soft soap. Beat well together and apply mixture to the corn on a small piece of linen (used as a poultice).

To *remove* corns, mix equal parts of olive oil and eucalyptus oil and massage into the corn. Or soak the foot in warm water and strap a piece of lemon on the corn, leaving it on overnight. These treatments should lift out the corn in three to four days.

Cough mixture

For a bad cough, put 1 teaspoon of Friars Balsam & Menthol in $1^1/_2$ cups of boiling water. Put mixture into an empty fruit tin, place a funnel into tin with the end of funnel covering the top of the tin. Wrap towel over tin and breathe in the vapour.

Honey added to warm milk helps prevent coughing.

Croup

Pound a piece of camphor and stir in some melted lard. Let the mixture set and then rub on the throat and chest for relief.

Alternatively, use 2 dessertspoons of vinegar, 1 dessertspoon of methylated spirits and 3 dessertspoons of water. Mix together and wring out a flannel in the

mixture, place around throat and then cover with another dry piece of flannel.

Cuts and wounds

To bathe cuts and wounds, use Epsom salts or boracic acid in warm water.

Cuts or scratches

Raw egg white or boracic acid added to water is good for a cut. Vaseline and eucalyptus oil blended together can be used as an ointment.

Dandruff

Collect 2 cups of lemon tree leaves. Cover with water and boil for 60 minutes. When cool, strain and rub into clean washed hair. Leave on for 20 minutes, then rinse. Another cure is to rub bicarbonate of soda into the hair, leave for an hour then wash hair as normal.

Dill

Use the seed in a salt-free diet as it is rich in mineral salts.

Make *dill water* for indigestion, flatulence, hiccups, stomach cramps, insomnia and colic. Infuse 1 tablespoon of bruised seeds in 1 cup boiling water. Strain. Take 1 tablespoon per adult.

Dog bites

Clean dog bites well and dab on some iodine. If you are concerned, or bites are deep, see your doctor. Also be sure that tetanus injections are up-to-date.

Earache

Use a solution of 10 per cent tea-tree oil in water for ear drops

Or make a sachet filled with salt then heat in the oven until the salt is very hot. Place a piece of material over the bag and lay it on the ear to help give relief.

Eczema

My mother suffered very much from eczema for many years of her life. It

can be so irritating, and of course the more you scratch, the worse
it is.

Many children who have asthma also have eczema. Use of the hints
below will do much to assist in the treatment of eczema.

A good remedy for eczema is to boil 1 cup olive oil, remove from heat
and add 30 mL of salicylic acid, stirring it in thoroughly. When cold
apply it with a piece of cotton wool, which should be burnt after use.
Don't use soap when washing the hands and avoid blood-heating foods.

Add *vinegar* to bath water or try a decoction of chamomile and dab over
the affected area.

Evening primrose oil

This is a very popular treatment for premenstrual tension. It also has
value to reduce breast pain.

Eyes

To relieve tired eyes, place used teabags on the eyes and rest. A
cold-water eye bath is also relaxing. Put water in an egg cup and open
the eye in it.

Fennel

Infuse the seeds as a tea to aid digestion and constipation. Chew fennel to
allay hunger and ease indigestion. (Note: Do not take excessive
amounts.)

Fish bone

A raw egg, if swallowed immediately,
will often detach a fish bone that has
stuck in the throat. Also try sipping
lemon juice.

Foot massage

Mix 2 parts glycerine, 1 part lemon
juice and 1 part methylated spirits.

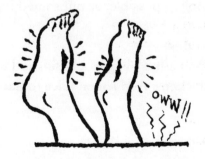

Place in a bottle, shake well and use after shower or bath, rubbing well into soles and between toes.

Foot bath

Add 1 to 2 tablespoons mustard to each litre of water. Water should be as hot as can be comfortably borne. Make a relaxing foot bath from 2 litres of water and a cup of bicarbonate of soda or salt.

Gargle

This is a very old recipe. A good gargle can be made by boiling $1^1/_4$ cups of sage leaves in $2^1/_2$ cups of water until the liquid is reduced by one half. When boiling keep the pan covered. Strain, then mix the liquid with an equal quantity of vinegar, port wine and $^1/_4$ cup of honey. Bottle it and warm when required.

Headache

A cloth rinsed in vinegar and placed on the forehead often helps. A brisk walk in the fresh air often clears the head; take a few deep breaths; or rub a little lavender oil on your temples.

Heartburn

Chamomile or peppermint tea can often help.

Heat rash

Rub cornflour into the affected area.

Hiccups

To help cure hiccups, sip a teaspoon of lemon juice or hold your breath as long as possible, or put something cold down your back.

Hoarseness

Beat a fresh egg in a basin, add 1 teaspoon castor sugar, beat until it thickens. Add lemon juice to flavour and drink.

Homemade liniment

> *2 eggs, well beaten*
> *4 dessertspoons of turpentine*
> *1 cup of vinegar*
> *4 dessertspoons of spirits of wine*
> *4 dessertspoons of camphor*

Beat all together, then pour into a bottle and shake. Keep bottled and use as required.

Insect bites and stings

When I put in my hint about bee stings, I recalled Joh's story of his bee-raising days.

When Joh was young he saw a book entitled *Making Money out of Bees in Australia*. As he was always trying to find ways to make money he just had to have that book.

It led him to having twelve bee hives and becoming an expert on the life of bees. However, he never made any money out of bees, he only received plenty of stings. Although we did have a good supply of honey for many years, but now it is much easier to go to the shop and buy a jar of honey.

Cold tea leaves applied to insect bites and stings relieve the pain and a paste of bicarbonate of soda and water painted on the area helps stop the itchiness.

Bee stings can be painful. Honey rubbed on the offending area after the sting has been pulled out will bring relief and slices of raw onion applied to the sting also often brings relief and helps to reduce swelling.

Also rub the affected area with fresh sage leaves, oil of lavender or eucalyptus oil to alleviate pain.

Lavender

Infuse the flower as a tea to soothe headaches, calm nerves, ease flatulence, fainting, dizziness and halitosis. Use neat essential oil as an antiseptic, or to relieve insect bites, stings and small burns. Add to bath water. Place one drop on the temple for headache relief.

Laxative (mild)

This is suitable for children.

315 g dates
125 g figs

Wash the dried fruit, stone the dates, mix dates and figs together and chop in a blender until mixture resembles breadcrumbs. Form the mixture into a sausage shape, pressing it together, chill in the refrigerator and cut into pieces about 2.5 cm long. Keep stored in refrigerator.

Lemon balm

Place fresh leaves directly onto insect bites and sores, or apply in a poultice. Infuse as a tea for relief from chronic bronchial catarrh, feverish colds, headaches, and nervous tension.

Marjoram

Infuse the flowering tops as a tea for colds, headaches, simple gastro-intestinal and nervous disorders. Add essential oil to bath water or make a compress for relief from rheumatic pains and tension.

Medicine

Always read the label carefully. Shake the bottle even if not directed. Use a graduated measure as spoons vary in size.

To *dull the taste* of nauseous medicine, put a little ice or peppermint in the mouth.

To *give medicine* to a resisting child, first try firm persuasion, otherwise hold the nose and put the spoon back far into the mouth. The child's arms can be held to the body with a towel.

Do not take medicine unless it is prescribed for that particular person.

Dispose of old or out of date medicine so children do not have access to it.

Methylated spirits

An excellent lotion for sprains and bruises when added to water and applied as a compress.

Midges

To prevent bites, rub the neck, wrists and other exposed areas with olive oil to which is added some oil of rosemary, lavender or eucalyptus.

1 teaspoon of any of these to 3 teaspoons of olive oil.

Mint (spearmint and peppermint)

Sprinkle on a handkerchief for relief from heavy colds. Infuse peppermint as a tea to help digestion, colds and influenza. Sip cold tea for hiccups and flatulence (spearmint and peppermint). Macerate leaves in oil then massage affected areas for migraines, facial neuralgia and rheumatic and muscular aches.

Mosquitoes

Oil of lavender often keeps mosquitos away if a few drops are sprinkled on bedclothes or on exposed parts of the body. Tea-tree oil or vinegar rubbed on the skin will also work.

Mouthwash

A few drops of vinegar in a glass of water is a good mouthwash.

Mustard plaster

To relieve heavy chest colds use the following:

1 heaped teaspoon of mustard
6 heaped teaspoons of flour
Water
Muslin
Brown paper

Mix mustard and flour with water until it has the consistency of peanut butter. Spread the mixture onto a piece of brown paper, approximately 20 by 25 cm. Cover with muslin. Place muslin side down on the patient's chest. Cover with a towel to keep the warmth in. Leave on for approximately 20 minutes.

Nerves

Thyme used as a tea will give relief to nervous people.

Nourishing drink

For someone who cannot retain food, add 2 egg whites to a glass of boiled water which has cooled. Add a pinch of salt.

Oregano

Infuse the flowering tops as a tea for coughs. Helps headaches and irritability, general exhaustion and menstrual pains. Drink as a sedative to prevent sea-sickness. Apply externally as an antiseptic poultice for swellings, rheumatism and stiffness.

Parsley

Chew raw leaves to freshen the breath and promote healthy skin. Infuse for a digestive tonic. Use in a poultice as an antiseptic dressing for sprains, wounds and insect bites.

Poultice (herbal)

Crush herbs and put in a muslin bag. Immerse bag in very hot water and squeeze out, then hold over inflamed area.

To *make an onion poultice*, roast onion and mash and spread on a piece of linen and apply to the spot.

To *make a poultice for splinters or boils*, soak bread in boiling water. Squeeze dry and saturate with castor oil or bicarbonate of soda. Apply to the affected area. When the bread is dry, reapply.

Poultices for boils
1/4 cup of honey
1/4 cup of plain flour
1 egg yolk

Beat together. Apply on a piece of lint using a bandage to keep in place.

Prickly heat

A tepid bath of 2 tablespoons bicarbonate of soda to each 2 litres of water helps prickly heat. A rub with lemon juice will also help.

Rosemary

Rosemary aids digestion of fat and is good for aching joints and rheumatic pains. Use as an antiseptic gargle and mouthwash.

Boil four branches of rosemary in water until water turns brown and use it to wash or rinse hair.

Sage

The leaf aids digestion and is antiseptic. Sage tea after a meal benefits digestion and is a nerve and blood tonic. Tea reduces sweating, soothes coughs and cold. (Note: Sage should not be taken in large doses for a long period.)

Scurf on babies' heads

Rub baby's head with vaseline or light oil 24 hours before bathing. Then wash out gently.

Snake bite

Don't wash the bite (a swab can be later taken to determine the species of snake). Bandage over the site first so that the tissue containing the poison is compressed. Then continue bandaging the whole limb. Restricting movement of the limb is important. Get to a doctor as soon as possible.

Sneezing

Sneezing can often be stopped by smelling camphor or pressing the tip of the tongue against the back of the central upper teeth.

Sore muscles

Massage sore muscles with a liniment made from the following:

1 part camphor
2 parts soft soap
10 parts water
12 parts methylated spirits

Sore throat

My mother's policy when my sister and I had sore throats as children was to get a mixture from the chemist of tannic acid and glycerine. She had a little brush with which she painted our throats. I also did this with my children, much to their horror. It didn't save my eldest daughter, Meg, from having her badly infected tonsils removed, but the other three children John, Helen and Ruth, still have their tonsils, and so have I.

Gargle with $1/2$ teaspoon of salt in a glass of warm water every 3 hours
Another mixture to gargle can be made from:

1 tablespoon of vinegar
2 tablespoons of honey
Juice of 1 lemon

Boil ingredients and bottle. When cool, sip as required.

Sterilising

If it is necessary to sterilise bowls or utensils quickly and there is no time to boil them, a little methylated spirits may be poured in and lighted. When it has burnt itself out the bowl is ready. Small instruments may be stored in the spirits for 30 minutes and they are then sterilised.

Sticking plaster

To remove easily, rub with olive oil and leave to soak for a few minutes.

Sunburn

A cooling application for sunburn is freshly sliced cucumber lightly rubbed on the skin.

Swollen feet

Rub a raw cut potato over the swollen feet. Leave it on overnight or alternate between hot and cold foot baths.

Tansy

Infuse the flower and leaf as a wash for bruises, rheumatism and sprains, but use with caution as tansy can irritate some skins. (Note: Use in moderation as it is potentially toxic. Do not use during pregnancy.)

Tarragon

The leaves are rich in iodine, mineral salts, vitamins A and C. Infuse as an appetite stimulant, digestive and general tonic.

Thrush

Thrush is the inflammation of skin or lining membranes by the fungus *Candida albicans*. The doctor will prescribe an anti-fungal drug but relief can be gained by having a bath in which 2 cups of cornflour has been added. Mix cornflour to a runny paste in a bowl before adding to the bath water.

Thyme

Infuse the leaf as a tea for a digestive tonic and for hangovers. Sweeten the infusion with honey for colds and sore throats. Apply infused thyme oil as a massage for headaches. It may also relieve insomnia, poor capillary circulation and muscular pain.

Tired feet

Rub methylated spirits into tired feet for relief and then dust with boracic powder before putting on stockings.

Toothache

Chew on an oregano leaf for temporary relief or rinse the mouth with bicarbonate of soda in water, then dip a damp piece of cotton wool into bicarbonate of soda and place in the cavity.

Placing a small piece of cotton wool dipped in *oil of cloves* in the cavity of the tooth will also reduce the pain. If toothache persists see your doctor.

Walking

A very good way of exercising. Try to walk at least 20 minutes, 3 times a week.

Water

Drink at least 8 glasses of water a day to keep the skin moist and supple.

Grooming

There are many helpful hints for your grooming in this book of classic country wisdom. We all want to look our best, but if you always have to go to the hairdressers and beauty consultants, it can become quite expensive.

The advice in this section is for all ages — care for the hair, for the eyes, for teeth, and a part very appropriate for me — aged skin! After all, if you brush up on your etiquette, it is important that you pay attention to your grooming, and the hints in this book will help you to do just that.

I travelled to Canberra once a week when the Senate was sitting, so I had to be very well organised. I tended to buy clothes that didn't crush and things I could wear a jacket with for the changeable Canberra weather. I always wear flattish shoes as they are much more comfortable when standing for long periods of time. It was important to look smart at all times, so I had my hair done once a week, which meant I could look after it during the week. I don't wear a lot of make-up, just a touch of lipstick. It is important to be well groomed and have a neat appearance at all times.

Adhesive plaster

To remove adhesive plaster, soak well in hot water first.

Aloe vera leaf

Use the leaf sap to make a soothing and healing moisturising cream, especially good for dry skin. Mix into shampoos to help dry or itchy scalp. Add to suntan lotions for its cooling and healing effect.

Aniseed

Ground seeds can be added to a face pack. Seed oil is used in toothpastes, soaps and mouthwashes.

Anti-freckle cream

2 tablespoons of lemon juice

$1/4$ teaspoon of borax

1 teaspoon of rosemary oil

Mix well and let stand for a few days before using. Always wear a hat outdoors.

Astringent (for acne and spots)

25 mL of witch-hazel

75 mL of rosewater

5 drops of lavender oil

5 drops of geranium oil

Let mixture stand for one month. Strain. Apply with cotton ball.

Or boil 2 cups of water and pour over a handful of lavender flowers and leaves. Leave for $1/2$ hour. Strain. Use as an astringent.

Basil

Add flowering top and leaf as a fresh infusion for an invigorating bath.

Bath oil

Put a light non-smelling oil in a bowl. Add your favourite herbs and flowers, perhaps lavender, roses or mint, covering completely with the oil. Leave to soak for 24 hours. Replace with fresh herbs and flowers.

Repeat process four times. Strain the liquid through muslin or cheesecloth and use for the bath.

Bathing

Add $\frac{1}{2}$ a cup of Epsom salts for a soothing bath or a few drops of your favourite oil.

Bathroom (sweet smelling)

Rub a few drops of a flower oil on to the spout of the hot tap and turn it on for a few moments to release the fragrance. The floral aroma will fill the room for some time.

Bay leaf

Add a bay leaf decoction to bath water to relieve aching limbs.

Caraway seed oil

Use caraway seed oil in mouthwashes and colognes.

Chamomile flower

Infuse chamomile flower as a facial steam and a hand soak to soften and whiten the skin. Make an eye bath or tea bag compress to reduce inflammation and eliminate fatigue shadows. Add an infusion for a reviving bath. Boil flowers for 20 minutes and use regularly as a rinse to lighten and condition fair hair.

Chervil leaf

Use chervil leaf in an infusion or face mask to cleanse skin, maintain suppleness and discourage wrinkles.

Cleanser (face)

Wipe over face with cotton wool soaked in milk. Rinse in warm water.

Cold cream

3 cups of olive oil
3 cups of rose petals
³/₄ cup of beeswax
Few drops of vinegar

Cut up rose petals finely. Cover with olive oil. Leave in a warm spot for 7 days. Strain. Heat olive oil in a saucepan. Heat beeswax in a separate container. Pour into one another several times, adding vinegar, until they blend.

Comfrey leaf and root

Infuse comfrey and add to baths and lotions to soften the skin.

Complexion

To improve your complexion, mix a level teaspoonful of salt with 2 tablespoons of milk, and rub it gently over the skin, allowing it to dry on and remain till morning.

Dentures

Soak dentures overnight in ¹/₂ cup of vinegar and ¹/₂ cup water.

Deodorant

2 tablespoons of vaseline
2 tablespoons of bicarbonate of soda
2 tablespoons of talcum powder
2 tablespoons of olive oil
1 teaspoon of lavender oil

Stir over low heat until a cream forms and store in a jar.

Or apply bicarbonate of soda with cotton wool after showering, while skin still damp.

Dill seed

Crush and infuse with hot water to use as a nail-strengthening bath.
Chew to sweeten breath.

Evening primrose

Use an infusion of leaf and stem to make an astringent facial steam or add to a hand cream as a softening agent.

Eye lashes

A touch of olive oil on lashes will give them lustre. A touch of olive oil on the eye lashes at night helps to darken lashes.

Eyebrows

To keep untidy brows in shape, a little dab of hair gel or mousse will keep the hairs in place.

Eyeglasses

To prevent eyeglasses steaming use a mixture of 1 part of glycerine to 6 parts of methylated spirits. Smear the lenses and leave them for a moment, then polish in the usual way. Repeat daily in cold weather and the glasses will not smear over. The mixture should be kept in a corked bottle or screw top jar and well shaken before use.

Face mask

Mash the flesh of an avocado to a pulp. Spread the pulp on the face and neck and leave for 20 minutes. Remove with tissues, then rinse in warm water.

Cleansing face mask (1)

2 tablespoons of green clay or fuller's earth

2 teaspoons of jojoba oil

1 teaspoon of yoghurt

3 drops of juniper oil or wheatgerm oil

3 drops of cypress oil or almond oil

Mix together and apply to the skin. Leave on for 15 minutes.

Cleansing face mask (2)

1 teaspoon of beeswax

1 tablespoon of lanolin

50 mL rosewater

1 tablespoon of fuller's earth

Melt the wax and lanolin, mix well. Remove from the heat and add the rosewater, stirring until it has cooled. Add in the fuller's earth, stirring until you have a smooth paste. Apply to face and neck (avoid the eyes), leave for 20 minutes, then rinse off with warm water, pat dry.

Rejuvenating face mask

2 tablespoons of green clay or fuller's earth

2 teaspoons of cornflour

1 egg yolk

1 teaspoon of evening primrose oil

1 drop of rosemary oil

1 drop of lavender oil

Mix together. Leave on the skin for 15 minutes then rinse in warm water.

Face mask for oily skin

Mix 2 tablespoons of honey and 1 cup of oatmeal to a paste and apply to the face. Rinse off when mask is dry.

Facial for aged skin

A good facial oil is made from 3 drops lavender oil and 1 teaspoon wheatgerm oil.

Facial cleansing oil

1 cup of olive oil

1 tablespoon of avocado oil

$1/2$ cup of apricot kernel oil

$1/2$ cup of walnut oil or almond oil

$1/4$ teaspoon of lavender, jasmine or violet oil

Pour all these ingredients into a screw top jar and shake. Keep in the refrigerator. Shake before using.

Facial oil

2 teaspoons of sweet almond oil

1 teaspoon of wheatgerm oil

3 drops of tea tree oil

3 drops of juniper oil or olive oil

3 drops of lavender oil

Blend all together.

Facial beauty pack

Fennel seed helps smooth lines away; chamomile is astringent and anti-inflammatory. Yoghurt and honey clear and stimulate the skin. Fuller's earth adds minerals. Chervil discourages wrinkles.

1 cup of water

2 teaspoons of any of the following herbs:

fennel seeds, chamomile flowers, sage leaves, chervil

100 g plain yoghurt

1 tablespoon of honey

1 tablespoon of fuller's earth

Simmer herbs in water for 15 minutes. Strain into a bowl (makes about 1 tablespoon strong liquid). Add yoghurt, honey and fuller's earth. Mix well together and cool in the refrigerator. Apply mixture over the face and neck and leave for 15 minutes. Rinse with warm water. Pat dry.

Fennel seeds

Chew fennel seed to sweeten the breath.

Fingernails

Stained or discoloured fingernails should be soaked in a 1 cup of warm water containing 1 teaspoon of lemon juice. To make nails less brittle, soak in a mixture of 1 cup of warm water, 1 teaspoon gelatine and 1 teaspoon of lemon juice.

Fresh breath

Chew on fresh mint to freshen the breath.

Garlic breath

To remove the smell of garlic from your breath, chew on some fresh parsley or juice if preferred.

Geraniums (scented)

Add the essential oil of scented geraniums to face creams.

Gums

For sore gums, gargle with $1/2$ teaspoon of salt dissolved in $1/2$ cup of warm water.

Hair

For *blond* hair, rinse with a little lemon juice strained and mixed with water.

For *dandruff*, rub bicarbonate of soda into the hair and rinse well.

A little vinegar added to the rinse water brings out the highlights in *dark* hair.

For *dry* hair, rub natural yoghurt into the scalp, leave for a couple of minutes and then rinse. *Or* rub a little warmed olive oil into the scalp the night before washing or rub in oil, warm a towel in hot water, wrap around the head for 20 minutes then shampoo hair.

For *white* hair, rinse in 1 part ordinary washing blue to four parts water.

For *brown to blond* hair, put chamomile flowers in a muslin bag and pour on boiling water. Rinse the hair with this infusion.

Add ammonia to water when washing *hair brushes and combs*.

To *clean combs quickly*, place them in a little warm water and sprinkle a heaped teaspoon of bicarbonate of soda over them. Remove after a few minutes.

For an *itchy scalp*, beat 1 egg then wet hair with warm water and wash scalp with the egg. Rinse with water and a small amount of vinegar. Rinse again in clean water.

Herbal hair rinses

Add 1 tablespoon selected herb to 3 cups of boiling water and
1 tablespoon cider vinegar (or lemon juice for fair hair). Infuse the herb
in water until cool. Strain well. Add the vinegar or lemon. Pour through
the hair.

Rosemary hair rinse

Gather about four to five leafy rosemary stalks and simmer them in
5 cups of water for 30 minutes. Keep the lid on the saucepan to prevent
the vapour from evaporating. Strain and use as a final rinse after washing
your hair, rubbing the mixture well into the scalp. This rinse will
revitalise the scalp and hair and will also help to prevent dandruff.

Hair shampoo

Beat 1 egg yolk in a little water then rub into hair and rinse well. Or
blend juice of 1 lemon with 1 egg yolk.

Hand lotion

Combine equal amounts of glycerine, honey, lemon juice and olive oil
together. Shake well in a bottle and use when necessary.

Herbal aftershave

1¹/₂ cups of apple cider vinegar

1¹/₂ cups of witch-hazel

1 tablespoon of chopped comfrey leaves

1 tablespoon of chopped sage or chervil leaves

1 tablespoon of rosemary leaves or lavender leaves

Put the herbs and vinegar into a jar and let stand for 1 week. Strain, then
stir in the witch-hazel. Keep in an airtight container in the refrigerator.

Herbal bath

Infuse a large handful of fresh herbs in 2 cups of boiled water. Leave for
10 minutes then strain and pour into the bath. Use any of the following:
chamomile, jasmine, basil, eucalyptus, lavender, lemon balm, mint,
rosemary, sage, comfrey, or spearmint.

Herbal saunas

Herbs rich in essential oils will release their
properties in the heat of a sauna. Sprinkle in
the water bucket a selection from basil,
eucalyptus, lavender, lemon verbena, pine,
rosemary, rose petals, sage, or thyme.

Herbal steaming facial

Thoroughly cleanse the skin before starting
this treatment. Now put 1 tablespoon of
mixed fresh herb leaves or flowers into 3 cups of water in a saucepan
(not aluminium) and, with the lid on, bring to boiling point. Lower the
heat and simmer the liquid for 5 minutes. Remove from stove. Cover
your head over the saucepan with a towel. If you have *fine* skin, allow 5
minutes. For *normal* skin allow 10 minutes. If you have *broken veins*, do not
use a facial steam, instead try cooled herb teas applied to the face with
cotton wool. For *dry* skin use chopped comfrey leaves and chamomile
flowers. For *problem* skin and *oily* skin use comfrey leaves, crushed fennel
seeds and lavender flowers.

Honey and milk rejuvenating lotion

1 cup of honey
1/2 cup of milk
2 teaspoons of rose water

Warm the honey in a saucepan. Add the milk and rosewater, turn off the
heat. Stir until the ingredients are mixed together. Allow to cool, then
pour into a container and keep it in the refrigerator. Before using, shake.
Ideal for fine skin.

Lavender flowers

Use lavender flowers as an antiseptic for acne. Add them to soap or use
the oil in massage for muscular aches.

Lavender sunburn oil

Lavender oil is healing and soothing. Add a few drops more to lessen the pain (for serious burns consult a doctor).

6 tablespoons of olive oil

3 tablespoons of cider vinegar

1/2 teaspoon of iodine

10 drops of lavender oil

Mix all the ingredients together and bottle. Shake before using.

Lemon balm leaf

Infuse lemon balm leaf as a facial steam and as a rinse for greasy hair. Add to the bath water for a scented wash.

Lemon cleansing cream (for oily skins)

1 tablespoon of beeswax

1 1/2 tablespoons of vaseline

3 tablespoons of olive oil

1 tablespoon of witch-hazel

1 tablespoon of lemon juice, strained

1/8 teaspoon of borax

6 drops of lemon essential oil

Melt the beeswax and vaseline together over a low heat. Warm the olive oil, then gradually add it to the wax mixture, beating for 3–5 minutes. Add the witch hazel to the lemon juice. Warm gently then stir in the borax until dissolved. Slowly add this to the wax mixture, beating steadily until it is creamy and cool. When cool, stir in the lemon oil. Store in jar.

Lip salve

1 teaspoon of beeswax

4 drops of lavender oil

1 teaspoon of almond oil

Heat all together gently and apply when cool.

Or mix equal quantities of glycerine and rose water and apply to lips.

Mascara

To prevent mascara drying out, stand dispenser in hot water for a few minutes.

Mint (spearmint) leaf

Decoct strongly to heal chapped hands. Add to bath water for an invigorating bath.

Mint and rosemary mouthwash

Both herbs sweeten the breath and rosemary has antiseptic properties.

2 cups of distilled or mineral water
1 teaspoon of fresh mint leaves
1 teaspoon of rosemary leaves
1 teaspoon of aniseed

Boil the water and add the mint, rosemary and aniseed. Leave for 20 minutes. When cool, strain and use as a gargle.

Moisturising cream (1)

A pleasant light cream for day-time use.

1 teaspoon of beeswax
1 teaspoon of lanolin
1 tablespoon of almond oil
$1/2$ teaspoon of wheatgerm oil
$1/4$ teaspoon of borax
3 tablespoons of rosewater or lavender water (warmed)
6 drops of essential rose oil, or lavender oil

Melt the beeswax and lanolin together, stirring constantly. Warm the oils gently and gradually beat them into the waxes. Dissolve the borax in the rosewater or lavender water and slowly add to the oil and wax mixture, stirring constantly until cool. Stir in the rose oil as the mixture begins to thicken. Store in jars.

Moisturising cream (2)

3 teaspoons of lanolin

3 teaspoons of beeswax

2 teaspoons of wheatgerm oil (or olive oil)

5 teaspoons of almond oil (or apricot kernel oil)

1 teaspoon of vitamin E oil or cream (oil can be obtained from a capsule)

3 teaspoons of boiling water

3 drops of lavender oil (or jasmine or violet oil)

Pinch of borax (to preserve ointment)

Melt beeswax and almond oil. Add borax to boiling water. Add to beeswax mixture with the rest of the ingredients. Beat together. Keep in fridge or cupboard.

Mouthwash

For a quick mouthwash, gargle with a peppermint infusion or use rosewater, lavender water, or dilute witch hazel (1 part witch hazel to 6 parts water).

Oils

Almond, avocado, wheatgerm, carrot, coconut and nut kernel oils are particularly skin-enriching. Castor oil disperses in water, making a good vehicle for scented bath oils.

Oregano leaf

Infuse oregano leaves for a relaxing bath. Infuse strongly to use as a hair conditioner.

Parsley

Infuse parsley as a hair tonic and conditioner. Add to facial steam and lotion for dry skin. Use an infusion as a soothing eye bath.

Revitalising mask

Beat 1 egg yolk with 2 teaspoons of lemon juice and 1 teaspoon of honey until thick. Apply to face. When dry, rinse.

Rosemary leaf

When added to a bath, rosemary leaves stimulate blood circulation. Use rosemary as a facial steam. Makes a rinse for dark hair.

Rough arms

Massage the arms with almond oil every night.

Sage leaf

Use sage leaf in facial steams and as an astringent cleansing lotion, and as a rinse to condition and darken grey hair. Rub on teeth to whiten. Use in a mouthwash.

Shaving cream

1 small packet of Lux flakes
1¹/₂ cups of boiling water
When dissolved add:
1 dessertspoon of olive oil or almond oil or wheatgerm oil
A few drops of perfume, e.g. lavender or eucalyptus oil

Beat until creamy and thick and put into wide necked jars.

Spots or blemishes: these can be dabbed with lavender oil or tea-tree oil (check for sensitivity on skin).

Strawberry mask

After cleansing the skin, cut up and mash enough strawberries to spread all over the face and neck. Leave for 20 minutes. Rinse with warm water.

Another method is to beat an egg white until stiff then add 6 very ripe crushed strawberries. Mix and spread on skin. Leave for 25 minutes then wash off with cool water. Pat dry.

Tansy

Use the flower and leaf in baths and facial steams for mature and sallow skins. Avoid tansy if you have sensitive skin.

Teeth

Clean teeth with bicarbonate of soda and a few drops of peppermint oil added for a minty flavour, or add a few drops of lemon juice.

Sage can be used to rub over teeth instead of brushing.

Chewing *strawberries* is helpful in removing plaque from teeth.

Also $^{1}/_{2}$ cup of bicarbonate of soda and 90 g of orris root can be mixed together to remove plaque.

Thyme

Use thyme leaf in baths, facial steams and ointments for spots. Infuse with rosemary as a hair rinse to deter dandruff.

Skin

To *unclog pores*, add 3 drops of cypress oil and 3 drops of geranium oil to hot water and steam face.

Toner

Put 2 tablespoons of Epsom salts in a bowl of hot water and 2 tablespoons in a bowl of cold water. Dissolve salts. Have 2 cloths and dip one in each bowl and apply to the face alternatively at least 6 times. Pat dry then apply your favourite moisturiser or cold cream.

Toothbrushes

To remove any stale odour, soak in a little lemon juice and water for 15 minutes and then rinse.

Vinegar

Vinegar is used in cosmetics to soften, cleanse and soothe the skin.

Vinegar baths

A vinegar bath soothes itchiness and aching muscles and softens the skin. Add a cupful of the following mixture to your bath. Bring 2 cups of cider vinegar and a handful of fresh bath

herbs slowly to the boil and then infuse overnight. Strain and bottle. Use as required.

Warts

Boil potatoes and use the potato water to bathe the warts.

Yoghurt mask

Apply natural yoghurt to the face and leave on for 20 minutes. Rinse face in warm water.

Etiquette

How I met Joh

When Joh took me to dinner for the first time, he brought along his sister, Neta. I wasn't sure if she was there as a chaperone but I must say we all had a lovely time. I was working as the Main Roads Commissioner's Private Secretary and every year he received deputations in his office from Councils from around Queensland to ask for money to build roads in their areas, and I had to take shorthand notes of the interviews.

Joh, as the local Member of Parliament, brought in deputations from the local authorities in the Barambah electorate in 1950. He tells people I caught his eye because I was bright and cheerful, and he eventually asked me had I ever been to Parliament. When I said I hadn't, we went to Parliament on our first date!

The engineers at the Main Roads who were at the deputations, told me 'Florence, if he asks you to go out, you go, because he's not married and has lots of money'. I accepted their advice but I always say that I didn't get rid of his money, he did, when we went in for aerial spraying of brigalow scrub to help develop Queensland and we lost 16 planes in crashes in 11 years.

Joh and I both are of a firm Christian faith and we were married in 1952 in the Presbyterian Church in Fortitude Valley in Brisbane, the Church I had attended all my life.

During my time as the wife of the Premier of Queensland, it was often my privilege to have dinner at Government House in Brisbane, where the rules of etiquette were faithfully observed.

With Joh, I attended dinners for the Queen and Prince Philip, for Prince Charles, and many other distinguished guests. It was also my privilege to escort the Duke of Edinburgh around garden parties held in honour of the Royal couple, and introduce him to the guests. Knowledge of etiquette for Royal occasions is most necessary.

When the Queen and the Duke of Edinburgh were in Queensland for the opening of Expo in 1988, Joh and I were allocated seats next to the then Leader of the Opposition and his wife.

At the opening of the new Parliament House in Canberra, I was standing behind the red ribbon waiting to see our Royal guests. The Duke walked towards us, and I was most surprised that when he saw me he came over and said 'I didn't see you at the opening of Expo' — what a wonderful memory he had! My reply was 'I was there, your Royal Highness, and I saw you'. He then said 'I did see Joh in the distance. He's an extinct volcano now!'

That's a term used for retired or defeated members of Parliament. Perhaps he meant that Joh can't blow up now!

A good restaurant

A good restaurant will only have prices on the menus supplied to the men.

Car

The gentleman always opens the door for a lady to enter first, then should alight first and open the door for the lady on arrival at the destination.

Dinner

When setting the table for a private dinner party, a tablecloth or placemats can be used.

Depending on how many courses, the knives and forks are placed as follows:

On the *right-hand side*, working in, one has the bread and butter knife, soup spoon, entree knife, main course knife and dessertspoon. The correct wine glasses should be placed on the right hand side of the plate above the cutlery.

On the *left-hand side*, working in, one has the entree fork, main course fork and dessert fork. The bread and butter plates are placed on the left hand side of the cutlery. Table napkins can be placed in napkin rings or folded and placed on the bread and butter plate.

Doorways

A lady precedes a gentleman through a doorway. A gentleman assists a lady up or down stairs by putting his hand under her elbow.

Drinks

Always serve from the right of the guest. Coffee and soft drinks are served on the left.

Giving up your seat

A gentleman should always give up his seat for a lady, or an elderly man. A young woman or man should give up his or her seat to the elderly.

Introductions

When introducing a person, always introduce by their title, that is Mr John Brown or Mrs John Brown. An acquaintance should be called by surname unless invited to do otherwise. If a man is sitting down, he should always stand when being introduced.

Invitations

To parties, weddings, etc. should be sent out three weeks in advance, and should be replied to within a week of receiving the invitation. Within a week of attending the function, the guests should ring and thank their hosts or send a thank you card.

Mail

When addressing envelopes a married lady should be addressed by her husband's initials and surname. Any person under 16 years should be addressed as Master or Miss. If you are not sure if a woman is married, the envelope is addressed Ms.

Order of the meal

Hors d'oeuvres such as nibbles, vol au vents, etc. are served before moving to the table. Then the first course is usually soup, followed by an entree. The next course consisting of fish, meat or poultry, then sweets, savoury dishes then cheese and biscuits. This meal can be simplified by having only two or three courses, which could consist of soup, main course and sweets.

Plates

Plates from each course are only removed when everyone has finished eating.

All plates are placed at the left-hand side of the person being served, and are removed from the right.

Port and liqueurs

Serve after a meal, preferably with coffee.

Red wines

Uncork red wine $^1/_2$ to 1 hour before drinking to let it breathe. Red wines are served with red meats.

Restaurants

Upon arrival, the man/host leads the way to the table and instructs his party as to where they are to sit. The gentleman also assists the lady into her chair. When ordering, the lady gives her order to her host who then gives it to the waiter. The host always advises the waiter as follows: 'the lady will have etc. etc.'

Seating

The ladies are always placed on the right-hand side of a gentleman at the dinner table. This was to enable the gentleman on her left to be in attendance to her using his right hand. When a lady arrives at a table, the men should stand, and the nearest man assist her with her chair. This also applies when she leaves the table.

Seating arrangements in a car

The most senior or important person should be seated behind the driver, and the others in the vehicle should be seated according to position, the youngest or lowest in rank to sit beside the driver.

Shaking hands

The most senior person should be introduced first. The right hand is used; the reason for this is that centuries ago a weapon was carried in the right hand and had to be put down when shaking someone's hand. A gentle handshake for ladies and a firm grip for gentlemen.

Walking in the street

A gentleman always walks on the kerbside of the woman. This is an old custom carried over from the days of unformed streets and the gentleman protecting the lady from being splashed by the carriages passing by.

When on a first date

On a first date, or having a business meal, the lady may offer to pay for half of the meal.

Wines

If a host is not sure what to order when dining out the waiter should be able to offer suggestions. When there is a choice of wines check with your guests to see which they prefer. If the host is pouring the wine, pour a few drops into your own wine glass first and taste, before you serve your guests. At family meals the lady of the house should be served first.

Chill and serve *white wines* with white meats, fish and poultry. Sweet white wines are served with desserts.

THE GARDEN

We live in the country, about 8 kilometres from Kingaroy, so we have a large area around our homes, fenced in, to keep the cattle out. We are fortunate to have a swimming pool between our two homes, which is used regularly by our grandchildren — though in winter we really need solar heating to encourage us to use it. In winter Kingaroy often has the lowest overnight temperature in the State.

Our pool area is surrounded by a lovely garden with roses, hibiscus, agapanthus and many shrubs, providing colour and shade. Joh has always loved trees and he has planted many pine trees in front of the scrub behind our homes.

We have one scrub tree at the corner of our house that we planted on our daughter Meg's fifth birthday which has grown into a huge tree over the past thirty-five years.

At 'Bethany' I have a stand that I call my greenhouse. Now that I have retired from the Senate and am home more, Joh has promised to make it into a proper greenhouse for me.

I had the loveliest small maidenhair fern, but because of the dry summer and the fact that I was away for a period, sadly it has died.

Now I am going to follow my helpful hint about potting mix for maidenhair, so that when I replace my dead fern, I will be sure that the new maidenhair fern will really do well — especially if Joh has time to make the proper greenhouse for me!

When I left Canberra I decided to buy a few deciduous trees — a Japanese maple, a claret ash and a golden ash — so that when autumn came I would still be able to watch the changing colours of the leaves.

I just loved the autumn colours on the Canberra trees, and had friends from Brisbane who enjoyed coming down regularly to see them — and me as well while I was there. In Queensland we don't have such vivid autumn colours.

We planted the trees in a corner of our front yard and in Kingaroy we have cool autumns and cold winters so I am looking forward, hopefully, to seeing a splash of colour soon that will remind me of my twelve and one-quarter years as a Senator in Canberra.

A slant-wise cut on the stems

Flowers will absorb a greater amount of water and this prevents the flower stems from sitting flat on the base of the vase.

African violets

African violets prefer to be grown indoors and need good light but not direct sun. Feed with a liquid fertiliser but at a weaker strength than for other plants. Feed fortnightly.

Aloe vera

Aloe vera should be grown in a well-drained soil, in full sun or light shade in a frost-free location. They will grow to approximately 30 cm in height. It is an evergreen perennial.

Animal manure

If allowed to rot, manure is good as a fertiliser.

Aniseed

Place aniseed in a sunny but sheltered position, in well-drained alkaline soil. Must be kept well weeded. They will grow up to 30–45 cm.

Ants

To keep ants out of fruit trees when the fruit is ripe, rub a ring of vaseline, about 10 cm wide, around the trunk of the tree.

Asparagus

Asparagus are fond of salt and a sprinkling may be laid along the rows of plants in their first and second year. When the plant decays at the end of the season it should be cut away and a dressing of manure spread over them.

Basil

Grow basil in a warm, sunny position protected from the wind, frost and extreme sun. Likes well-drained and moist soil. Will grow up to 45 cm in height.

Bay tree

A bay tree requires full sun but protected from wind. Grow these trees in a rich, moist and well-drained soil. They grow up to 7 metres.

Before weeding

Rub fingernails across a cake of soft soap to keep them free from dirt.

Bulbs

To check if they are sound, press the thumb on the hollow at the base; this will be firm if the bulb is sound, and soft if the bulb is unsound.

Caraway

Caraway requires a rich loam soil in full sun and will grow up to 60 cm in second year.

Caterpillars

A spray of flour and water will kill the caterpillar in a couple of days.

Chamomile

Grow chamomile in full sun in a light and well-drained soil. It grows to 30 cm. Grown near a poor plant, it will help revive it. Infuse and spray on seedlings to prevent 'damping off' and on compost to activate decomposition.

Chervil

Prefers light and well-drained soil. In hot conditions it quickly runs to seed. It is a hardy annual that grows 25 cm in height.

Clay soil

Improve clay soil by adding lime, leaf mould or sand.

Coffee grounds

Coffee grounds make excellent mulch for indoor plants.

Comfrey

Plant comfrey in full sun, but be careful as it is difficult to eradicate if it gets 'out of control'. It requires soil rich in nitrogen. Grows up to 1 metre.

Compost

Dig a hole in the garden, fill with peelings and organic waste, then cover and leave to rot.

Coriander

This plant requires full sun in a rich and light soil. It will grow to 60 cm in height and is an annual.

Cottage gardens

Leave some of the dying flowers to seed for next year, for example forget-me-nots, alyssum, primula, hollyhocks.

Cushion

Fill an old hot-water bottle with sand and use to kneel on when gardening.

Delphiniums

These will last much longer with sugar
added to the vase water.

Dill

Dill prefers rich and well-drained soil in
full sun, but needs to be protected from
wind. A hardy annual, it grows to 1 m.

Eggshells

Save eggshells when cooking, soak in
water. Use water to water pot-plants.

Placing *crushed eggshells* around plants will help produce glossy leaves,
especially on an African violet.

Ends of woody or semi-woody stems of flowers

These should be crushed or split before putting in a vase so that the
water intake is greater.

Evening primrose

Evening primrose grows in a sunny and open position in well-drained
soil. It will grow from 1 to 2 metres in height.

Fennel

Grow fennel in a full sunny position (to ripen seed) and a well-drained
loam soil. Avoid clays. It grows to 2 m in height.

Flowers (cut)

A little salt placed with the water in a vase will lengthen the life of cut
flowers. They will also last longer in a vase of water to which drops of
eucalyptus oil have been added.

Gum tips will keep much longer if a little washing blue is put in the vase
with the water.

Rose stems should be scraped for about 1 cm and then split. Stand them
in shallow hot water for 30 seconds, then place them into deep cold
water.

Cut off a small piece of the stem every day; if the stalks are hard and woody, the ends should be split for an inch or so from the bottom.

The ends of the stems of flowers such as poppies should be closed by dipping them into melted wax or by burning them.

Foliage

To preserve foliage, dissolve 3 teaspoons shellac in 5 tablespoons methylated spirits and leave it for several days. Strain the liquid and spray on to autumn foliage or berries to retain the colour.

Garden spray

1 onion

3 cloves of garlic, unpeeled

1 teaspoon of chilli powder

1 teaspoon of soap powder

Put into a blender and mash. Add to 1 litre of hot water. Stir. Cool. Then strain through a stocking and use. This is harmless to cats and dogs.

Garden spray (garlic)

This spray can be used against aphids, snails, cabbage moth, caterpillars and mosquitoes.

3 knobs of unpeeled garlic

6 tablespoons medicinal paraffin oil

1 tablespoon oil-based soap, grated

500 mL hot water

Chop garlic, put into a blender with paraffin oil and mash. Put pulp into a bowl, cover and leave for 2 days. Add grated soap to hot water, stir until melted, then add to garlic mixture. When cool, strain into jars and store in refrigerator. Use 2 tablespoons of garlic solution to 2 litres of water when spraying in the garden.

Geraniums (scented)

These are also known as pelargoniums, they require a sunny position in well-drained soil. They are perennials and will grow up to 1 metre in height. They can be grown in pots.

Ground-covers

Ground-covering plants reduce the need to weed as weeds find it harder to establish themselves.

Herbs

Grow in pots or hanging baskets.

House plants

A piece of *charcoal* in the soil of pot-plants will keep the soil sweet.

To *revive*, water occasionally with lukewarm tea or coffee.

Hydrangeas

To grow *blue hydrangeas*, add rusty nails or 1 teaspoon of alum to 24 cups of water or feed with iron pills.

To grow *pink or red hydrangeas*, add 2 teaspoons of Epsom salts to 24 cups of water. Treat the soil occasionally with lime also.

Lavender

There are several varieties of this plant and most prefer a sunny and open position in well-drained sandy soil with lime content. Lavender can grow up to one metre in height.

Lavender bags

1 cup of dried lavender flowers

2 tablespoons of common salt

1 tablespoon of dried thyme

1 tablespoon of dried mint

Mix together.

Leaves

To press leaves, simply place them in layers, separated with absorbent paper. Weigh down evenly and allow to remain for about a month.

Lemon balm

Grow lemon balm in full sun with midday shade. They will grow in any moist soil. A hardy herbaceous perennial, it will grow up to 1 metre. Plant around beehives and orchards to attract bees.

Marjoram and oregano

These are very similar to each other so plant both in full sun, but where they will get midday shade, in a well-drained, dryish, alkaline, nutrient rich soil.

Mealy bug

An effective remedy is to paint the limb with a brush dipped in methylated spirits or paraffin oil.

Mint

Various types of mint are available but most prefer partial shade or sunny site and a moist, well-drained, alkaline soil rich in nutrients. Mint can grow up to 1 metre in height and it needs to be watched as it can spread. It can also be grown in pots.

Grow mint near roses to deter aphids.

Mint grown around paths or stepping stones gives out a lovely aroma.

Nasturtiums

Nasturtiums thrive in full sun or partial shade, in well-drained soil.

Oyster shells

Heat oyster shells until they crumble, then add to potting composts.

Palms

If grown in pots, palms will remain a moderate size.

Parsley

Plant in full sun or light shade. Requires rich, moist soil. Hardy biennial, grows to 38 cm. Plant near roses to improve their perfume.

Potpourri

Dry rose petals, lavender, lemon verbena leaves for at least 2 hours in the sun and add to them all or any of the following:

200 g powdered orris root

4 tablespoons of cloves

1 stick of cinnamon (powdered)

2 tablespoons of allspice

Juice and grated rind of 2 lemons

Lavender oil or any other essential oil can be added

Mix together in a large container. Seal or cover and leave for at least two to three weeks, stirring occasionally. Place quantities in a bowl throughout the house and you will have a lovely lingering fragrance.

Potpourri (lavender)

1 cup of lavender flowers

$1/2$ cup of marjoram leaves

1 tablespoon of thyme leaves

1 tablespoon of mint leaves

1 tablespoon of orris root powder

2 teaspoons of ground coriander

$1/4$ teaspoon of ground cloves

A few drops of lavender oil

Mix the flowers and leaves together. Blend the orris powder, coriander and cloves separately, then stir in the lavender oil and add to the dried material. This mixture may be used in sachets or as potpourri.

Potpourri (another recipe)

4 cups of rose petals

2 cups of geranium leaves

2 cups of lavender flowers and leaves

1 cup of lemon verbena leaves (optional)

2 tablespoons of orris root powder

1 teaspoon of rose geranium oil

1 teaspoon of lavender oil

1 teaspoon of ground cloves

1 tablespoon of ground cinnamon

Several pieces of cinnamon bark

12 whole cloves

Dry the flowers and leaves. Put all the flowers and leaves into a large jar. Put the orris powder, ground cloves and cinnamon into a small bowl and blend, then add the essential oils, combining them into the powder. Add the mixed powder to the dried material in the container, thoroughly mix all the ingredients together. Cover and leave for at least one month. If faded mixture needs revitalising, add a few drops of your favourite flower oil.

Potting mix

A good potting mix for *maidenhair fern* is $2/3$ loam, $1/3$ peat and leaf-mould with sand added freely.

For *palms* a good potting mix is $2/3$ loam and $1/3$ peat with sand added freely.

Pruning

Summer pruning is important. If you neglect pruning spent blooms on shrubs it will cause plants to become more leggy and sparse and produce fewer flowers. To prolong flowering period of plants, remove spent blooms regularly.

Pyrethrum

Plant pyrethrum in a sunny and open position in alkaline and well-drained soil. They can grow up to 75 cm.

Rosemary

There are several varieties of this plant. It prefers a sunny position but should be protected from cold winds. Grow in a large pot. Needs drainage. In limed soil, rosemary is a smaller but more fragrant plant. To provide additional lime, apply eggshells or wood ash. It grows up to 2 metres in height.

Roses

A solution of soapy water thrown over roses deters aphids. A mixture of 1 part white flour mixed with 5 parts of milk and 20 parts of water can also be used and hosed off later.

Sage

There are several varieties in this group and they prefer full sun in a light, dry, alkaline and well-drained soil. Sage grows up to 75 cm in height.

Secateurs

Sharpen along the outside edges only.

Seeds

Tie paper bags over vegetables going to seed to collect the seeds.

Shears

Sharpen along the bevel on the outside face of the blades only.

Soot

After exposure to the air for a few weeks, soot is an excellent fertiliser for plants. If placed in a bag and suspended in a drum of water, soot makes a useful liquid manure for ferns, chrysanthemums and other pot-plants.

Sorrel

Plant in sun or light shade. Requires moist, rich well-drained soil with iron. Sorrel is a hardy perennial and grows up to 45 cm.

Spade

Use a file to sharpen a spade on the bevel edge of the surface only. A few light strokes of the file on the front of the blade will bring up a sharp cutting edge.

Sugar

Add sugar to the water of strong-smelling flowers, such as marigolds, to remove the strong odour, while dropping a piece of charcoal into the water will keep it sweet.

Watering

Water your garden in the evening or early morning. This lessens evaporation.

Weeds

Sprinkle kerosene or salt on paths and prevent tedious weeding.

When picking roses

Hold the stems with a spring clothes peg to save being scratched by the thorns.

When storing gardening gloves

Fold the tops of gardening gloves over twice and secure with a clothes peg. It keeps out any creepy crawlies.

White pepper

Sprinkle white pepper on plants to stop caterpillars.

Worn-out household sponges

These are excellent drainage material and help hold moisture in bottoms of pot-plants.

Glossary

Allspice
A pea-like berry that when dried and crushed seems to combine a flavour of cinnamon, cloves and nutmeg.

Alum
Sold as crystals and as a powder. The kinds sold are potash and ammonia alum. Both have the same properties.

Ammonia
A strong alkali and on this account is used as a cleansing agent. It is poisonous and must not be inhaled.

Arrowroot
A pure starch powder. It is a valuable invalid food and is easily digested.

Beeswax
Obtained from bee hives and is used extensively for floor and furniture polish.

Bicarbonate of soda (bicarb soda)
With cream of tartar, it is used to make baking powder. It is useful for cleaning, removing stains, as a water softener, for medicinal purposes and to remove odours. Can be purchased in bulk at health food stores.

Boracic acid
A very useful mild antiseptic.

Borax
A white powder used as a water softener and as a mild antiseptic and bleach. Can be bought through pharmacies.

Bran
Used in face masks, soaps and body scrubs as a cleanser.

Camphor
Obtained from distillation of the

wood of the camphor laurel; it is a pungent crystalline substance.

Camphorated oil

The liniment of camphor. To make a camphorated oil use 30 g of camphor dissolved in $\frac{1}{2}$ cup of olive oil. This can be used as a liniment.

Cream of tartar

Used in cooking and can be used for cleaning stainless steel, etc.

Decoction

A process of boiling down so as to extract some essence.

Epsom salts (sulphate of magnesium)

Can be used as a purgative.

Essential oils

The chief flavouring part of vegetable substances is known as essential oil and one of the characteristics is that it retains the odour, for example lavender oil retains the perfume.

Eucalyptus oil

Obtained by distillation from the leaf of the gum tree. It is a strong antiseptic and disinfectant.

Fuller's earth

A mineral used as a dusting and cleansing powder. It is a fine grey powder derived from single-cell algae found on sea beds. Its absorbent properties and mineral richness make it an excellent face mask. It can be bought at pharmacies.

Gelatine

A colourless, odourless and tasteless glue which is a rich source of water-soluble protein, obtained by boiling animal bones. Used in eye ointment and nail hardening lotions. Agar agar is a vegetable substitute.

Glycerine

A thick, colourless and odourless syrup and a by-product of soap manufacture. It mixes with water, is soluble in alcohol and has softening properties.

Honey

For softening and healing and binding other ingredients together.

Infusion

A liquid extract which is obtained by steeping or soaking the substance in boiling water.

Kaolin

The purest form of clay, useful in face masks.

Kerosene

Oil obtained from bituminous coal and petroleum. It is used in cleaning and also for heating and light.

Lanolin

Obtained from sheep's wool and used as a base for ointments. It penetrates the skin, so is good for wrinkle-removing creams, etc.

Lemon

Lemon juice can be used as a mild bleach and an effective stain remover.

Liniment

A liquid preparation usually containing oil or spirit, to be rubbed into or applied outwardly to the skin for sprains, etc.

Linseed oil

Used particularly for polishing furniture.

Liquid paraffin

A mineral oil which is not absorbed by the skin, making it useful in barrier cream.

Methylated spirits (metho)

Alcohol which is unfit for use as a beverage by a process of denaturising. It has many uses in the home but is *highly inflammable.* It is used for cleaning glass, removing stains from boots (but dries leather, so use sparingly) and can also be used to sterilise instruments.

Mustard

Is a hardy annual plant. The seed is powdered for commercial use. Used as a condiment or can be used to make a mustard poultice.

Oleic acid

An emulsifying liquid that can rescue separated creams.

Olive oil

Obtained by pressing the ripe fruit of the olive tree. It is a valuable food source and is often taken for mild constipation.

Onion

A bulb which is used as a vegetable as well as a condiment. It can also be used as a poultice for boils.

Orris root

The root of the iris. Its scent resembles that of violets and it can be bought from health food shops.

Paraffin oil

Also known as kerosene.

Peroxide of hydrogen
When diluted with equal parts of water, it can be used to bathe wounds. It was once used as a bleach for hair.

Petroleum jelly (vaseline)
A pale yellow translucent mineral jelly insoluble in water. It does not turn rancid when exposed to air. Used in lip salves.

Poultice
A means of applying heat to any part of the body.

Pumice
Used in soaps and cleansing mixtures. Pumice stone is good for removing stains from hands and produces a gloss on unpolished marble.

Putty
Is composed of whiting and linseed oil. It is used for sealing windows, etc.

Salt
It is used in cooking and is an excellent cleanser in the house as an abrasive scouring powder and for removing stains on baths, enamel, etc. Salt is also mildly antiseptic.

Shellac
A fine resin which is soluble in methylated spirits and is used as a French polish. Shellac can be obtained from hardware stores.

Soda
Used for removing grease and dirt from pots and pans and cloths, soda should not be used on aluminium or enamelled saucepans. It is often used to soften hard water.

Steep
To soak or saturate.

Turpentine (Turps)
Oil of turpentine is a colourless liquid with a strong odour and bitter taste. It has many uses in the home; its odour keeps away ants, flies, mice and moths. Paint stains can be removed from clothes and it has antiseptic properties.

Vanilla essence
Obtained from the vanilla plant and used in cooking and confectionery as a flavouring. It can also be used to eliminate unpleasant odours in the house.

Vinegar
A solution of acetic acid in water. It may be prepared from malt, wine, cider and sugar. It is used for

cooking, cleaning and lots of
household chores.

Washing soda

Ideal for washing floors and walls.
Added to the washing water it helps
clean really dirty clothes and is a
water softener, but use in
moderation.

Whiting

Made from the well-washed residue
of chalk. It is used for making
whitewash and also for polishing and
cleaning in the house, such as
pewter.

Index